Official Microsoft® Image Composer Book

Microsoft® Press

PUBLISHED BY
Microsoft Press
A Division of Microsoft Corporation
One Microsoft Way
Redmond, Washington 98052-6399

Copyright © 1998 by William Tait and Stephen W. Sagman

All rights reserved. No part of the contents of this book may be reproduced or transmitted in any form or by any means without the written permission of the publisher.

Library of Congress Cataloging-in-Publication Data
Tait, William, 1959–
Official Microsoft Image Composer Book : an example packed guide to designing and enhancing graphics using Microsoft Image Composer 1.5 / William Tait, Stephen W. Sagman.
p. cm.
– Includes index.
ISBN 1-57231-593-8
1. Computer graphics. 2. Microsoft Image Composer. 3. Web sites––Design. I. Sagman, Stephen W. II. Title.
T385.T34 1997
006.6'869--dc21 97-44406
CIP

Printed and bound in the United States of America.

1 2 3 4 5 6 7 8 9 WCWC 3 2 1 0 9 8

Distributed to the book trade in Canada by Macmillan of Canada, a division of Canada Publishing Corporation.

A CIP catalogue record for this book is available from the British Library.

Microsoft Press books are available through booksellers and distributors worldwide. For further information about international editions, contact your local Microsoft Corporation office. Or contact Microsoft Press International directly at fax (425) 936-7329. Visit our Web site at mspress.microsoft.com.

FrontPage, Microsoft, Microsoft Press, Windows, and Windows NT are registered trademarks of Microsoft Corporation. This product contains images from PhotoDisc Collections. Images © 1996 PhotoDisc, Incorporated. Photos and artwork copyright © Will Tait. Other product and company names mentioned herein may be the trademarks of their respective owners.

Acquisitions Editor: Kim Fryer
Project Editors: Laura Sackerman, Victoria Thulman
Manuscript Editor: Gail Taylor
Technical Editor: Jean Hollis Weber

Dedicated to our parents, John and Anne Tait, and David and Audrey Sagman, and to Alvy Ray Smith for making possible the tools we use.

Contents

Acknowledgments

The authors would like to gratefully acknowledge the Image Composer team at Microsoft for their immeasurable assistance during the development of this book. Joel Singer, Susan Pappalardo, Craig Murphy, Jonathan Fay, and John Bronskill met with us and offered valuable information about the inner workings of Image Composer. Terri Sharkey reviewed each chapter as we completed it and gave us the immense benefit of her experience.

The authors also wish to thank our friends at Microsoft Press who faithfully guided us during the project. Kim Fryer, Lucinda Rowley, Laura Sackerman, Victoria Thulman, Mary DeJong, and Bill Teel gave us the opportunity and led us to fruition.

We'd also like thank Jean Hollis Weber for her careful technical review of every procedure and for her providing us with valuable suggestions from a locale down under in Ryde, New South Wales, Australia. We also were lucky to have Gail Taylor of Taylor Wordsmiths, in Cowichan Bay, British Columbia, Canada, on our international team. She performed delicate surgery on our sentences and nursed our language to good health.

Will Tait and Steve Sagman

Foreword

One key idea made Image Composer inevitable. In 1990 at Pixar, the computer animation company that I cofounded, I wrote a prototype application to demonstrate a new imaging language. I quickly determined that it wasn't the language that amazed people. It was the non-rectangular floating images I used in the prototype. The idea then was this: *Images can have any shape!* I had overthrown the tyranny of the rectangle in imaging. Shaped images, which we now call sprites, could be handled just like the geometrical shapes in drawing packages; they could float, have depth order, be grouped, aligned, etc. I know it's hard to believe such an obvious idea had to be invented, but it did.

With this insight I started a company, Altamira Software Corporation, and created an imaging application called Altamira Composer, on the Windows platform, that combined the familiar user interface to objects from the drawing world with the editing capabilities from the imaging world. I called this new type of picture-creation tool an image-composition application, because sprite arrangement is just as easy as sprite editing and often more important. To be brief, Microsoft bought my startup, and Image Composer is a direct descendent of Altamira Composer.

The notion of image sprites was a natural one for me. I and three of my colleagues from Pixar and Lucasfilm before that (I co-started computer graphics there in 1980) had invented a notion called the *alpha channel*. To the three well-known color channels of an image—red, green, and blue—we added a fourth channel to carry the pixel-by-pixel partial transparency information of an image. This is now the way that full-color images are represented in Hollywood, a fact for which we received a technical Academy Award in 1996. Image Composer is a full flowering of the alpha channel technology.

Will Tait is in many ways the perfect author for this book on Image Composer. First, he is a practicing, accomplished artist, independent of the computer. Second, he creates real Web sites, posters, and artworks. But, third, and most important to you, is the fact that he knows Image Composer as a user better than almost all others. This is because he has used all versions of the product all the way back to Altamira Composer. In fact, he was one of my first, and best, testers—a so-called beta tester—for the original product. And he has beta tested every version of the product since then! Many of the ideas in Image Composer are a direct result of his input. Oh, by the way, Will is one of the few people I like to go to the top of mountains with and stretch my brain. I think you will like his and Steve's book.

Alvy Ray Smith, PhD
Microsoft Graphics Fellow
October 16, 1997

Introducing Image Composer

Microsoft Image Composer gives you a remarkably easy-to-use set of tools for creating sophisticated images with one-click ease. It offers all the painting and photo-editing features you'd expect in a world-class image editing program, and it offers a powerful new concept in working with graphics—image objects called sprites.

Sprites are the basic building blocks of Image Composer compositions. Each image you draw, import, extract, or scan is a sprite you can work on individually. Because you can work with and store a number of sprites in a single Image Composer file, you can arrange them into overlapping groupings easily by moving them about freely and directly. You can also smoothly blend sprites into seamless image montages and transfer the properties of one sprite to other sprites, which gives you tremendous power to bring your visions to life.

Image Composer is just as powerful in working on a single sprite as it is in creating compositions of them. It lets you start with scanned photos or pictures you've taken with a digital camera, color tune them, apply any of hundreds of visual effects with a single click, and retouch photos, even extracting and re-combining their elements to create your own virtual reality.

The sprites you make or the compositions you compose will be well-suited for Web pages, as Image Composer is fine-tuned for creating Web graphics. However, the images you create with Image Composer are just as suitable for printed publications, electronic presentations, and multimedia applications.

Working in Image Composer is somewhat like performing traditional paste-up, the method that has been used to combine images into final designs for decades. Image Composer provides a central area on the screen, called the Composition Space, where you work with images, try "what if I did this" scenarios, develop visual concepts, and work out your ideas with the tools from the adjacent toolbox. On the surrounding Workspace, you keep all the bits and pieces and visual elements that you can pull in as you work, trying different combinations until you've worked out the right visual solution to your design challenge.

But where Image Composer far exceeds traditional paste-up techniques is in its unique application of alpha channel and sprite technologies. As you'll learn in this book, these two technologies enable you to make any changes you can imagine with amazing speed, almost as quickly as you can think them up. For anything less than a dedicated graphics workstation, Image Composer is the most useful and versatile composition tool available to meet your creative needs.

The Power of Sprites

Because each image or portion of an image in an Image Composer file is a separate sprite, you can work on a collection of images as a composition and still work on the individual elements of the collection as separate entities. Even after you have saved a composition as a single bitmap graphics file suitable for a Web page, the sprites remain separate elements within the Image Composer file. You can select any sprite, apply effects to change its appearance, remove it, replace it with a different sprite, or pass its properties to another sprite. Figure 1-1 shows a collection of individual sprites of various types.

In most other graphics programs, you work on each image in a separate file and window before combining them into one large file. The individual components you've combined often lose their identity as discrete, editable, and reusable objects.

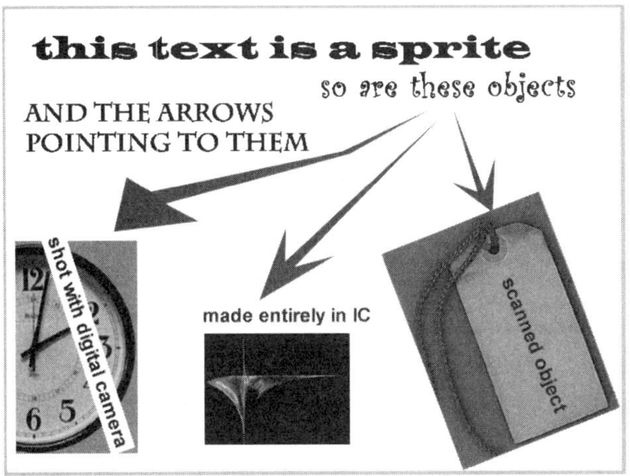

Figure 1-1
Several sprites of different types.

A Bridge Between Raster and Vector Graphics

Graphics programs are generally categorized as either raster or vector programs. Image Composer is a raster program that has many of the benefits usually ascribed to vector programs.

Raster programs work with pixels, the tiny squares or rectangular areas of the computer screen. The word pixel comes from Picture Element or Pix El. A PC graphics card and monitor suitable for working with graphics shows thousands of pixels, often 800 pixels across by 600 pixels down or 1024 pixels across by 768 pixels down.

Vector programs, on the other hand, work with shapes modified by mathematical formulas. You can freely move these shapes in front of or behind each other, and move them anywhere on the screen by simply dragging them around.

Image Composer lets you directly manipulate the pixels in sprites like a raster program, and move the sprites as separate objects anywhere on the screen, just like a vector program. This provides a freedom to work that you won't find in many other graphics programs.

The Image Composer Window

Centered in the Image Composer window is the Composition Space, the area on which you place and work on sprites. When you save an Image Composer composition as a bitmap graphics file that you can use on the Web or in an electronic presentation, Image Composer saves a snapshot of everything within the Composition Space. If a sprite is half in and half out of the Composition Space, only the half that is within the Composition Space appears in the bitmap file, as shown in Figure 1-2.

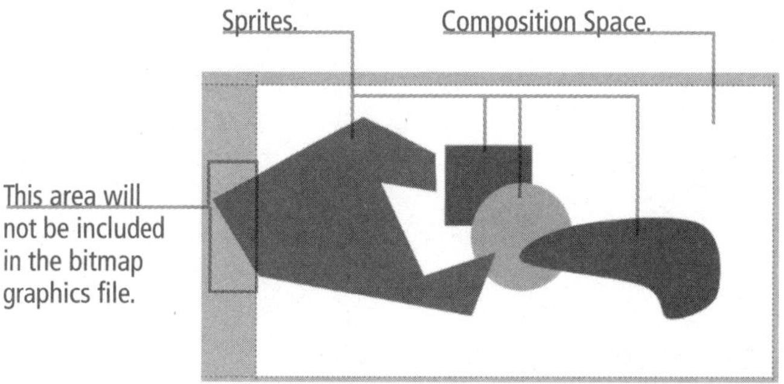

Figure 1-2
Portions of images that hang outside the Composition Space will be chopped off in a bitmap graphics file.

Surrounding the Composition Space is the Workspace, a vast, open area upon which you can throw all the bits and pieces of images—sprites in themselves—that you might want to use later. It's also an ideal place to explore experimental tangents and put copies of sprites that you're about to modify so you have a backup handy in case things don't work out as well as you might have hoped. In fact, it's so simple to make backup copies of sprites that it's a good idea to keep at least one incremental copy of every sprite you change. If you decide to try a different modification, you have another copy of the sprite with which to experiment. This gives you an enormous amount of freedom to explore without having to save a new file every time you want to save an image in its current state.

In addition to the Composition Space and the Workspace, the Image Composer window contains these elements, all shown in Figure 1-3:

Toolbar	The Toolbar contains shortcuts to frequently used commands.
Toolbox	The Toolbox holds buttons that perform specific tasks, such as zooming in on an image, or that open palettes, such as the Shapes palette that is shown in Figure 1-1.
Color Swatch	The Color Swatch displays the currently selected color. Clicking the Color Swatch opens the Color Picker dialog box, which lets you choose a different color.
Status Bar	The Status Bar shows helpful information about the current status of your work, such as the exact location of the mouse pointer and the size of the object you have selected.

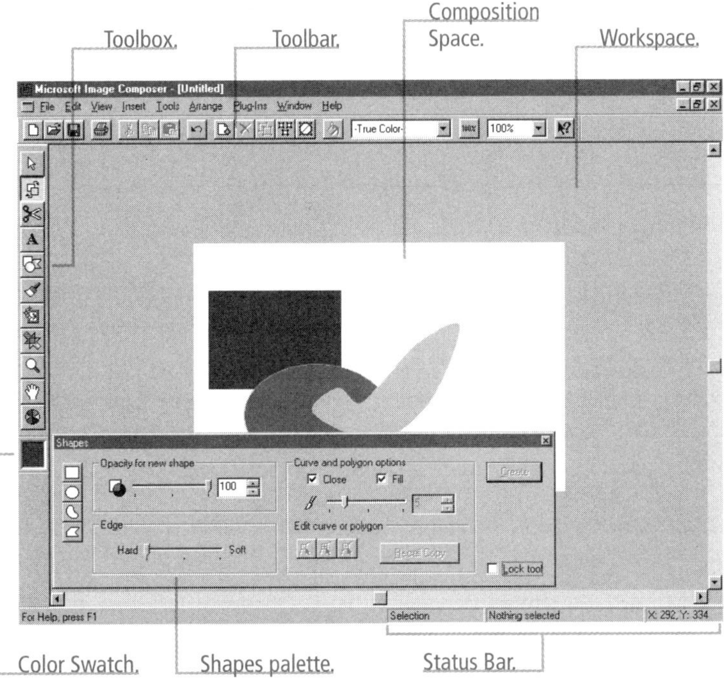

Figure 1-3

The Image Composer window.

The Composition Guides

The Composition Guides are the dotted lines that define the boundaries of the Composition Space. If you do not see these lines, click the Composition Space with the right mouse button and click Composition Guides on the shortcut menu that appears.

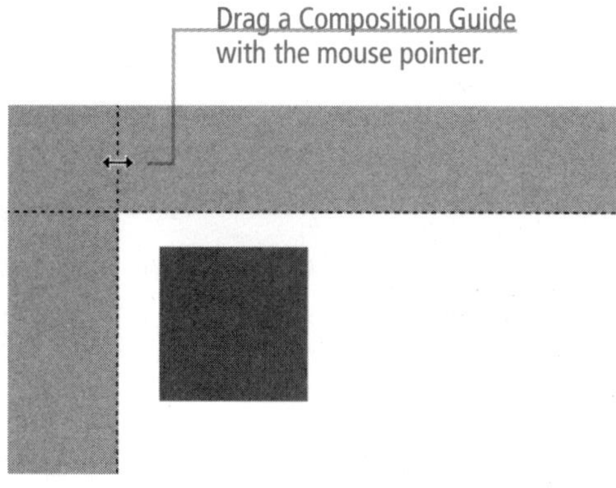
Drag a Composition Guide
with the mouse pointer.

Figure 1-4
The Composition Guides.

You can drag these Composition Guides to interactively change the size of the Composition Space. You can also lock them so they will not move accidentally while you are trying to move something else on the screen. To lock the Composition Guides, right-click the Composition Space and choose Lock Composition Guides from the shortcut menu.

Especially when you are developing graphics for the Web, you will plan your projects so they have a specific composition size, so the composition guides are unnecessary. Unless you have a specific reason to use them, we recommend that you turn them off and forget about them. Again, right-click the Composition Space and click the Composition Guides selection.

The Toolbox

The buttons in the Toolbox provide the main controls you use to work with images. A few of these buttons actually perform direct actions, such as the Selection button at the top of the Toolbox, which returns the mouse pointer to a Selection tool after you've been using it to do something else. The Pan button lets you drag the work area around within the Image Composer window, and the Zoom button zooms in and out on particular spots.

The rest of the buttons open palettes, which hold the tools and controls you use to make most changes to images. For example, clicking the Arrange button on the Toolbox opens the Arrange palette. Figure 1-5 shows the functions of the toolbox buttons.

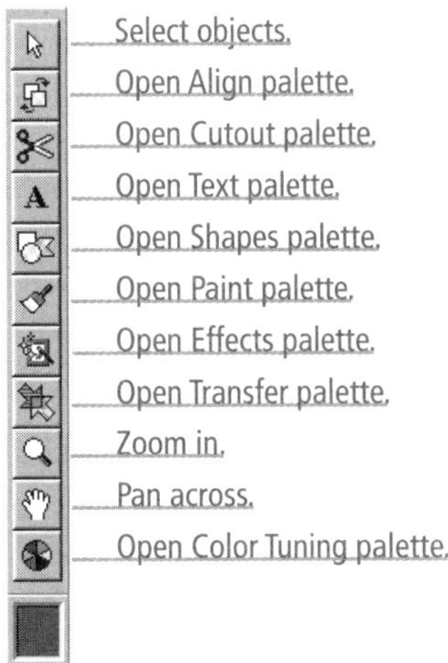

Figure 1-5
The Toolbox buttons.

As you work through the projects in this book, you will get to know which button to click to open each palette. Until then, we will show you the button to click, like this:

Shapes button

1. Open the Shapes palette.

Whenever we ask you to open a palette, you can assume there is a button on the Toolbox for it.

TIP

To identify a Toolbox button, move the mouse pointer onto the button and pause. After an instant, a little Tooltip appears, showing the button's name. Tooltips also help you identify Toolbar buttons and buttons within palettes.

Color Swatch

The Color Swatch

The Color Swatch, just below the Toolbox, displays the current color that will be used by the tools you select. To change the current color, you can click the Color Swatch to open the Color Picker, a dialog box that displays the color space. The standard color space, True Color, shows 16.7 million colors, but you might want to use one of the custom color palettes that are available on the Custom Palette tab of the Color Picker dialog box. The Web-specific palettes contain only 216 colors, the common colors that Web browsers can display without dithering, which is mixing dots of other colors to try to approximate a color that is not in the palette.

If you are making a Web site, perhaps for a company intranet, and you know that your intended users all have 24-bit color graphics systems, you can make highly customized palettes suited to a particular look. For instance, you can create and use a palette that contains 150 shades of blue, 50 reds, and a variety of gold tones. But images created with this palette would not look very good displayed in 8-bit color on a public Web site.

TIP

The Color Swatch is actually its own tiny little toolbar, as you can see when you click on its edge, just outside the display of the current color, and then drag the Color Swatch somewhere else on the screen. The Toolbox is also moveable, but we recommend leaving it at the left edge of the Image Composer window for now.

When you click the Color Swatch, you can select a color by clicking anywhere in the color matrix, the rainbow display of colors on the True Color tab. The color you've chosen is pinpointed by a small circle on the color matrix, as shown in Figure 1-6, and it's also displayed in the New Color (right half) portion of the color display at the top right. The left half of the color display is the Original Color.

To make minor adjustments to the color, you can drag the small circle on the color matrix left or right to change the hue, or you can drag it up or down to change the degree of black in the color. To add white to the color, you can click and drag within the Whiteness slider next to the color matrix.

The three sliders on the right side of the dialog box let you set the current color by changing the Red, Green, and Blue levels, or the Hue, Saturation, and Value levels depending on whether the RGB or HSV button is selected. Using these sliders, or entering an exact number for each level, gives you the precision to select a color accurately. The default color mode is RGB. This is what will be used throughout this book.

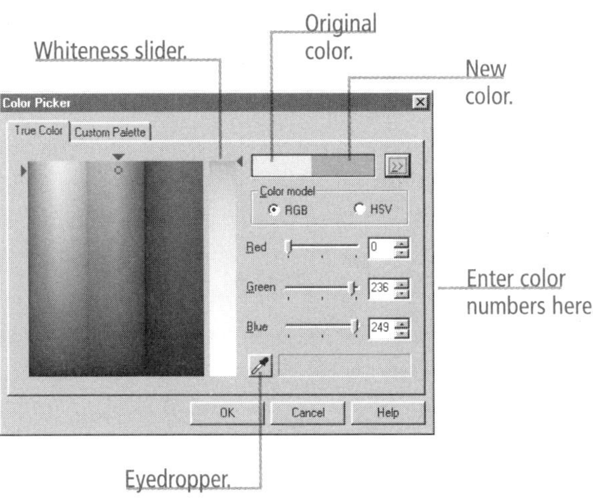

Figure 1-6
The True Color tab of the Color Picker.

NOTE

To specify the color we'd like you to use throughout this book, we will supply the RGB levels of the color in this format: 0, 236, 249. This translates to settings of Red 0, Green 236, and Blue 249.

A special tool on the True Color tab of the Color Picker, the Eyedropper, lets you click any spot on the screen and pick up the color at that spot. To see the eyedropper in action, click the Eyedropper button and move the Eyedropper across the color matrix. Watch the numbers in the RGB fields of the Color Picker dialog box as you go. To choose the color under the Eyedropper, click the mouse, and then click OK. To dismiss the Eyedropper without choosing a new color, press Esc on the keyboard.

No matter how you choose a color, whether you use the color matrix, the RGB sliders, or the Eyedropper, clicking OK sets the current color, and shows it in the Color Swatch.

Try setting the Red, Green, and Blue sliders each to 200 and clicking OK. Setting all three sliders to the same number always produces a gray, so we can be confident that you will see a gray in the Color Swatch when you click OK in the Color Picker dialog box.

You can right-click the Color Swatch (click it with the right mouse button) to open the color matrix and select a basic color by clicking it there. For accuracy however, you will want to use the Color Picker.

Working in Image Composer

As you use Image Composer, you'll need to perform certain tasks no matter what project you're working on. Here are some of the basics that apply.

Setting up the Composition Space

Although you can drag the Composition Guides to change the size of the Composition Space, you can set the size of the Composition Space to the exact pixel by choosing Composition Setup from the File menu. The Composition Setup dialog box, shown in Figure 1-7, allows you to enter the precise width and height of the Composition Space. It also lets you set the default size for new files, and change the color of the Composition Space, as you will see in Chapter 3. Changing the color of the Composition Space can be helpful when you have chosen the color for the background of a Web page or presentation and you'd like to view the same background color while working in Image Composer.

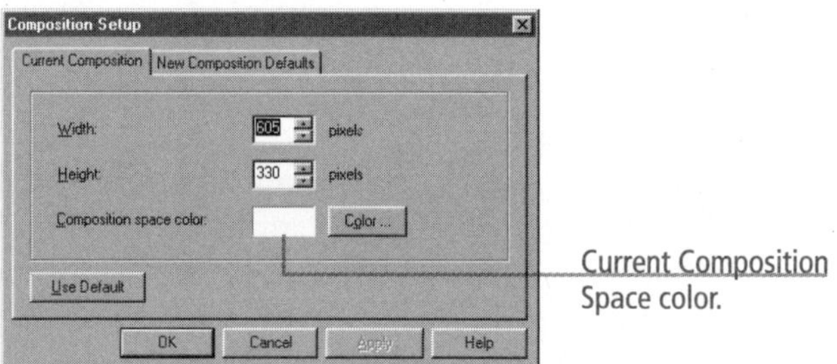

Figure 1-7
The Composition Setup dialog box.

Moving Around

As you work in the Image Composer window, you can move up, down, left, or right by dragging the scroll bars along the right and bottom edges of the Workspace.

Pan button

Another option is to use the Pan tool, which lets you drag the entire composition around within the Image Composer window. To try it, click the Pan button in the Toolbox, place the mouse pointer (which now looks like a hand) on the Composition Space and drag it around. Once you get used to it, this is an easy way to move around the screen.

At any time, you can press the Home key to center the Composition Space in the Image Composer window.

Zooming In and Out

Zoom button

To zoom closer on a composition, click the Zoom button on the Toolbox, place the magnifying glass cursor over the area you want to Zoom in on, and click the composition. To zoom back out, hold down the Ctrl key when you click.

The Zoom Percent control on the Toolbar, shown in Figure 1-8, shows the current zoom level and lets you jump multiple levels in or out. But unlike the Zoom tool, it doesn't let you zoom in to a particular spot. Instead, it zooms in on whatever is at the center of the Image Composer window. To quickly return to 100% zoom, click the 100% button on the Toolbar.

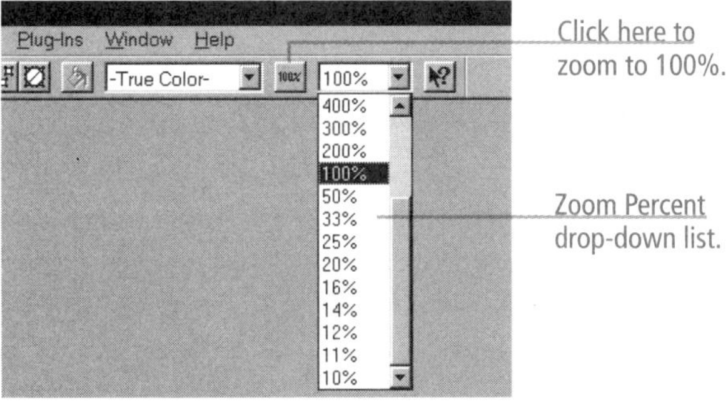

Figure 1-8
The Zoom Percent drop-down list and the 100% button.

To zoom in or out on whatever is centered in the Image Composer window, press the plus or minus keys next to the numeric keypad on your keyboard. For this to work, you must click the Composition Space with the Selection tool to give it focus.

Using Multiple Views

Image Composer allows you to open two views on the same subject by selecting New Window from the Window menu. Unfortunately, you cannot open a second file in the second window to transfer graphics back and forth between projects. If you want to work between files, however, you can open two instances of Image Composer and copy and paste between them using the Windows Clipboard.

A second view on a composition allows you to view a different color palette applied, or zoom in closely for fine-tuning in one window and still get a broader view of the entire design in another window. Figure 1-9 shows two views of a composition. The left window uses the True Color palette. The right window uses the Web (Solid) palette and it's zoomed in. You can work in one window and observe the changes in the other.

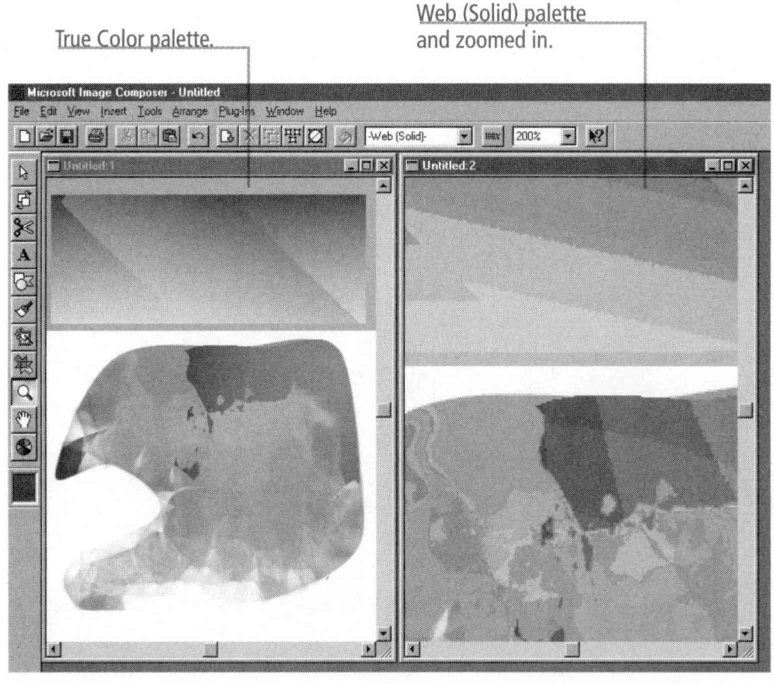

Figure 1-9

Using two views to look at a composition at two zoom levels.

Image Composer's Working Method

Image Composer follows the same basic work method that all Windows programs employ. It's referred to as "Select, Do." You select something, and then you do something to it. In Windows itself, for example, you select files and then drag them to a folder. In Microsoft Word, you select text and then format it. In Image Composer, you select a sprite and then modify it.

To show you this, we'd like to take you on a very brief excursion that will have you create a sprite and then make some quick changes to it.

Shapes button

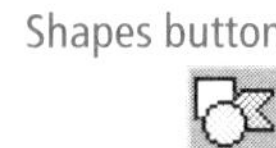

1. To begin, open the Shapes palette by clicking the Shapes button in the Toolbox. The Shapes palette appears, as shown in Figure 1-10.

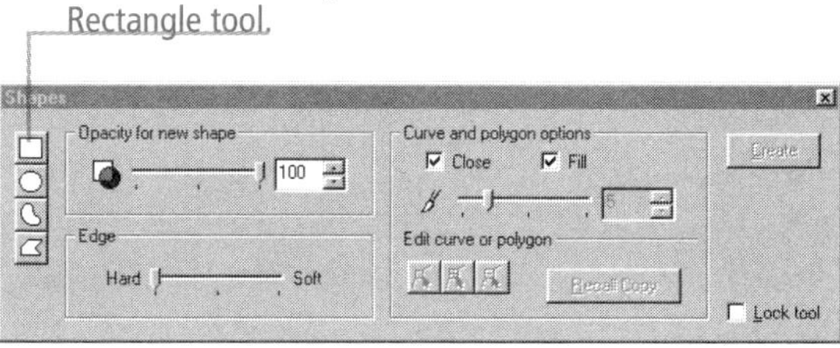

Figure 1-10
The Shapes palette.

2. On the Shapes palette, click the Rectangle tool, the top-most button on the left side of the palette. This tells Image Composer what kind of shape you want to make.
3. Move the mouse pointer onto the Composition Space, press and hold the mouse button, and drag diagonally down and to the right. The outline of a rectangle appears.
4. To set the rectangle in place, release the mouse button, then click the Create button on the Shapes palette. The rectangle appears in the current color, the medium gray you set earlier in this chapter.

   The rectangle sprite you've drawn is selected. The control handles at its sides and corners tell you so. To deselect the rectangle sprite, click elsewhere on the Composition Space or the Workspace.

Now trying modifying the rectangle sprite by changing its color.

5. Click the rectangle sprite to select it. The control handles return.
6. Click the Color Swatch to open the Color Picker.
7. On the color matrix, select a light blue and click OK. This sets the current color to light blue, as shown on the Color Swatch.

Color Fill button

8. Click the Color Fill button on the Toolbar. The selected sprite, the rectangle, fills with the current color, light blue.

A Project-Oriented Approach

Using Image Composer creatively requires more than simply understanding the function of each of the program's tools and effects. Image Composer's comprehensive online help system can give you all the technical information you'd ever want about every setting for each tool. What you will learn in this book, instead, are techniques that you can use in Image Composer to create useful and attractive designs and visual effects. These techniques use combinations of Image Composer tools in creative ways to accomplish particular graphics tasks. You'll find out what you can really do with Image Composer's tools, not just how the individual tools work.

The best way to demonstrate techniques is within the context of projects. These projects set out typical goals for graphics projects, such as creating a set of onscreen elements for a Web site home page. They show both an approach and a set of techniques you can use to fulfill those goals.

The first projects explore basic concepts and demonstrate the most fundamental tools and techniques. They also employ a set of effective working methods you can use while creating your compositions. Later projects in the book build on the concepts and techniques you learn early on, and tackle more complex design challenges and real-world scenarios. They also demonstrate how to use tools and effects together in a truly synergistic relationship.

The fundamentals you'll learn are making shapes, transferring properties among sprites through mapping, using the alpha channel for transparency mapping, using the Cutout tools to extract pieces of images to use in compositions, applying effects effectively, and creating collage effects by composing pieces of several images.

Although we know that the essence of using a graphics tool is to create a design, we also know that the topics of design and designing cannot be the subject of this book. During the course of the projects, we will instruct you to choose colors, create shapes, and modify sprites in ways that we know will produce effects that either demonstrate a technique or create a harmonious design. Whenever possible, we will explain the graphic decisions we've made, but many simply grew from experimentation, from hours of exploring the possibilities, and settling on one permutation among many possibilities that we found worked well.

We ask you to go with us for the ride. Try our suggestions and see the results we found. Along the way, you'll learn to master the tools and you'll become prepared for your own explorations.

What You Will Need

To use Image Composer effectively, you'll need to have a few things:

Image Composer 1.5: You'll find a trial version of Image Composer 1.5 on the Official Image Composer Book CD-ROM that is included with this book. You'll also find the full version of Image Composer 1.5 on the FrontPage 98 CD-ROM. An earlier version of Image Composer, Version 1.0, is available in FrontPage 97, but you'll notice a number of differences in the user interface and you won't find the new features of Image Composer 1.5.

24-bit graphics card: We assume that you have a graphics card capable of displaying 24-bit color at a minimum screen resolution of 800 x 600. If your graphics card will handle it, run your graphics system at 24-bit color and use a high resolution, such as 1024 x 768 or 1280 x 1024. This will offer you additional screen space on which to work.

At least 16 megabytes of memory: 16 megabytes is a practical minimum for using Image Composer. On Windows 95, 32 megabytes is much faster. On Windows NT, 64 megabytes is even better. Don't even shy away from considering 128 megabytes. When it comes to graphics, you can never have enough memory and hard disk space.

Familiarity with basic Windows operation and conventions: We assume you know how to use the mouse to do things like click and drag, and how to use Windows 95 toolbars, dialog boxes, and drop-down menus.

Small Fonts: To reproduce the results you'll see in the book's projects exactly, you must have Small Fonts set in your system's Display Properties, not Large Fonts. To check the current setting, open the Control Panel and choose Display. The Font Size setting is on the Settings tab of the Display Properties dialog box.

Hard Disk Maintenance: It is a good idea to defragment your hard disk regularly. If you don't know how to do that, look in your Windows documentation or online help. Also, keep plenty of space free on your hard disk with which Image Composer can work when your image files become larger than the amount of available memory. 100 megabytes of free space is a reasonable minimum amount.

You're Ready to Begin

You are now ready to begin working on projects. Each project walks you through step-by-step procedures to achieve a goal. If you are a beginning computer graphics artist, working through the projects will help you to use Image Composer to create graphics that you might never have thought you could create. If you are an intermediate or advanced user, the projects will demonstrate Image Composer's unique tools and techniques and point you in the direction of fruitful exploration.

Have fun.

About Anti-Aliasing

If you look closely at the edges of curves, lines, and especially text in Image Composer, you'll notice that they are smoothed with a technique called anti-aliasing. Anti-aliasing adds semi-transparent pixels to the edges of an object or a text character to create a cleaner looking edge. Anti-aliasing, called Smoothing in Image Composer, is necessary when the resolution of an image is not high enough to allow smooth-looking edges. Without anti-aliasing, the edges of text look jagged or stairstepped, as you can see in Figure 1-11.

Smoothing is turned on by default when you create text. To turn it off, clear the Smoothing checkbox on the Text palette before typing text onto a composition.

Figure 1-11
Text with Smoothing on (top) and turned off (bottom).

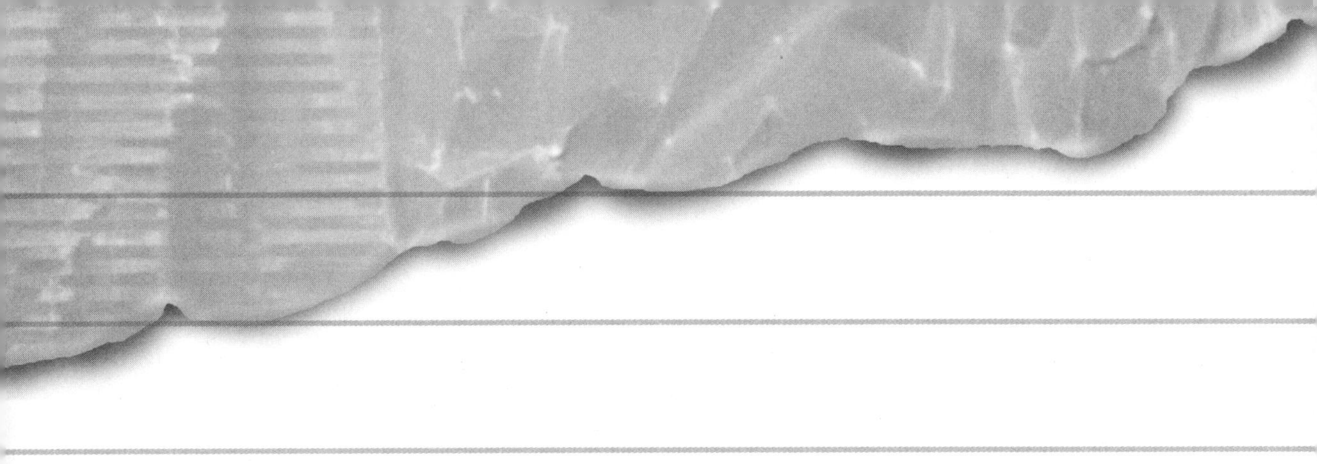

CHAPTER 2

Button Boogie: Web Buttons, Bullets, and Rules

Your hands-on learning begins here. In this overview chapter you will learn a set of basic Image Composer working techniques by creating some generic graphic elements. In later, project-oriented chapters, you will focus more closely on particular aspects of Image Composer, and you will work toward specific goals, such as the design of a Web site.

In this chapter, you use the Button Wizard and the Shape tools to create some of the fundamental elements common to most Web pages—buttons, bullets, and rules. As you work, you also get the chance to try out several other tools located on the Arrange, Texture Transfer, and Effects palettes. You'll see that working on any composition in Image Composer requires borrowing tools from many different palettes and using them in combination.

Making Buttons with the Button Wizard

So many people have used Image Composer to create so many buttons that the program now gives you a special wizard just for making Web page buttons. The Button Wizard guides you step-by-step through the button-making process, asking for the information it needs along the way, and delivering just the buttons you want in the form of ready-to-use sprites.

If the Button Wizard can't give you exactly what you need, you can also make buttons from scratch, as you will see later in this chapter, in the section named "Building Buttons from Scratch."

Preparing an Image for the Button Face

When the Button Wizard creates a button, it asks for text or an image to put on the button face and it sizes the button to fit the text or image you provide. So, before you start the Button Wizard, you should have the text or image you need ready and the image needs to be saved in a file.

Here's how you can quickly create a bitmap file to have on hand when you begin making a button. Try these steps:

1. Begin a new Image Composer composition by choosing New from the File menu.

Color Swatch

2. Click the Color Swatch on the Toolbox to choose a color. On the True Color tab of the Color Picker Dialog box, you can choose a color by pointing to it on the color matrix or by entering the exact numbers that will make up the color.
3. If it is not already selected, click RGB for the Color Model on the True Color Tab.
4. Set Red to 96, Green to 70, and Blue to 214, and click OK to see the blue you've chosen appear in the Color Swatch.

Shapes button

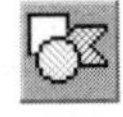

5. Click the Shapes button on the Toolbox to open the Shapes palette, and select the Oval tool on the Shapes palette. Leave the other settings as they are.

Oval tool

Take a look at the indicators at the right end of the status bar, which reads "Nothing selected" until you select a sprite or begin drawing.

When drawing an object, you can tell its size by watching the status bar, which shows the X and Y position of the spot at which you clicked the mouse pointer, and the width and height of the sprite you are making, as shown in Figure 2.1. The last X and Y numbers indicate the exact mouse pointer position at all times.

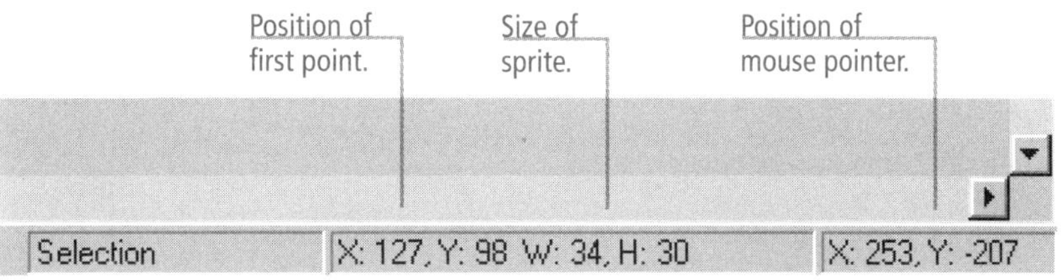

Figure 2-1
The indicators on the status bar.

6. Place the mouse pointer in the middle of the Composition Space, the area within the Image Composer window.
7. Hold down the Shift key while holding down the mouse button, and drag the mouse pointer in any direction to draw a circle that is 25 pixels across. When the circle is the correct size, release the mouse button and the Shift key.

If you have trouble sizing the circle exactly, you can gain finer control by clicking the Zoom tool on the Toolbox and then clicking a spot on the Composition Space. To zoom back out, click the Zoom tool, hold down the Ctrl key and click again on the same spot on the Composition Space.

8. Click Create. A blue circle appears and it's surrounded by a bounding box that has arrows on each side and at each corner. The first X, Y indicator on the status bar identifies the position of the upper left corner of this bounding box relative to the upper left corner of the Composition Space.

To constrain rectangles and ovals to exact squares and circles, press and hold down the Shift key as you draw.

9. Choose Save Selection As from the File menu to begin saving the image.

10. On the Saves the Current Selection dialog box, make sure Keep Transparency is checked so that the bounding box around the circle doesn't fill with color.
11. Make sure the Save As Type setting is TIFF (*.tif,*.tiff) and enter the file name BLUDOT.
12. Check to see where you are saving the file (you'll need to retrieve it soon), and click Save.

Now, create a red dot TIF file, too, by following these steps:

1. Click the Color Swatch again and choose these colors: Red 255, Green 0, and Blue 0.
2. Click OK to close the Color Picker dialog box.
3. Click the Color Fill button on the toolbar to apply the new color to the circle.
4. Choose Save Selection As again from the File menu, use the same settings as earlier, and save the file with the name REDDOT.

Color Fill button

You have now created a pair of button decals that you will place on the faces of buttons in the next section.

Using the Button Wizard

Unlike many other tools in Image Composer, the Button Wizard doesn't have its own toolbar icon or Toolbox button. To start the Button Wizard, choose Button from the Insert menu. The Wizard opens and offers a menu of button styles, as shown in Figure 2-2.

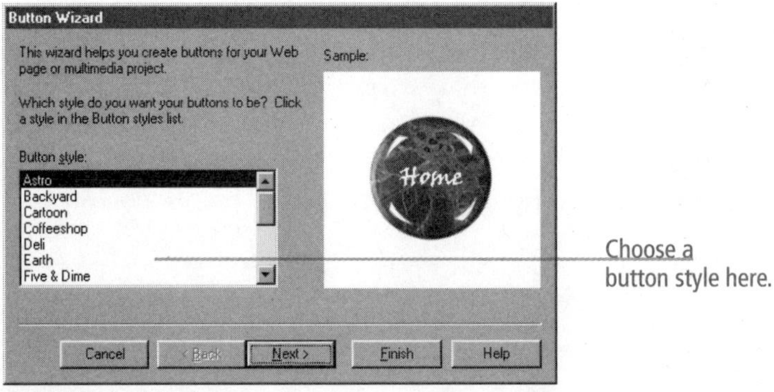

Figure 2-2

The first page of the Button Wizard.

In general, to use wizards like the Button Wizard, you make a choice or two on each wizard page and then turn to the next page by clicking Next. To back up one step, you click Back. After you click Finish on the last page, the button you have created appears on the Composition Space.

To try out the Button Wizard, follow these steps:

1. Start a new Image Composer composition without saving the changes you made to the first file.
2. Open the Button Wizard by choosing Button from the Insert menu.
3. On the first page of the Button Wizard, choose Astro from the list of button styles and click Next.
4. On the second page of The Button Wizard, shown in Figure 2-3, enter the number 3 to create three buttons, and then click Next. By making a full set of buttons, you can easily give them the same look.

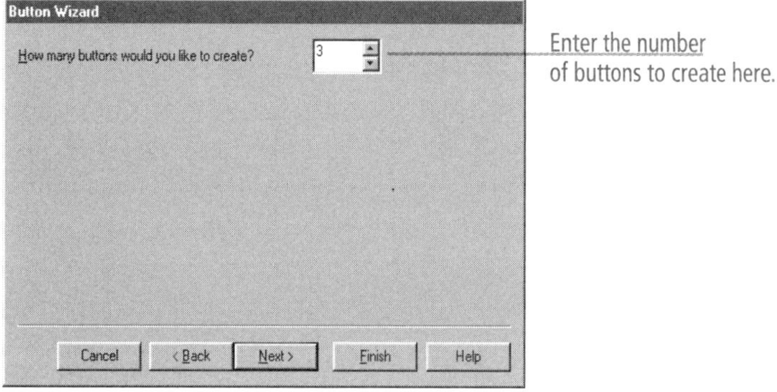

Figure 2-3
The second page of the Button Wizard.

The third page of the Button Wizard, shown in Figure 2-4 on the next page, asks for the text and images to place on the first button. After you enter information for the first button, this page will return to solicit information for each button you've requested.

5. For the first button, enter "First" in the text label box and click the Image checkbox to choose an image for the button face decal.
6. Click Browse to locate BLUDOT.TIF, the file that you created earlier.

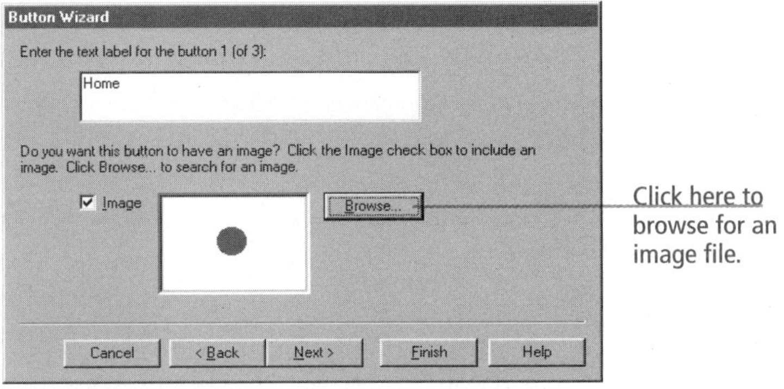

Figure 2-4
The third page of the Button Wizard.

7. When you locate BLUDOT.TIF, double-click it to return to the Button Wizard, and then click Next.
8. For the second button, enter "Second" as the text label and choose the same image file, BLUDOT.TIF, for the image. Click Next to go on to the third button.
9. Enter "Third" as the text label for the last button and choose the REDDOT.TIF file you created. Click Next once again.

   On the last page of the Button Wizard, shown in Figure 2-5, the Button Wizard now wants to know how large to make your buttons. The default choice, Exact Fit For Each Button, makes each button just large enough to fit its own text label or image, but for now, go ahead and make them the same size.
10. Click Same Size For All Buttons to make all the buttons the size of the largest button. To see this size, click Size Preview.

That's it. You've supplied all the information the Button Wizard needs, so click Finish and then Finish again at the last screen to see the final product, a pile of button sprites one on top of the other. You'll see only the top sprite, but you can separate the pile by clicking anywhere away from them, and then clicking the topmost sprite and dragging it away from the pile.

Notice that all three buttons are sized to fit the largest text and image, just as you requested. To learn how the size of the image you choose for a button will directly affect the size of a button, try making a few images like REDDOT, but at larger sizes, such as 35 by 35 and 45 by 45 pixels square.

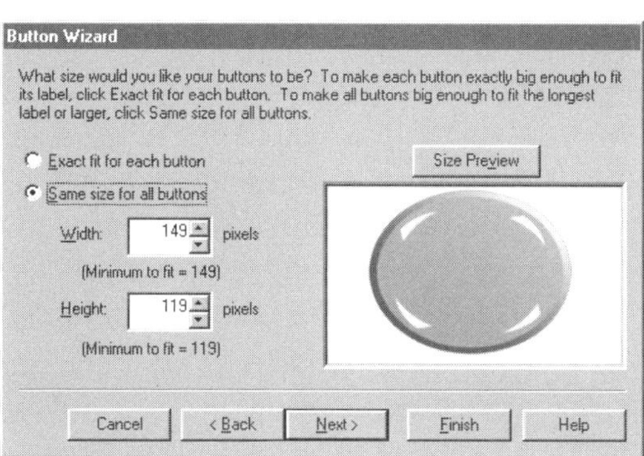

Figure 2-5
The last page of the Button Wizard.

Here's something to take note of because it's so central to the power of Image Composer. Notice how the surface of the button shows through all around the circular shape of the blue and red dots? That's because all the pixels in the REDDOT and BLUDOT sprites that aren't red or blue are transparent. It's this transparency (provided by something called the alpha channel) that will make it so easy to compose parts of photos together and create tons of additional special effects.

Planning Bitmap Images for Buttons

When you plan the size of buttons and other graphic elements for the limited space of a Web page, first consider the minimum text that can appear on each element. This produces the smallest elements and tells you whether there's room left over with which to make the design more interesting. It also helps you decide whether you can create single screens of information or whether you need to create scrolling pages or frames.

If your design for the Web page requires images on buttons, you might want to make up a few in advance to see how the images will affect the size of the buttons. This will let you know whether your design concept will work.

Using the Save For The Web Wizard

Now that your buttons are done, you can take advantage of another wizard, the Save For The Web Wizard, which saves single sprites or arrangements of multiple sprites as GIF files that Web browsers can display. To try the Save For The Web Wizard, follow these steps:

1. Select the three buttons you've just created by Shift-clicking them (holding down the Shift key and clicking each button), and choose Save For The Web from the File menu.
2. Click The Selected Sprite Or Group on the first wizard page and click Next.
3. On the next Wizard page, which asks how to handle transparent areas, choose Let The Web Page Background Show Through, and click Next.

   On the third Wizard page, you can specify a solid color that matches the background color of the Web page. This blends the sprite edges with the background color so that the sprites look natural on the page.
4. For this example, click Color, choose any color with the Color Picker (normally you'd choose the same color as the Web page background), click OK to return to the Wizard, and click Next.
5. The final Wizard page provides a summary of your choices. Click Save to create the GIF file.

If your Web page background uses a tiled bitmap, you might consider selecting the color that is most prevalent in the bitmap and specifying it here as though it's the Web page background's solid color. This will help the button blend with the surrounding tiles.

Refining with the Button Editor

After making basic buttons with the Button Wizard, you can refine them in the Button Editor, which gives you much more flexibility in designing exactly the button styles you'd like. The Button Editor lets you change your mind and choose a different overall button style. But it also lets you make a handful of fine-tuning adjustments; you can change the button shape, apply a different texture to the surface, or even change the apparent light source direction, which determines how the button is shaded.

To open the Button Editor, select a button and choose Button from the Edit menu. The Button Editor dialog box opens, as shown in Figure 2-6.

You can also right-click a button and choose Edit Button from the shortcut menu.

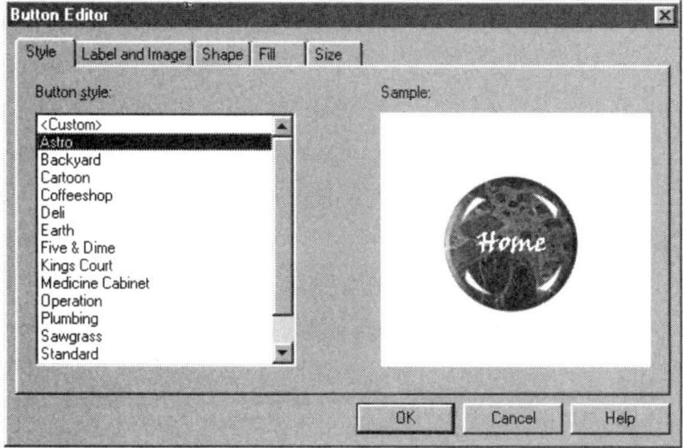

Figure 2-6
The Button Editor.

On the Style tab of the Button Editor dialog box, you can choose a different preset style, or you can change settings on the other four tabs. The Label and Image tab allows you to change the text font, the label text, the button face image, and the alignment of items on the button face.

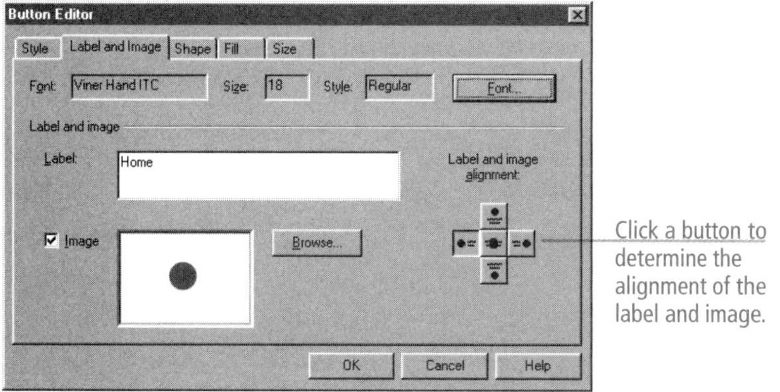

Figure 2-7
The Label and Image tab of the Button Editor.

The Shape tab of the Button Editor dialog box lets you choose a direction from which the button appears to be lit. The Fill and Size tabs enable you to change the button surface and size.

Building Buttons from Scratch

Although the Button Wizard produces truly sensational buttons in an incredible array of shapes and styles, it's still limited to its built-in palette of designs. For unusual or unique shapes, such as the shape of a company logo, you'll still have to construct buttons from scratch, building them piece by piece. This section covers building buttons from the ground up, too, so you'll be prepared for any button-making challenge thrown your way. The button projects that follow will also help you to become familiar with more Image Composer tools and basic image construction techniques.

Setting the Size of the Composition Space

Although some people will view your Web pages at higher resolutions, a Web page size of 640 by 480 pixels is the least common denominator for which you should plan. Taking into account the screen space occupied by the browser software, 605 by 330 is an ideal size for the Composition Space. This leaves enough room on the page for scroll bars and other interface items.

To set this size for your Web page compositions, choose Composition Setup from the File menu. Then, on the New Composition Defaults tab, set the width to 605 and the height to 330, as shown in Figure 2-8. Click OK to exit and save these settings.

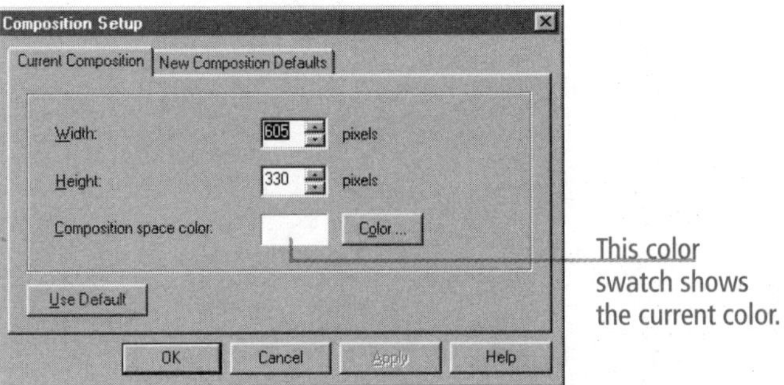

Figure 2-8
The Composition Setup dialog box.

From the File menu, choose New. If you are asked whether to save the changes you've made, click No. The new Composition Space is now the shape and usable size of a browser screen on a machine running at 640 by 480 screen resolution. To confirm this, place the mouse pointer at the lower right corner of the Composition Space and check the status bar. For the projects in this book, you will use this new size as the default Composition Space size unless a specific project calls for a different size.

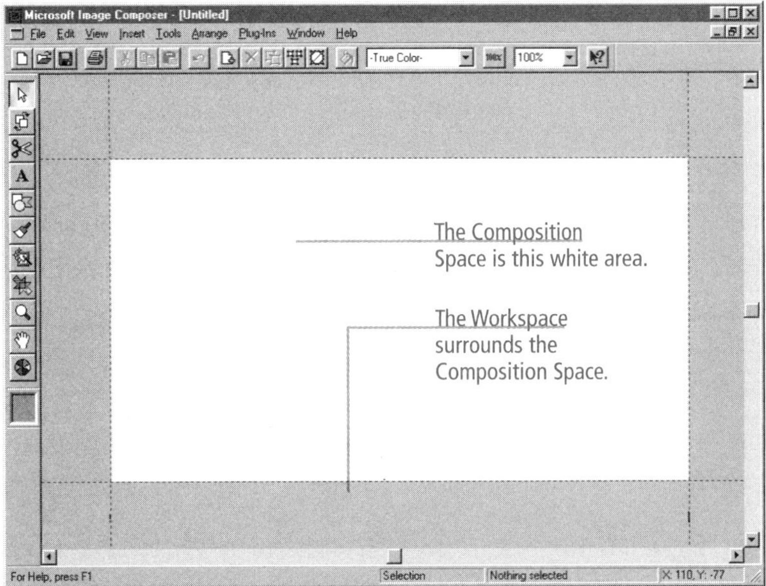

Figure 2-9
The Composition Space.

Recording What Works

As you experiment with design ideas, you might want to stop and take notes when a particular venture works out well. You can always save the end product of a successful experiment as a sprite, but you can't capture the successful sequence of steps that led to that end product without recording them manually somehow. The tried-and-true method is to write down what you've done on paper, while it's still fresh in your mind.

Starting the Button

You'll begin your exploration by creating the button face.

1. Click the Color Swatch, and then, on the True Color tab of the Color Picker dialog box, make sure RGB is selected

rather than HSV. RGB will be the default throughout the book. Set Red to 100, Green to 100, and Blue to 100.

Color Swatch

Shapes button

Rectangle tool

2. Click the Shapes button on the Toolbox.
3. Click the Rectangle tool on the Shapes palette and then draw a rectangle in the Composition Space that is W=130, H=40 in size. Remember to check the W and H indicators in the status bar for those numbers.
4. Click Create on the Shapes palette. A gray rectangle appears.
5. Click the Color Swatch and set the current color to Red 153, Green 101, Blue 219. You'll see the new purple color appear next to the old gray color on the color swatch near the top of the Color Picker dialog box.
6. Click the Shapes button on the Toolbox again, select the Rectangle tool on the Shapes palette, and draw a rectangle next to the gray rectangle that is W=120, H=30. Remember to click Create on the Shapes palette.
7. With the purple sprite selected, Shift-click the gray sprite. Then, without the Shift, click the gray sprite again. The gray sprite is now the "source" sprite, so it can pass an attribute to another sprite or it can be used as a reference for another sprite. You can confirm that the gray sprite is the source sprite by examining its handles. Notice that the handles of the gray sprite are solid. The handles of the purple sprite are hollow, instead. Figure 2-10, on the next page, shows the source sprite in two sprite pairs.

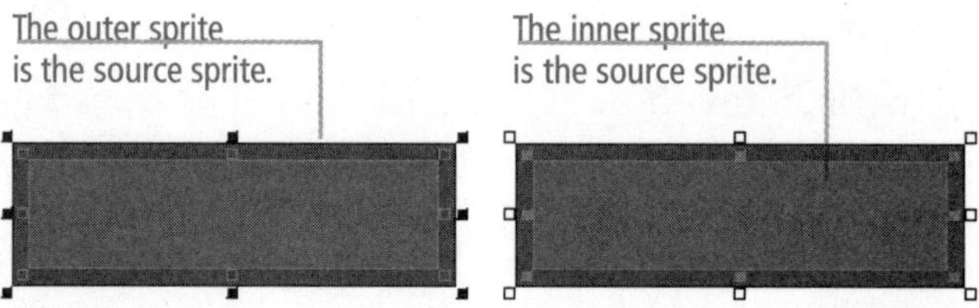

Figure 2-10

The source sprite has filled handles.

Arrange button

Centers Align button

8. Click the Arrange button on the Toolbox to open the Arrange palette.
9. On the Arrange palette, make sure that Relative To Composition Space is unchecked. Click the Centers Align button.

The gray sprite is the source sprite, so the purple sprite becomes centered on it. You can think of it this way: the gray sprite's center attribute has been transferred to the purple sprite.

Zooming In and Out

Now try the Zoom tool to zoom in on your composition.

1. Click the Zoom button on the Toolbox.
2. Place the mouse pointer on the sprites and click.
3. Click again to zoom in closer.

Zoom button

The spot you click with the Zoom tool becomes the center of the zoomed view.

To see the current zoom level, you can check the Zoom Percent control on the toolbar, shown in Figure 2-11. You can also jump directly to a zoom level by clicking the Zoom Percent control and choosing a zoom percentage from the drop-down list. Now try pressing the Ctrl key and clicking to zoom out. Again, the zoomed out view will center on the pointer position.

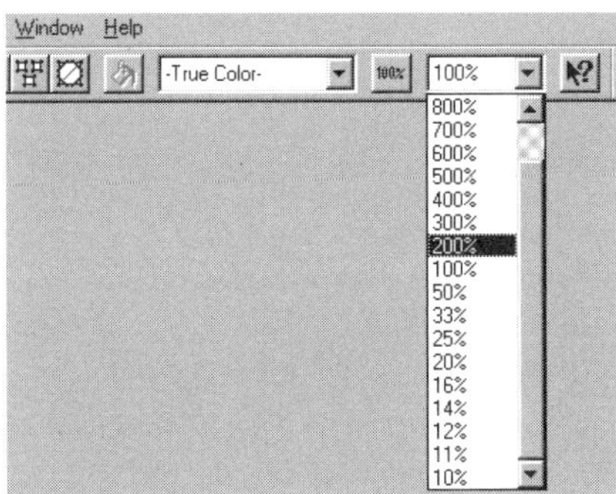

Figure 2-11
The Zoom Percent drop-down list.

To return to 100% zoom, click the 100% button next to the Zoom Percent control on the toolbar.

Setting the Home Position of a Sprite

You'll often find it handy to set the home position of a sprite, because this will establish a position to which you can return the sprite by clicking a single button. You will use home position over and over to do things like position sprites in a particular way or move a sprite away to make modifications to it and then return it to its precise original position. To set the home position of a sprite, follow these steps:

Selection tool

1. Click the Selection tool at the top of the Toolbox and position the pointer slightly above and to the left of the two sprites. Then click and hold the mouse button and drag a selection box around the sprites. Release the mouse button.

2. Drag the two sprites to the approximate center of the Composition Space. You may want to zoom out to accomplish this.

Set Home Position button

3. While the sprites are still selected, click Arrange on the Toolbox and then click Set Home Position on the Arrange palette.

TIP

Home position is the location on the Composition Space to which the sprite's X=0, Y=0 pixel will go if you select the sprite and click Return To Home.

4. Click elsewhere on the Composition Space to deselect all the sprites. Then drag the sprites to another location in the Composition Space.

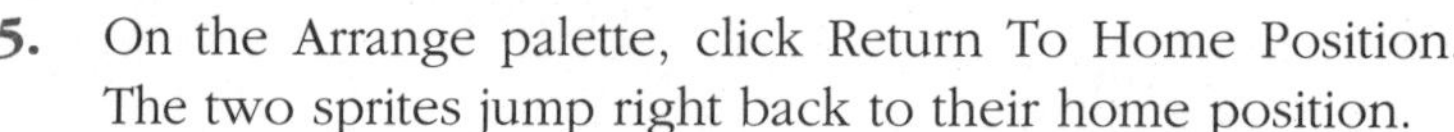

Return To Home Position button

5. On the Arrange palette, click Return To Home Position. The two sprites jump right back to their home position.

TIP

Selecting one or more sprites and pressing Ctrl + Home also sends the sprites to their home position.

Now try one more exploration into home position by following this procedure:

1. Use the Rectangle tool on the Shapes palette to draw a square about 100 pixels across, then right-click the square and click Create.

2. Open the Arrange palette again.
3. Move the new sprite and then click the Return To Home Position button on the Arrange palette. The sprite moves to the upper left corner of the Composition Space.
4. Move the sprite somewhere else on the Composition Space and click Set Home Position on the Arrange palette.
5. Move the sprite once again and click Return To Home Position on the Arrange palette.

You've seen that the initial home position of each new sprite is the upper left corner of the Composition Space until you set a new home position for it. Explore home position a bit more on your own. Try making several sprites, selecting them all, setting their home positions, and moving each one to a different place on the screen. Then select them all and click Return To Home Position.

Locking Sprites in Place

Another useful tool is Lock/Unlock Position, also on the Arrange palette. To see how Lock/Unlock Position can help you avoid moving carefully placed sprites accidentally, try these steps:

1. Delete all sprites except the gray and purple rectangles near the center of the Composition Space.
2. From the File menu, choose Save As, and save the composition with any file name you'd like. The extension .MIC is added automatically.
3. Select the two sprites and click Lock/Unlock Position on the Arrange palette or choose Lock/Unlock Position from the Arrange menu. Try to move the sprites. Notice when you move the pointer over one of these sprites, the pointer displays a small lock icon.
4. Click Lock/Unlock Position again and try to move the sprites.

Lock/Unlock Position button

Creating a 3D Look with a Bevel

A bevel gives a button a raised, three-dimensional look. To see how to create a bevel easily, follow these steps to first create the hollow rectangle:

1. Click Return To Home Position on the Arrange palette to move the sprites back into position.
2. Click anywhere on the Composition Space or the Workspace to deselect all the sprites, and then use the Zoom button on the Toolbox to zoom in on the sprites.

3. Select the gray and purple sprites. Make sure that the purple sprite's control handles are solid so that it is the source sprite. If it is not, click the purple sprite again.

Texture Transfer button

4. Click Texture Transfer on the Toolbox to open the Texture Transfer palette.
5. On the Texture Transfer palette, click Snip.
6. Make sure the Opacity slider at the upper right corner of the Texture Transfer palette is set to 100, and click Apply.
7. Click away from the sprites to deselect them all, and then move the purple sprite next to the gray sprite. Notice that the shape of the small sprite has been removed from the larger sprite and is now transparent. This hollow rectangle is vital to creating the bevel.

Here's a minor digression that will show you the effect of changing the order of sprites that overlap one another. While the purple sprite is selected, try this:

1. Move the purple sprite so it partially overlaps the transparent area of the gray sprite.
2. While the purple sprite is selected, open the Arrange palette and click To Back, as shown in Figure 2-12.

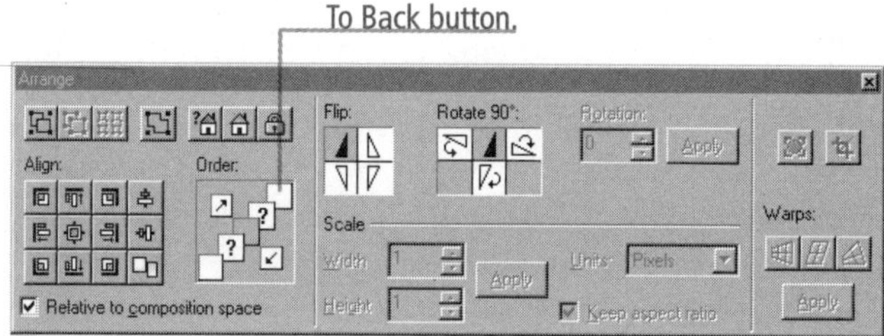

Figure 2-12
Click To Back on the Arrange palette.

The gray sprite now overlaps the purple sprite.

3. Click To Front on the Arrange palette.

Now, carry on by duplicating the sprite. Follow these steps:

Duplicate button

1. Move the purple sprite away from the gray sprite, select the gray sprite, and click Duplicate on the toolbar.
2. Move the copy aside and select the original.

3. Click the Color Tuning button on the Toolbox to open the Color Tuning palette.
4. On the Color Controls tab of the Color Tuning palette, drag the Brightness slider to –60, as shown in Figure 2-13, and click Apply.

Color Tuning button

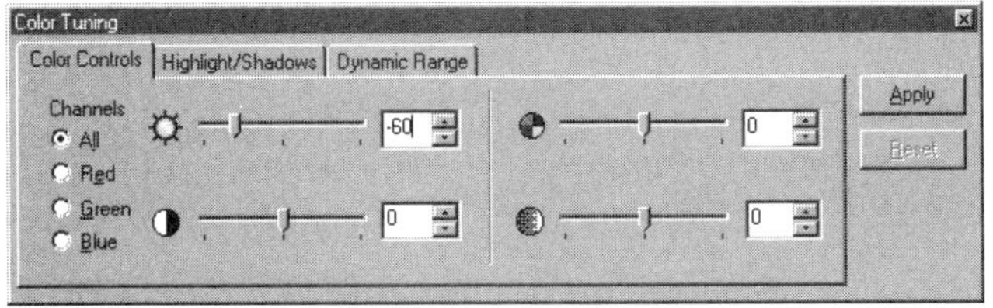

Figure 2-13
The Color Controls tab of the Color Tuning palette.

5. Duplicate this sprite three times and move the copies outside the Composition Space into the Workspace. Zoom out to 100 percent, if necessary.
6. Move the remaining dark sprite near the left or right edge of the Composition Space.
7. Select the original, lighter gray rectangle sprite, open the Arrange palette and click Return To Home Position.
8. Open the Color Tuning palette, set the Brightness slider to 60 and click Apply. The sprite becomes lighter gray.
9. Duplicate this sprite three times and move the copies onto the Workspace.

TIP: Making copies of sprites as you work through a project builds a small library of spare parts that are specific to your project.

Creating the Shadow

Now you are ready to create the unique shadowing effect of the bevel.

1. Use the Zoom tool to zoom in on the light gray sprite to 300 percent, or whatever zoom level makes the rectangle sprite nice and large on your screen.
2. Select the sprite.

You must always select a sprite before you can do something to it. Use the Selection tool to select a sprite.

Cutout button

3. Click Cutout on the Toolbox and select the Polygon tool on the Cutout palette, as shown in Figure 2-14.

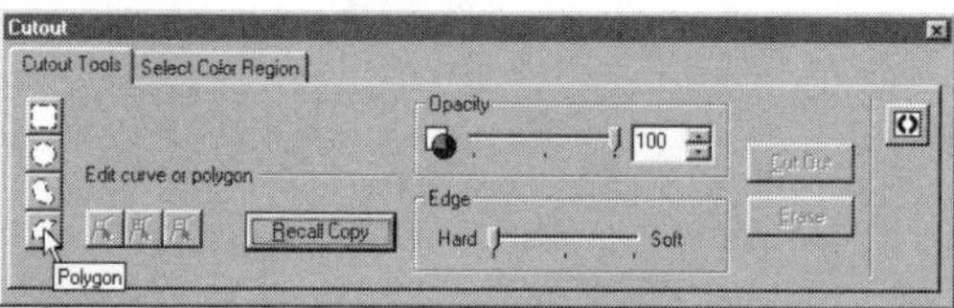

Figure 2-14

Selecting the Polygon tool on the Cutout palette.

4. Use Figure 2-15 as a guide to draw a polygon on top of the gray rectangle. Start by clicking at number 1 and then click at 2, 3, 4, and 5. You want the lines between 1 and 2, and between 3 and 4 to cut directly through the inside and outside corners of the hollow rectangle. If you make a drastic mistake while clicking, don't worry; you can always press Esc and start again.

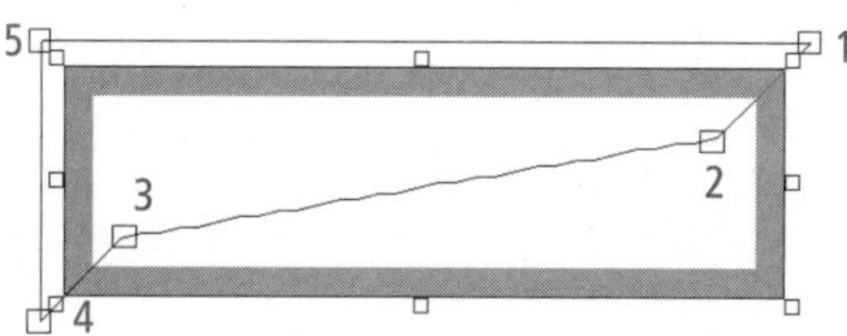

Figure 2-15

Drawing the polygon.

5. Click the Move Points button on the Cutout palette.

   As you move the pointer over the polygon, control points become visible when the pointer comes near. When a control point is visible, you can drag it to adjust the shape of the polygon. Go ahead and adjust the shape of the polygon, if necessary, so it matches the polygon in Figure 2-15.

6. On the Cutout palette, click Cut Out. It won't look like anything has happened, but try deselecting all the sprites, clicking the gray sprite and then dragging it slightly above and to the left of its current position. You will drag away a new sprite. Now you want a lower right sprite.
7. Repeat Steps 1 through 6 above, but use one of the dark gray hollow sprites as the source sprite. This time, drag a polygon which encloses and selects the bottom and right sides only.
8. Move the new sprite near the first sprite you cut out.

Move Points button

Now you can align the two sprites and complete this portion of the exercise by following these steps:

1. Zoom out to 100 percent centered on the middle of the Composition Space. Pressing the Home key will center the Composition Space in the Image Composer window.
2. Move the two sprites you just made near each other and select them both.
3. On the Arrange palette, click the Align button that is labeled Upper-Left Corners. Depending on how precise you were when cutting out the two sprites, the two bevels will jump into position with their upper left corners more or less aligned. You may have to use the arrow keys on one sprite to move it more precisely into position. Remember to deselect all the sprites and re-select the sprite that you want to move.
4. Select both sprites if they are not already selected.
5. Click Set Home Position on the Arrange palette.
6. Duplicate the two sprites by clicking the Duplicate button on the toolbar, and move the copies near the left edge of the Composition Space.

   You will no longer need the upper and lower bevels in two separate sprites, so you can convert them to a single sprite by flattening them.
7. Select the original two bevel sprites and click the Flatten Selection button on the Arrange palette or choose Flatten Selection from the Arrange menu.
8. Zoom in centered on the newly flattened sprite so that it nearly fills the screen.

Flatten Selection button

Light and Dark

Your newly cleaned up bevel sprite is light on the top and left sides, and dark on the bottom and right sides. This visual effect suggests a light source from the upper left shining down and to the right. Although each sprite can have its own light source direction, maintaining a consistent light source on all objects in a composition enhances the feeling that they work together spatially. Of course, there are times when light, as a design element, needs multiple sources for drama or other reasons. The banner in the last project in the book has multiple light sources that enhance the spatial quality of a multi-image composite. However, unless you have a specific reason to use more than one light source, you should keep to a single light source direction to maintain the realism of the final composition.

100% button

It's housecleaning time. Move all the sprites you've made outside the Composition Space except one of the purple buttons and the new beveled sprite. If you only have one purple rectangle, duplicate it and move the copy. You can quickly zoom out to see the entire Workspace and Composition Space by clicking the 100% button on the toolbar.

Creating the Button Edges

The next pieces your button requires are a pair of edges to define the button face and the button base. First, though, you'll arrange the pieces you've already created.

1. Select the purple button face and move it to the center of the Composition Space.
2. Center the bevel on the purple button face.
3. With the bevel still selected, click the To Back button on the Arrange palette and then use the arrow keys on the keyboard to fine-tune its position. After you click To Back, you may need to click elsewhere to deselect all the sprites and then select the bevel again before you can move it with the arrow keys.
4. Now select the bevel and purple button face sprites, move them all to the center of the Composition Space, and set their home position.
5. Click the Composition Space to deselect all the sprites, select the purple sprite, and then duplicate it.

6. Drag the duplicate purple sprite down below the composite sprite so you can work on it separately later.

Now you're ready to begin enhancing the button edges. You'll want to create a rectangular outline that is one pixel smaller all around than the button face. In other words, you will end up seeing one pixel of the button face showing all around the rectangle you've drawn.

1. Zoom to 400 percent centered on the purple and bevel sprites, or as high as your screen resolution will allow.
2. Use the Color Swatch to set the current color to Red 199, Green 247, and Blue 255. You'll get a light blue.
3. Click the Rectangle tool on the Shapes palette and draw a rectangle near the purple rectangle that is exactly 118 pixels wide and 28 pixels tall.
4. Right-click the rectangle outline and choose Create from the shortcut menu.

   Now move the rectangle on top of the button and create the outline.

5. With the new rectangle selected, Shift-click the purple sprite that is on top of the composite sprite. Then click it again without Shift. The purple rectangle is now the Source sprite.
6. Click the Align Centers button with Relative To Composition Space unchecked on the Arrange palette. This centers the light blue sprite on top of the composite button sprite.
7. Click elsewhere in the Composition Space to deselect the purple sprite, and then select and set the home position of the light blue sprite.
8. With the light blue sprite still selected, click the Effects button on the Toolbox.

9. On the Effects palette choose Edge Only from the scrollable display of effects.
10. On the Details tab of the Effects dialog box, set Thickness to 1 and use the Color Picker that is on this tab (not the main Color Picker on the Toolbox) to set the color to the same light blue: Red 199, Green 247, Blue 255.
11. Click Apply on the Effects palette.

    You now have a single-pixel line whose corners are still transparent. You need to fix that.

Over button

1. Zoom in to any corner of the line sprite, click the Paint button on the Toolbox, and set the tools on the Paint palette to match those shown in Figure 2-16. Make sure the Over button is selected. It enables you to paint on transparent pixels.

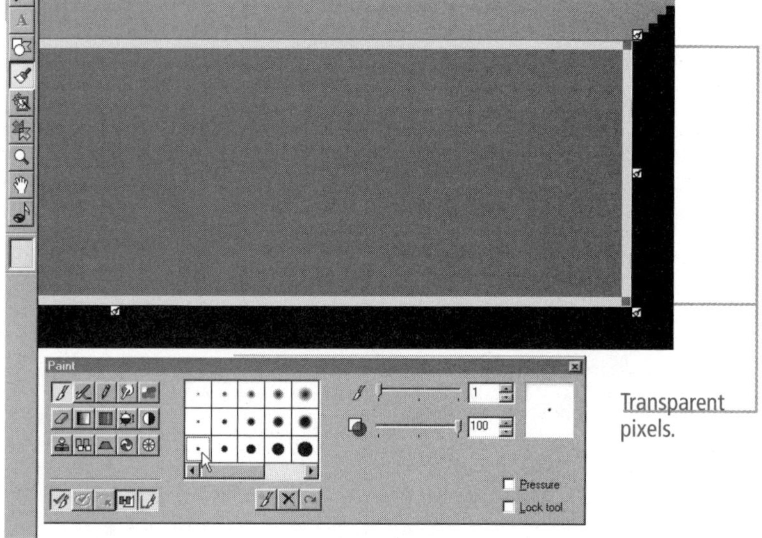

Figure 2-16
Duplicate these Paint palette settings.

Pan tool

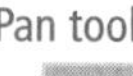

2. With the Paintbrush tool, paint each corner pixel of the line sprite by clicking it. While you're so closely zoomed in, you can use the Pan tool to drag the other side of the button into view by clicking the Pan button on the Toolbox, placing the pointer on the composition, and dragging the pointer left or right while holding down the mouse button.
3. Zoom out to 100 percent and save the file.

The next task is to create the edge for the button base.

1. Drag one of the dark gray rectangle sprites onto the Composition Space near the composite button.
2. With the dark gray rectangle still selected, click the Effects button and click Edge Only on the Effects palette.
3. On the Details tab of the Effects palette, set the current color to Red 199, Green 0, Blue 28, and click Apply.

4. Send this new, red sprite to the back and then move it onto the composite button and center it so it fits all around. You need to send it to the back because each new sprite that you create goes on top of sprites that are already present. In other words, each new sprite automatically becomes the front sprite in the Z order, and is on top of all the other sprites.
5. Paint the corner pixels of the red outline as you did with the light blue line sprite, but use 199, 0, 28 as the color by clicking the main Color Swatch again. Figure 2-17 shows the current composition.

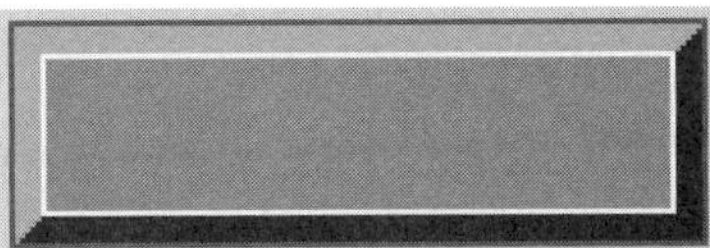

Figure 2-17
The current composite button sprite.

Now you've built all the basic elements for a button, so zoom out to 100 percent and move any unused sprites outside the Composition Space and onto the Workspace, except for the purple rectangle. Tidy them up a bit, if necessary, and save the file.

Enhancing the Buttons You Have Built

A gradient is a color wash, a gradual transition from one color to another. Image Composer's gradients can span four different colors. Of course, not every gradient requires four colors, but Image Composer gradients give you the power to create subtle lighting effects.

Applying a gradient to just about any surface can give the illusion of light striking the surface from an angle. Applying such a gradient to a button face makes the button look more realistic, natural, and most important, three-dimensional. Depending on the direction of the light, the button face can be made to appear hollowed out (concave) or protruding (convex). To try applying a gradient to the button face, follow these steps:

1. Select all the sprites of the composite button by drawing a selection rectangle around them with the Selection tool. Then duplicate them and drag the duplicate button a little to the left of the original. Deselect all the sprites.

2. Zoom in on the duplicate and select the purple rectangle sprite. To be sure you've selected the purple sprite rather than another in the pile, press one of the arrow keys a few times to move it. You should see the purple sprite shift position. Press the opposite arrow key a few times to move the purple sprite back in place.
3. Open the Effects palette and select Gradient and then click the Details tab on the Effects palette.
4. To create a light-to-dark gray gradient, click each of the four small color swatches surrounding the gradient sample on the Details tab and set their RGB colors according to the settings shown in Figure 2-18. (Set the upper left color to 30, 30, 30, the upper right and lower left colors to 100, 100, 100; and the lower right color to 192, 192, 192.)

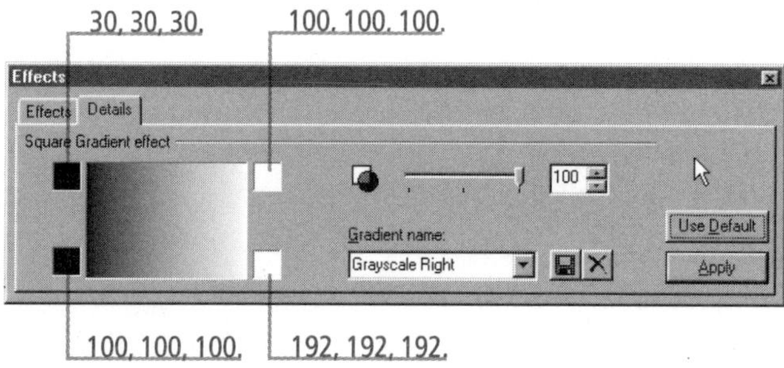

Figure 2-18
The Details tab of the Effects palette.

5. Click the Gradient Name text box and enter "button gray ramp," and then click the small disk icon to save the gradient. By saving a gradient with a name, you create a reusable gradient that can be applied to other sprites. In fact, applying the same gradient to several sprites in a composition can create a uniform lighting effect. This creates continuity that is important for the naturalism of the final piece.
6. Click Apply to apply the gradient to the button face.
7. Select the composite button by drawing a rectangle around it with the Selection tool, and then click the Group button on the Arrange palette. Grouping sprites locks them together into an object that has a single set of selection handles.

Group button

A single grouped object can be easier to work with, easier to move and resize, for example, than multiple objects.

Now you'll duplicate the composite button that has a gradient face, and use color tuning to modify the color of the gradient.

1. Duplicate the composite button and move the copy above the original, and then, with the duplicate still selected, click the Ungroup button on the Arrange palette. Set the home position of the selected sprites in the duplicate after ungrouping.

Ungroup button

2. Click away from the sprites to deselect them, and then select the gradient sprite on the duplicate.
3. Click the Color Tuning button on the Toolbox to open the Color Tuning palette.

Color Tuning button

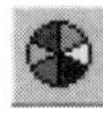

4. On the Highlight/Shadows tab of the Color Tuning palette, make sure Red is selected and use the mouse pointer to drag the three handles along the curve into the configuration shown in Figure 2-19. By dragging these handles, you change the amount of red that is applied to highlighted and shadowed areas within the image.

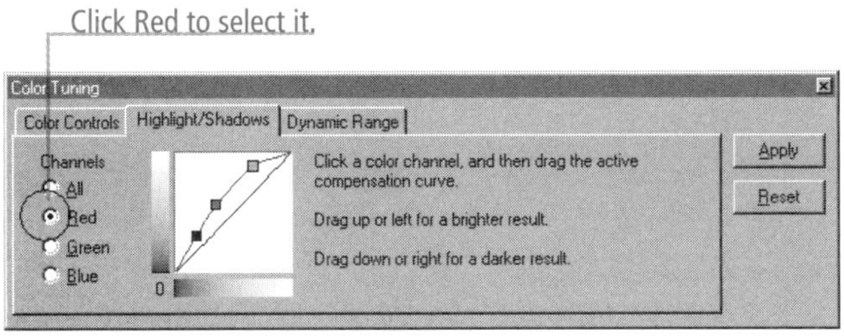

Click Red to select it.

Figure 2-19
The Highlights and Shadows tab of the Color Tuning palette.

5. Click Apply to see the enhanced redness in the image. Then save the file to update it.

Applying a Photo Portion to the Button Face

Even gradient surface buttons are not nearly as interesting as buttons that show a pattern, texture, or photo on their surface. In this procedure, you'll extract a portion of one of the sprites that is provided with Image Composer, and use it to adorn the button face.

1. From the Insert menu, select From File.
2. Open the TUTORIAL folder within the Microsoft Image Composer folder on your system—by default, the Microsoft Image Composer folder is set up within the PROGRAM FILES folder. Select HIBISCUS, and click OK. If the TUTORIAL folder is not present, you can also find HIBISCUS in the PLANTS folder within the PHOTOS folder on the Image Composer CD.
3. Move the hibiscus image onto the Workspace, duplicate it, and move the duplicate beside the original so you can work on the duplicate.
4. Select the copy and drag out its lower right corner handle to stretch the sprite to make it about 50 percent larger in both width and height. Then duplicate the sprite and arrange the original and the duplicate together so one is just a little above the other, as shown in Figure 2-20.

Figure 2-20
Two stretched sprites that have been composed together.

5. Select both sprites and choose Flatten Selection from the Arrange menu to turn them into a single sprite.

Now you'll use the purple rectangle sprite to isolate an area of the image that is sized perfectly for the button face.

1. Duplicate the purple rectangle sprite and move the copy onto the flattened hibiscus sprite to the position shown by the black rectangle in Figure 2-20 above. If the purple rectangle sprite doesn't quite fit inside the hibiscus, stretch the hibiscus sprite a bit more to make room.

2. Deselect all the sprites, and then select the hibiscus sprite and then the rectangle sprite to make the hibiscus sprite the source.
3. Open the Texture Transfer palette and click once on Transfer Shape. You may need to scroll to the right to find it. Transfer Shape transfers the surface of the source sprite onto the shape of the second, selected sprite.
4. Click Apply, deselect all the sprites by clicking elsewhere in the Composition Space, and then move the hibiscus sprite aside. You'll see that the purple sprite now shows an interesting portion of the hibiscus image. Deselect all the sprites.

Now you can place the new sprite with the hibiscus texture on one of the composite buttons.

1. Move the new sprite near the three composite buttons in the Composition Space, and zoom in to 300 percent with the composite buttons centered.
2. Select the sprites of the composite button that has the reddish gray surface, duplicate them, and move the copy above the original on the screen. If the composite is a group (if it has a single set of control handles), ungroup it by clicking Ungroup on the Arrange palette.
3. Move the light blue line sprite and the reddish gray surface sprite off this composite button and drag the new hibiscus button face onto the button in their place. You may need to bring the hibiscus button face to the front by using To Front on the Arrange palette.
4. Finally, save the file to update it.

Adding Text to the Button Face

The crowning touch will be a text label, carefully rendered to fit the button face style.

1. Use the Color Picker to set the current color to Red 108, Green 39, Blue 28 and then click OK and zoom out to 100 percent.

NOTE

The Text tool only works at 100% Zoom.

2. Click the Text button on the Toolbox and draw a text entry box to the right of the button. A text entry box appears and the Text palette opens, as shown in Figure 2-21.

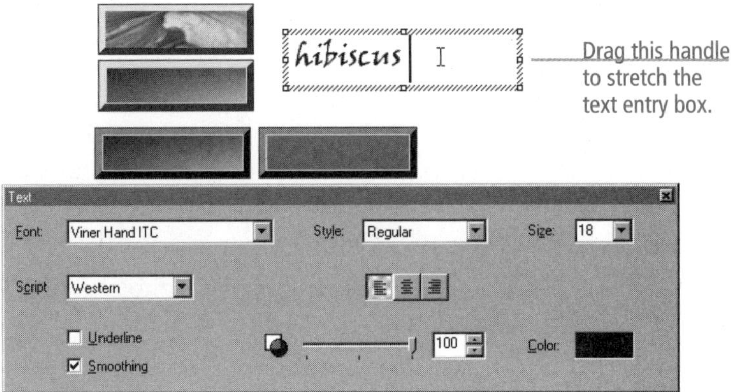

Figure 2-21
A text entry box appears next to the button.

3. On the Text palette, choose Viner Hand ITC for the font, and 18 for the size.
4. Click in the text entry box and type "hibiscus."

While typing in a Text entry box, you may need to widen the box to fit the text. Simply stop typing and stretch the box as wide as you need, and then continue typing.

5. Click elsewhere in the Composition Space to set the text and then zoom in to 300 percent.
6. Select the text sprite, click Set Home Position on the Arrange palette, duplicate the sprite and click Return To Home Position.
7. Select the sprites that are one on top of the other, and choose Flatten Sprites from the Arrange menu. This technique helps counteract the normal text anti-aliasing which softens the edges of text characters. The result is text with sharper edges.

Now apply a gradient and outline to the text.

9. On the Effects palette, select Gradient.
10. On the Details tab, set the two left gradient colors to Red 169, Green 253, Blue 241. Set the two right colors to Red 123, Green 220, Blue 170. Click Apply to apply the gradient to the text.
11. Duplicate the text sprite, move the copy above the original, and select the copy.
12. On the Effects palette, select Drop Shadow as the effect, and set the current color on the Details tab of the Effects palette to Red 117, Green, 0, Blue 21. See Figure 2-22 for the rest of the Drop Shadow effect settings.

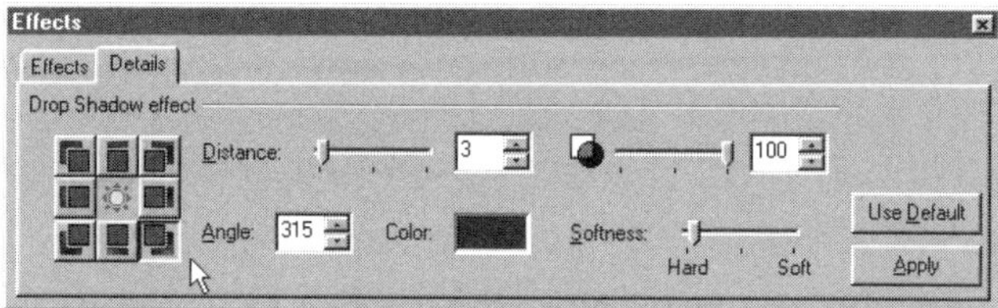

Figure 2-22
Drop shadow settings.

13. Click Apply to apply the drop shadow and use the Pan tool to move the composition over enough to see all of the button that has the hibiscus surface.
14. Move the text onto the button and center it.
15. Set its home position, duplicate it, and send the copy home. Select and flatten the two text sprites. That makes a nice strong text element against the button face image.
16. Finally, with the flattened text still selected, click the Color Tuning button on the Toolbox, and set Saturation to 15 on the Color Controls tab of the Color Tuning palette. This intensifies the color of the text just a bit and makes it easier to read against the colorful button face. Click Apply and zoom out to 100 percent to see the final button.
17. Save the file to update it with the new hibiscus button.

Saturation icon

To summarize this section, you have learned the basic procedures for creating rectangular buttons that have both beveled edges and gradient faces. (You might also try applying a gradient to the beveled edges for a great effect) You extracted a sprite from a photographic image and applied it to the button face, and you used the automatic Drop Shadow effect to give text a raised appearance. You even did a little color tuning to enhance the appearance of the sprites.

Although that's quite a handful of tasks in one exercise, we wanted you to see how you use different palettes of tools in combination to create graphic effects. It's this integrated approach to creating graphics with Image Composer that we hope you will learn in the many projects that will follow.

In the next exercise you will apply the principles you have learned in this chapter to creating shaped buttons.

Creating Shaped Buttons

To create more unusual shapes for buttons, you can use the Curve tool on the Shapes palette. With a few simple steps, as you'll see in this example, you can give curved buttons a bevel too, which will give them the same raised look you've given to rectangular buttons.

To try creating a non-rectangular button, open a new Image Composer file and then set the current color to 80, 150, 220, a middle blue. Then follow these steps:

1. Open the Shapes palette and click the Curve tool.
2. In the Composition Space, click a spot to create the first control point for the curve.
3. Use Figure 2-23 as a guide and move your way around the shape shown in the figure, clicking at each black dot to produce a control point.

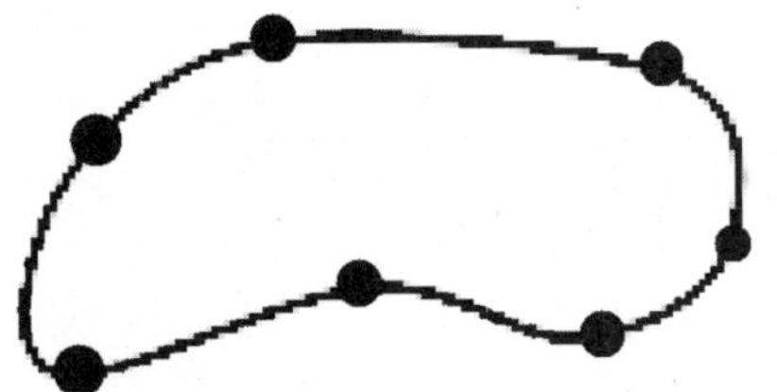

Figure 2-23
Click at the black dots to draw this curve.

As you make the shape, you will see only an outline, not the filled shape. To fine tune the outline, right-click it and choose Move Points from the shortcut menu. As you move the pointer onto the outline, the nearest control point appears. Drag the control point into position and then move to the next control point along the outline.

4. When you are satisfied with the shape, right-click the outline and choose Create. A blue shape appears.

Adding Bevels to the Button

To create the bevels for the edge of the irregular shape, follow these steps:

1. Click anywhere in the Composition Space to deselect all the sprites.
2. On the Shapes palette, click Recall Copy. A curve with the same control points as the original appears over the blue shape. Move Points is activated, as you can see by positioning the pointer on the new curve.
3. Move the control points to create the shape in Figure 2-24.

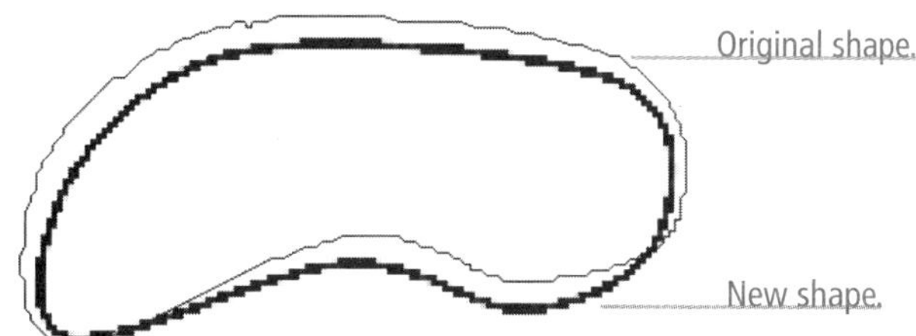

Figure 2-24
Move the control points of the copy to create this shape.

1. Right-click and choose Create from the shortcut menu.
2. Move the sprite off to the side.
3. On the Shapes palette, click Recall Copy again. A copy of the most recent curve you created appears.
4. Move its control points to create the shape in Figure 2-25.

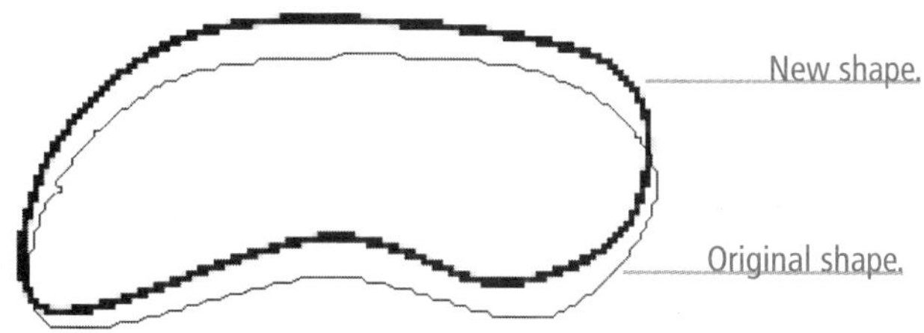

Figure 2-25
Move the control points of the second copy to create this shape.

5. Move this shape to the side also, below the second shape.

Now you can give the bevels their proper colors and move them into position.

1. Set the current color to 179, 195, 236, and then select the upper of the two new sprites and click Color Fill on the toolbar to change it to a lighter blue.
2. Set the current color to 53, 53, 204, and then select the lower sprite and click Color Fill to give it a darker blue.
3. Move the bevel shapes near the original sprite and send them to the back by clicking To Back on the Arrange palette.
4. Position the light blue shape so it extends a little above and to the left of the original. You can use the arrow keys to fine tune the placement of the sprite.
5. Position the darker blue shape so it extends a little below and to the right of the original. Figure 2-26 shows the button with the two bevels in place and a gradient applied to the button face for a little extra dimensionality.

The final tasks are to group the shaped sprite, clean up the Composition Space, and save your file.

Figure 2-26
The completed non-rectangular button.

Creating Bullets and Rules

On Web pages, bullets call out items of interest and rules separate functional areas. In this exercise, you will create a few bullets and rules to get a sense of the possibilities.

Creating a Gradient Rule

To create a basic gradient rule, try these steps:

1. Create a rectangle that is 230 pixels wide by 100 pixels tall.
2. Choose Gradient from the Effects palette, and on the Details tab, set the two left colors of the gradient to 43, 0, 195. Set the two right colors to 0, 156, 39. Click Apply, and set the home position of the sprite.
3. Duplicate the sprite, select the duplicate, and click Flip Horizontally on the Arrange palette.
4. Drag the copy to the right of the original.
5. Select both sprites and with Relative To Composition Space turned off, click Align Tops on the Arrange palette. Then click Align Touch Edges, also on the Arrange palette. The two sprites should now be side by side with their edges touching, blue on the outside and green in the middle.
6. Select both sprites, flatten them, duplicate the flattened sprite, and put the copy aside temporarily on the Workspace.

   Now you will reduce this large sprite to a thin rule.

1. Select the original, flattened sprite and make sure Keep Aspect Ratio is unchecked on the Arrange palette.
2. Set the Width to 415 and the Height to 20 in the Scale section of the Arrange palette, and click Apply.
3. Duplicate the resulting sprite and set aside the copy.
4. Scale the 415 by 20 sprite down to 320 by 6.

Adding Transparency to the Rule

You now have a standard, two-color gradient rule. You can make it a bit more interesting by adding transparency to the ends of the rule.

1. Draw a 75 by 75 pixel square.
2. On the Effects palette, select Gradient again and then select Grayscale Right from the list of gradients on the Details tab.
3. Send the square to the back and move it over the left side of the blue-green rule that you just created.
4. Roughly line up the left ends of the square and the rule and then move the square one or two pixels to the left. A pixel or two of black should extend beyond the rule.
5. Select both sprites and click the square to make it the source.

6. On the Texture Transfer palette, select Map Transparency and click Apply. The left end of the rule is now transparent, becoming opaque toward the center.
7. Use Flip Horizontally to flip over the square and then position it at the right end of the rule. Use Map Transparency again to add transparency to the right end of the rule.

Creating a Tapered Rule

In addition to giving a rule a gradient and transparency, you can taper the end of a rule to a point. Here's what you do:

1. Duplicate the original, flattened sprite that you put aside and move the duplicate onto the Composition Space.
2. On the Cutout palette, click the Oval tool, and draw a 400 by 90-pixel oval centered on the blue-green sprite. You can drag the control point at the center of the oval to center the oval exactly on the blue-green sprite.
3. Click Cut Out on the Cutout palette and then drag the newly created oval sprite aside.
4. Duplicate the oval and move the copy onto the Workspace. Move the rectangle sprite onto the Workspace, too.

To make a pointed rule, you must start with a small oval. You created a larger oval to start in order to have a nice gradient.

1. Scale the oval down to 230 by 20 pixels using the Scale control on the Arrange palette to make it wide and flat. (Make sure Keep Aspect Ratio is unchecked).
2. Scale the oval back up to 300 by 7 pixels. This scaling from small height to large width creates the point.

Here are some permutations you might want to try on your own: start with different sized ovals to see the variety you can create; apply transparency to the pointed ends; start with a gradient that runs from top to bottom rather than left to right.

Making 3D Bullets

Here's a quick and easy procedure for creating a neat 3D bullet.

1. Draw a pair of circles. Make one 20 pixels in diameter and the second 30 pixels in diameter. It doesn't matter what color you use. Remember to hold down the Shift key while using the Oval tool on the Shapes palette to create a perfect circle.

2. Apply a Grayscale Left gradient to the large circle and a Grayscale Right gradient to the smaller circle.
3. Select each circle, enter 45 in the Rotation control on the Arrange palette, and click Apply. The large circle is light at the upper left. The small circle is dark at the upper left.
4. With the small circle selected, Shift-click the large circle.
5. On the Arrange palette, make sure Relative To Composition Space is unchecked and click the Align Centers button. The circles are centered one on top of the other.
6. Select them both, flatten them, and zoom out to see them.
7. Move the blue-green rectangle onto the Composition Space and move the bullet onto the blue portion of the rectangle.
8. On the Color Tuning palette click the Highlight/Shadows tab.
9. Click the Blue Channels button and then drag the three boxes on the curve to adjust it to the shape shown in Figure 2-28.
10. Click the Green Channels button and adjust the green curve to the shape shown in Figure 2-28. Click Apply.

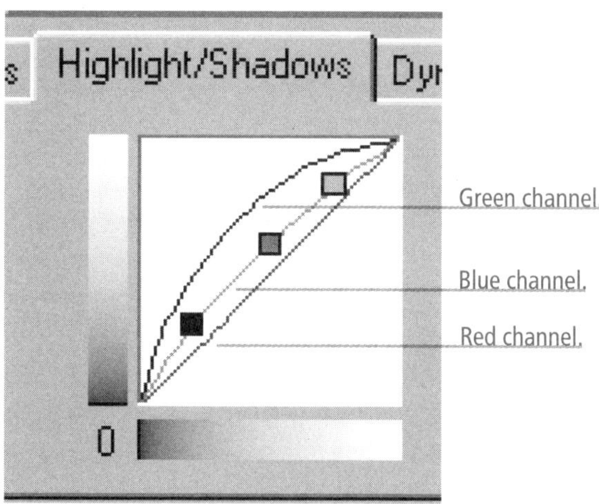

Figure 2-28.
The Highlight/Shadows control on the Color Tuning palette.

The button now has a diagonal dark to light blue-green gradient.

In the next chapter, you will have the chance to explore more thoroughly some of the techniques you've tried here: you will use shapes to create a set of elements for a Web page.

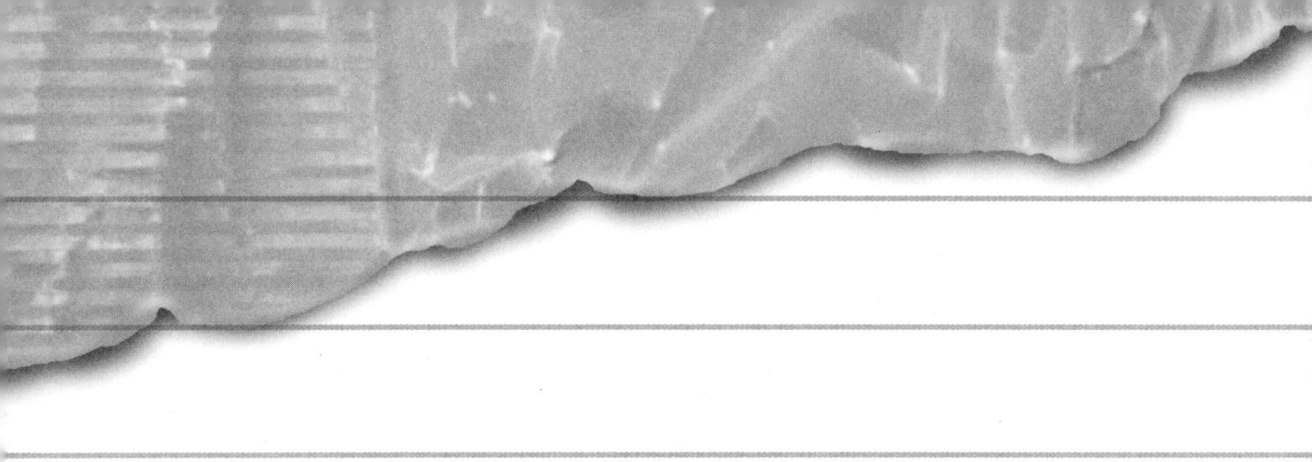

3
CHAPTER

Rolling Your Own: Drawing Shapes and Making Them Work Together

Much of the work that you will do in Image Composer will focus on manipulating images and composing photos and portions of photos into compositions. For this, you will use scanned photos or stock images tiat you've acquired from a variety of sources. But Image Composer also allows you to draw a basic set of shapes from scratch. You can use these shapes to help apply effects to other sprites, or you can employ them as basic elements within compositions.

In this chapter, you will create an end product, a Web site design, that begins with a few basic shapes as its essential building blocks. Along the way, you will get the chance to create shapes, modify their basic attributes, and apply techniques that combine them in particular ways to produce interesting and helpful results, such as a subtle, but useful, three-dimensional effect.

About the Project: A Web Page Design with Non-Rectangular Shapes

For this project, you will design the look of an imaginary Web site "Shape World," which uses non-rectangular shapes to define its banner and navigation areas and controls. For a sneak peek at the final result, choose From File from the Insert menu and insert the file CHAPTER3.TIF from the PROJECTS folder of the CD-ROM. After you've taken a look, move the image out onto the Workspace, away from the Composition Space so that you have plenty of room in which to work.

On many Web pages, the banner area crosses the top of the page and holds a logo and a set of buttons that lead to the primary sections of the Web site. The navigation area runs down the left side of the page and holds another set of buttons for navigating the current section within the site.

Defining the Banner and Navigation Areas

Before you begin working, you can mark off the banner and navigation bar regions for reference. This preliminary layout will give you an idea of how big each shape can be, and how the vertical and horizontal shaped elements relate to each other.

To begin, set the current color to a medium blue-green (0, 133, 140) and draw a large, 605 by 120-pixel rectangle that starts at 0,0 and crosses the entire top of the Composition Space. This gives you enough space in which to place the logo and some navigation aids, and it still leaves enough room for some meaningful content. Don't worry if it's not positioned precisely. You'll fix that in a minute.

To mark off the navigation area on the left, choose a complementary color, such as 130, 240, 240, and draw a rectangle against the left edge of the Composition Space that is 95 pixels wide by 210 pixels high. Position its top edge against the bottom edge of the first sprite.

Upper-Left Corners Align button

Left Sides Align button

To make sure these two rectangles are positioned properly, open the Arrange palette and make sure the Relative To Composition Space check box is selected. Then select the horizontal rectangle and click the Upper-Left Corners Align button. Next, select the vertical rectangle and click the Left Sides Align button.

To position the vertical rectangle neatly below the horizontal rectangle, turn off Relative To Composition Space on the Arrange palette and select both rectangles. Click the horizontal rectangle again to make it the source sprite and click the Touch Edges Align button on the Arrange palette. The vertical rectangle jumps into position so that its edge touches the edge of the source sprite, as shown in Figure 3-1.

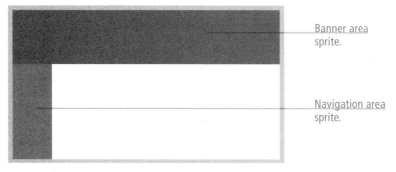

Figure 3-1
A pair of sprites mark off the banner and navigation areas of the Web page.

Select both rectangles and click Lock/Unlock Position on the Arrange palette to prevent them from moving.

You can also right-click a sprite and choose Lock/Unlock Position from the shortcut menu.

Creating Curved Shapes for the Banner and Navigation Areas

Now for the non-rectangular shapes we promised you. First, set the current color to 222, 170, 101, a warm golden-brown tone that contrasts well with the cooler blue-green tone that you will use in the banner area.

Drawing a Curve for the Banner Area

Begin by using the Curve tool on the Shapes palette to click the approximate control points shown in Figure 3-2, on the next page. You don't have to be absolutely precise and you can even use a different number of control points. Just aim for the same general shape, which extends well beyond the edges of the Composition Space to enable the curve to flow smoothly as it passes in and out of the Composition Space. Then click Create on the Shapes palette to convert the outline to the shape.

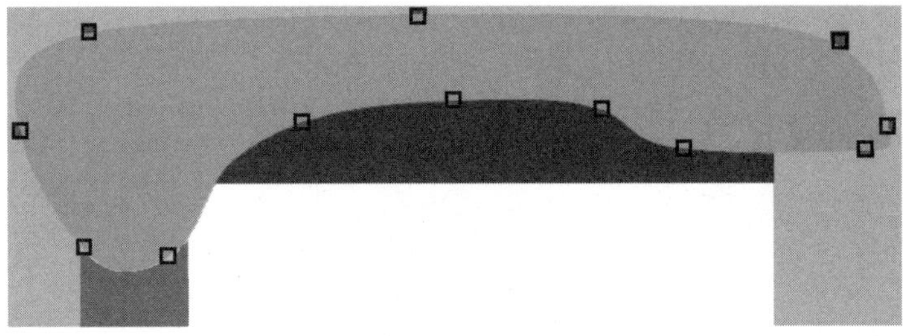

Figure 3-2
The control points for the Banner area curve.

After you click Create to commit the outline of a sprite to a shape, you can no longer change the shape of the object by moving its control points. You can resize it, rotate it, stretch it, and apply effects from here to eternity, but you can't simply reshape it, because its control points are no longer present. What you can do, though, is to move the current copy out of the way and click Recall Copy on the Shapes palette. Go ahead and try it. This brings back the original set of control points to work with. You can then reposition them, right-click and turn on Add Points to add new points, and right-click and turn on Delete Points to delete others before clicking Create again.

Once you have a shape you like, set the home position of the shape before proceeding.

When the control points of a shape are visible, you can position the mouse pointer anywhere on the line and press the "I" key to insert a new point or the "D" key to delete a point.

Cropping the Curve

Although only the areas within the Composition Space will be included when you save the final result to a Web-ready bitmap file, cropping the curve removes the excess areas outside the Composition Space so that you can see exactly how the Web page will look. To crop the curve, right-click it and select Crop from the shortcut menu. Crop is also available on the Arrange palette.

1. Drag the crop handle on the left side of the bounding box containing the shape to the right so it aligns with the left edge of the Composition Space, as shown in Figure 3-3.

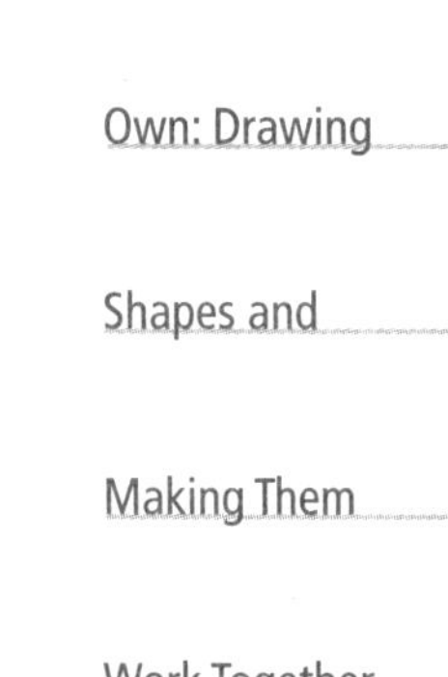

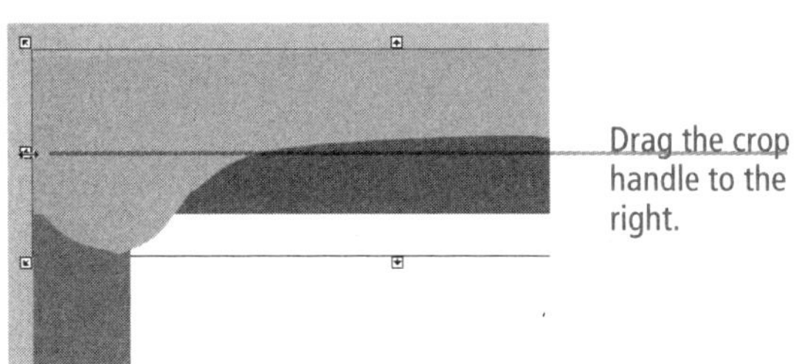
Drag the crop handle to the right.

Figure 3-3
Cropping the left edge of the top sprite.

2. Drag the right crop handle to the left so it aligns with the right edge of the Composition Space. While dragging the right crop handle, watch the status bar to see the sprite's size. Stop dragging when the size of this sprite is 605 pixels wide, the width of the Web page.

If the sprite is not quite lined up with the Composition Space, you can use the Align tools to align the sprite with the upper left or right corner of the Composition Space. This ensures that the sprite is the proper size and shape.

1. Drag the top crop handle down far enough so you can see the top of the Composition Space, and then drag the handle back up again to align it with the top of the Composition Space.
2. Click the Selection button on the Toolbox and click on the Workspace, away from any of the sprites, to deselect the curved golden sprite.

You want to crop the bottom edge of the curve, too, but here's a different way to do it that gives you a lot more precision.

1. Draw a rectangle across the lower portion of the Composition Space that is wide enough to extend out onto the Workspace on the right and left. The rectangle should also be tall enough to cover the bottom of the curved golden sprite that extends below the blue-green sprite.
2. Shift-click the blue-green, horizontal rectangle to select it, too, and then click the blue-green rectangle again to make it the source sprite.

3. On the Arrange palette, make sure Relative To Composition Space is turned off and click the Touch Edges button.
4. Click elsewhere to deselect both sprites.

When a composition becomes complex with lots of sprites, you may want to use a contrasting color to differentiate sprites used just for snipping.

Now you can use the rectangle to snip the bottom edge of the curved golden sprite.

5. Click the rectangle sprite and Shift-click the curved sprite. The rectangle sprite should be the source sprite.
6. On the Texture Transfer palette, select Snip, and set the Opacity to 100.
7. Click Apply to snip away part of the curved sprite. You can deselect all the sprites and then delete the rectangle sprite to see the result. Your Composition Space should now look something like Figure 3-4. Set the sprite's home position.

Whenever you change the shape or size of a sprite with the Crop/Extend tool, you must reset the sprite's home position.

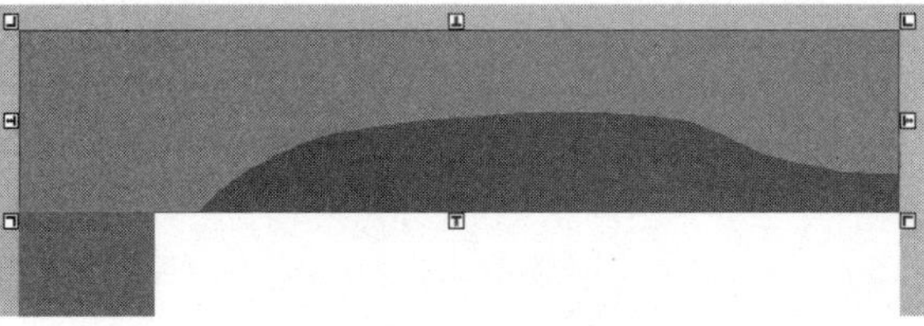

Figure 3-4
The neatly cropped and snipped golden sprite.

Creating the Curve for the Navigation Area

Now that you've got such a lovely, flowing curve for the banner area, you will want to create a complementary shape for the navigation area. In fact, with little effort, you can add a curve to make the navigation area non-rectangular, too.

Later on in the project, you'll need a copy of the original brown, vertical sprite. So duplicate it now and move the copy aside and out of the way.

1. Draw an oval whose right and left sides align with the top corners of the brown, vertical sprite, as shown in Figure 3-5.

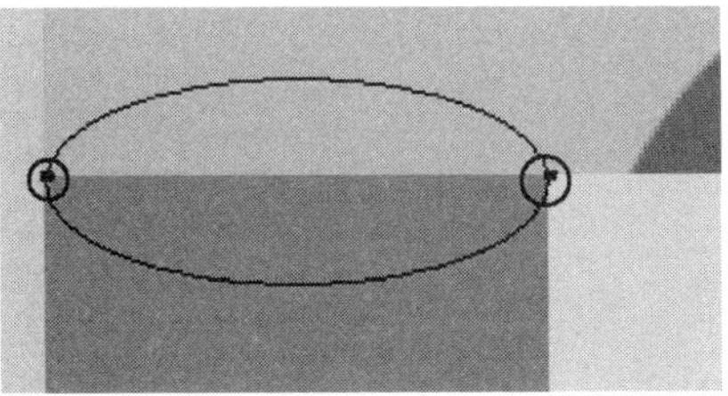

Figure 3-5
Align the left and right control points of the oval with the top corners of the vertical sprite.

2. With the oval sprite still selected, Shift-click the vertical sprite and flatten both sprites into a single sprite. Set the home position of the newly flattened sprite

To flatten selected sprites, you can press Ctrl + F.

Removing the Overlapping Areas

The remaining shape you need is the piece that fits inside the bottom curve of the curved sprite and defines the straight-edge bottom of the banner area and the top edge of the content area. At the moment, the blue-green sprite is filling this position, and rather than use something else, you decide to use it (with a few modifications, of course). So now the areas of the Web page are defined by three sprites: two in the banner area and one in the navigation area.

Before you go on to the next step, you need to cut out any portions of sprites that are overlapped by other sprites. This gives you three sprites that fit together like a jigsaw puzzle and whose edges you can modify to create the final effect.

A side result of performing the cut out is that a thin space will appear between the golden, horizontal sprite and the blue-green horizontal sprite. This space is caused by anti-aliasing that the cut out procedure produces. To eliminate this space, you want to have a copy of the blue-green sprite to place under the banner area later, so duplicate the blue-green sprite now, and put the duplicate aside on the Workspace, alongside the copy of the brown vertical sprite.

To cut out the overlaps, follow these steps:

1. Select the vertical sprite and Shift-click the gold banner area sprite. The vertical sprite should now be the source sprite.
2. On the Texture Transfer palette, use Snip with Opacity set to 100. This cuts the shape of the curve at the top of the vertical sprite from the gold banner area sprite.

   You will be using the blue-green sprite underneath the gold sprite, so you want to snip the same piece from it.
3. Deselect all the sprites and then re-select the vertical sprite and Shift-click the blue-green sprite that is under the horizontal gold sprite.
4. Use Snip again, at an Opacity of 100.

   Now snip the shape of the horizontal golden sprite from the blue-green sprite beneath it.
5. Deselect all the sprites, select the gold banner area sprite again, and Shift-click the blue-green sprite.
6. Use Snip again to cut the shape of the gold banner area sprite from the blue-green sprite.

Fit Bounding Box button

After snipping the sprites, you should select each sprite and click Fit Bounding Box on the Arrange palette. This reduces the bounding box size to the new, outside dimensions of the sprite. You also need to set the home position of each sprite again after fitting its bounding box.

TIP To set the home position of a selected sprite, press Alt + Home on the keyboard.

To see what you've done, unlock the position of the blue-green sprite and drag all the sprites apart, as shown in Figure 3-6. When you click Return To Home Position, the sprites jump neatly back into position.

Figure 3-6
Drag the shapes apart to see how they fit together neatly.

Now would be a good time to save your work, so choose Save As from the File menu, and save everything in an Image Composer file.

Adding Three-Dimensional Effects

The three sprites you've created clearly delineate the areas in which you'll add a logo and navigational controls, but they look flat and uninteresting. To enhance their appearance, you can give them a three-dimensional look by shading their edges with an open curve and a texture transfer procedure.

The open curve you are about to draw will be used to create a shading effect, so it must be a bit darker than the other two sprites.

1. Set the current color to 64, 0, 116—a dark violet.
2. Open the Shapes palette and clear the Close checkbox in the Curve and Polygon Options. You want to draw an open curve.
3. Set Line Width to 20 and drag the Edge slider about a quarter of the way to the right so the line edge has ten pixels of blur. (Five outside the edge of the curve and five inside.)
4. Select the Polygon tool on the Shapes palette.
5. Click a sequence of control points along the top edge of the blue-green sprite, exactly where it meets the curved banner area sprite, as shown in Figure 3-7 on the next page, and click Create.

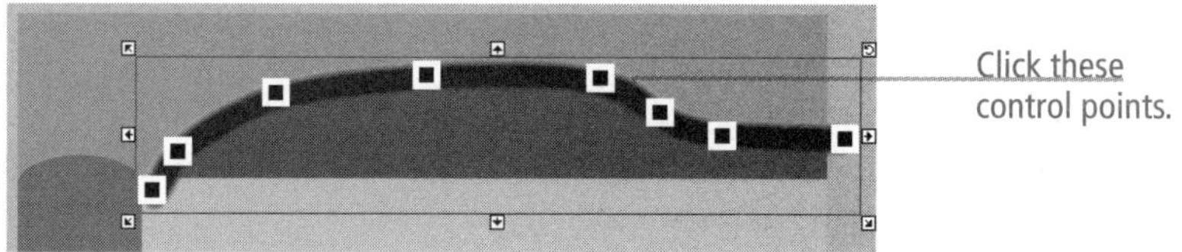
Click these
control points.

Figure 3-7
The curved line with approximate placement of control points.

6. The curve needs to be softer and more subtle, so choose the Blur effect on the Effects palette and apply it to the curve at a setting of 7 (both Horizontal and Vertical) to blur the line.
7. Choose the Transparency effect on the Effects palette and apply it to the curve at a setting of 90 to make the edge more natural. This lets some of the color from the underlying sprites mix with the color of the curve.

About Edges

The Edge control on the Shapes palette allows you to specify the softness of a shape's edge, but it also affects the overall size of a sprite in the process.

Take a look at the three squares shown below with their bounding boxes. All three squares were drawn to be 150 pixels across, but the second and third squares were drawn with the edge slider set 25 percent to the right and 50 percent to the right, respectively.

To soften the edge of a shape, Image Composer creates an opaque to transparent gradient (also called feathering) that crosses the original edge of the sprite. Half of the gradient is inside the original edge and half is outside the edge. As a result, the overall size of the sprite grows, as shown by the position of its bounding box. When the precise size of a sprite is important, you'll want to keep this in mind.

Now you can use this curve to transfer shading to the curved golden-brown and blue-green sprites.

1. Select the curve and Shift-click the horizontal, golden, curved banner area sprite.
2. On the Texture Transfer palette, use Transfer Shape with Opacity set to 100. This transfers the purple of the curve to the curved sprite.
3. Deselect the sprites, select the curve again, and then Shift-click the blue-green sprite.
4. Use Transfer Shape again and move away the curve.

Notice that you see a very thin line of light color between the light-brown sprite and the blue-green sprite. This line is caused by the anti-aliasing that occurred along the edge of the shapes when you cut them out. Here's where you can use the duplicate of the blue-green horizontal sprite that you made a while ago. Select the duplicate on the Workspace and send it home.

To apply the same shading effect to the intersection of the light, golden brown, banner area sprite and the vertical navigation area sprite, repeat the same procedure, drawing an open curve and transferring its shape to both sprites. Refer to the finished piece, if necessary, to see how it should look. The blue-green sprite underneath will take care of the one-pixel problem.

To complete the three-dimensional illusion, you can apply a texture to the blue-green sprite that will make it appear to recede a bit.

1. Select the blue-green sprite, choose Rough Texture from the Effects palette, and set Opacity to 60.
2. Click the Texture Controls button on the Effects palette and then choose these settings: Type=Sandstone, Light position=Bottom Left, Scaling=110, Relief=4 and Invert Texture=on. Click OK, and then click Apply; you will notice the difference immediately.

When you invert the texture, the relative amount of light and dark surface area is weighted toward dark and reinforces the illusion of the sprite receding from the light-brown banner area sprite.

A finishing touch is to lower the saturation and brightness of the blue-green sprite. This serves to add a little more visual separation between the blue-green area and the light-brown sprite. On the Color Controls tab of the Color Tuning palette, set both Saturation and Brightness to –10.

Repeat the Rough Texture and color tuning procedures on the vertical brown sprite.

When you want an area of color to recede visually from another, lower the saturation and brightness.

Before you go on, take a moment to save your work, updating the current Image Composer MIC file.

Adding a Logo

In the next few sets of steps, you'll create a simple but effective logo and set of buttons for the banner area of the page. After that, you'll create the navigation buttons that will appear in the navigation area on the left.

Preparing the Background Shape for the Logo

The logo for the Web site will consist of the Web site name superimposed on an oval graphic element. By using a set of ovals flattened into a single sprite, you will be able to give the logo a three-dimensional effect that suits the effect you applied to the background.

Before you draw the ovals, set the current color to 167, 118, 72, the color of the vertical sprite before it was textured. This darker earth color contrasts nicely with the light brown of the banner area and harmonizes well with the rest of the design. Open the Shapes palette, drag the Edge slider all the way to the left (to Hard), and make sure Close and Fill are checked in the Curve And Polygon Options area of the Shapes palette.

1. Draw a 160 by 50-pixel oval and position it near the upper left corner of the banner area, as shown in Figure 3-8. Set its home position.

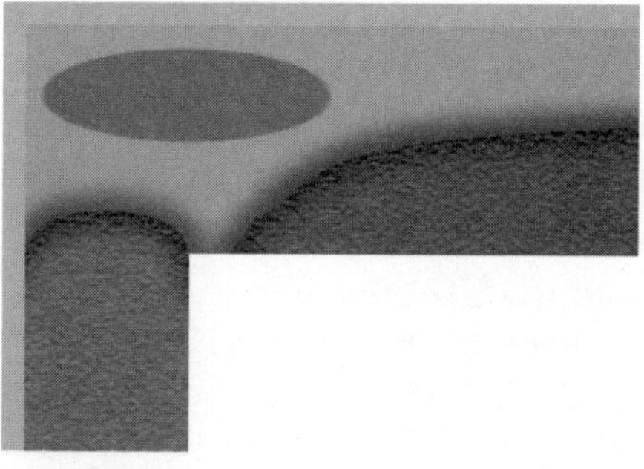

Figure 3-8
Oval in position.

2. Duplicate the oval and leave the original in place to mark the location for later use.
3. Make two copies of the duplicate, and place all three side by side so you can make color changes to them.
4. Apply the same texture that you applied to the blue-green sprite to one of the duplicate ovals. Here are the settings to use on the sprite: Rough Texture: Opacity=60. Texture Controls: Type=Sandstone, Light position=Bottom Left, Scaling=110, Relief=4 and Invert Texture=on.
5. Fill the second oval with 150, 95, 55—a darker brown.
6. Fill the third oval with 140, 85, 55—an even darker brown.

   Now you can use these three ovals to create a shape whose color is lightest at the center and darkest at the outer edges.
7. Select the lightest oval, which is textured, and apply the Bulge effect with Warp Direction set to In.
8. Position this oval over the middle oval and make sure the lighter oval is on top by bringing it to the front, if necessary. Notice that some of the second oval shows through.
9. Select both ovals by drawing a selection box around them and flatten them.
10. Apply the same Bulge effect to the flattened sprites and then make a duplicate and set it aside for the moment.
11. Position the flattened sprites on top of the darkest oval.
12. Select all the sprites and flatten them.

Now turn your attention to the sprite you just put aside, which will become the background for all the other sprites. By using the effect called Recess, you will create a final sprite that seems to sink into the banner sprite.

1. Apply the Recess effect to the sprite you put aside.
2. Position this sprite on top of the placeholder oval you left at the upper left corner of the banner area and set its home position.
3. Move the sprite aside and remove the placeholder, and then send the recessed oval home.
4. With the recessed oval still selected, Shift-click the banner sprite and click it again to make it the source sprite.

5. On the Texture Transfer palette, select Transfer Shape with an Opacity setting of 40. The recessed oval takes on some of the coloring of the banner sprite, so it blends into its background better.
6. Now for the final touch, position the flattened oval on top of the recessed sprite so that the top left and bottom right edges of the recessed oval are still visible, select both sprites, flatten them, and set the home position of the final sprite.

   For a quick check on how the sprites should look, see Figure 3-9.

Figure 3-9
Logo background ready for text.

Adding the Text

The logo text should be easy to read, so you'll use bold text and choose a light color that relates to the blue-green color of the design and also contrasts well against the darker oval background.

Open the Text palette and set the color on the palette to a light blue-green (0, 215, 225). Choose Viner Hand ITC for the font, Bold, 24 points, and set the Opacity to 100. Also, make sure Smoothing is turned on, which causes anti-aliasing to smooth the rounded edges of the characters.

NOTE

For your results to exactly match ours, you must be using Small Fonts as the Font Size in your Windows display settings. To change the Font Size setting, open the Display settings in the Windows Control Panel. The Font Size setting is on the Settings tab of the Display Properties dialog box.

Make two text sprites, "Shape" and "World", and position them as shown in Figure 3-10. Flatten them and set their home position.

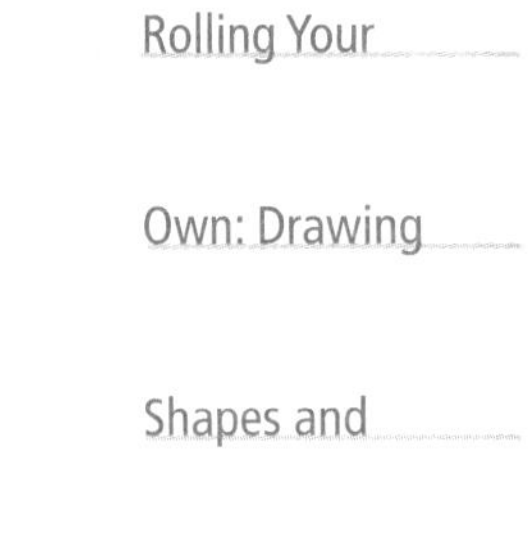

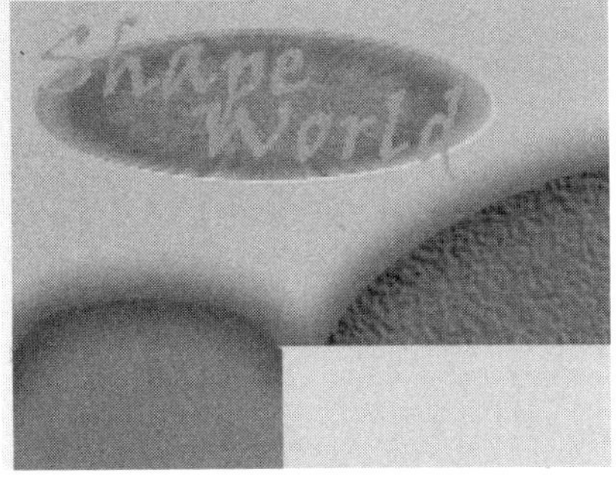

Figure 3-10
Shape World sprites in position.

To offset the text from the background even more, apply the Drop Shadow effect with the settings shown in Figure 3-11 and the color set to 125, 0, 0.

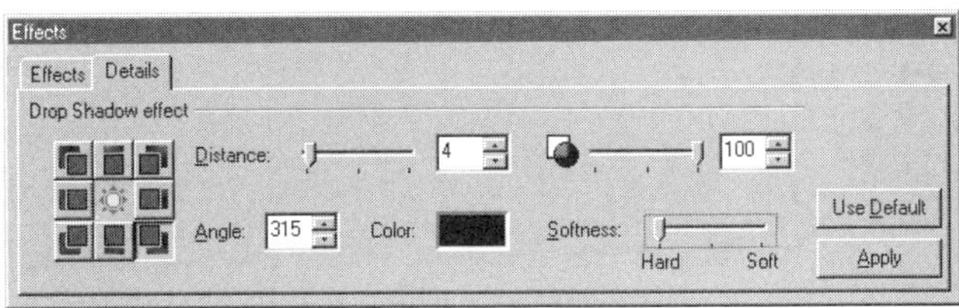

Figure 3-11
Drop Shadow palette setup.

Adding Navigation Buttons

To enable visitors to navigate to the main sections of your Web site, you can now make a set of buttons for the banner area. You have just a few requirements for these buttons: first, you need four of them, but you also want them to fit the blue-green portion of the banner area, and you'd like them to echo the oval shape of the logo. Suppose you experiment with a few oval button sizes and settle on a size of 105 by 40 pixels for each button.

NOTE

Although you want the oval buttons to fit the blue-green area, you also want them to appear to float above it. To achieve this effect, make the ovals somewhat overlap the banner sprite where it meets the blue-green sprite.

Here's how you make the buttons:

1. Set the current color to 0, 64, 117—a dark blue that complements the lighter blue-green.
2. Draw a 105 by 40-pixel oval shape and duplicate it twice.

Press Ctrl + M to apply Color Fill to a selected sprite.

3. Change the color of one duplicate to 55, 0, 105, and change the color of the other to 0, 165, 175. You have created a darker and lighter oval you can use to simulate bevels for the buttons.
4. Send the original dark blue oval to the front.
5. Place the light oval under it and move it two pixels up and to the left.
6. Place the darkest oval under it and move it three pixels down and to the right.
7. Select all the ovals by drawing a selection box around them and flatten them.
8. Finally, duplicate the flattened oval three times and position the duplicates as shown in Figure 3-12.

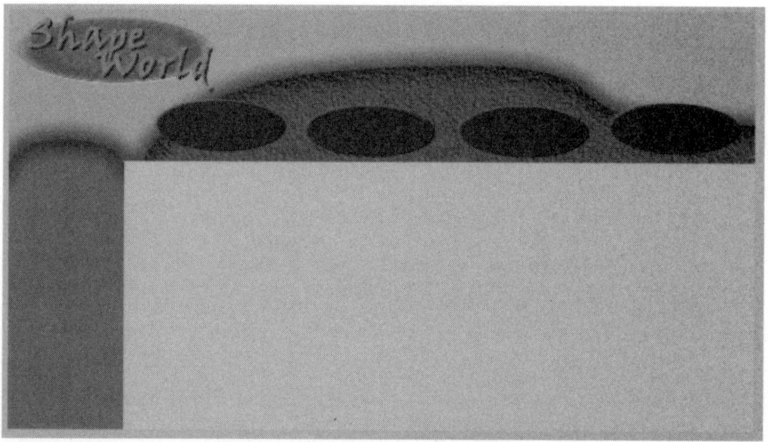

Figure 3-12
Main navigation buttons in position.

9. On the content area of the Web page, make a brown oval (125, 85, 70) that is 90 by 40. This is four pixels wider than the rectangle you will join to it. You want the additional four pixels of size because the outermost pixels of the oval are anti-aliased, making the actual oval look a little smaller.
10. Move the oval onto the navigation area and position it below the top curve, as shown in Figure 3-13, so that you can see the relationship between the oval, the oval logo shape, the oval buttons, the curve of the horizontal sprite, and the upper curve of the vertical sprite.

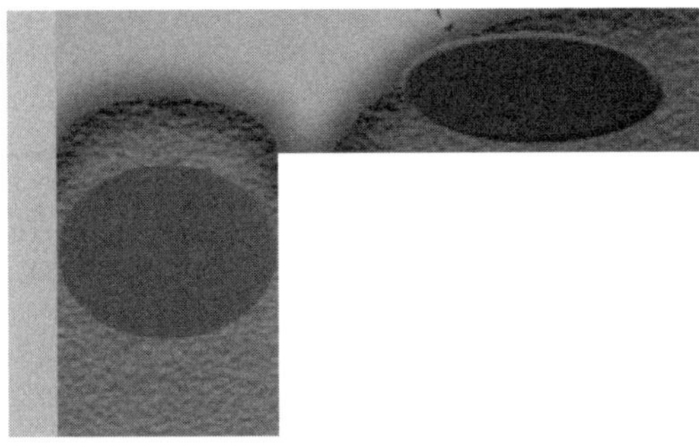

Figure 3-13
The top of the oval closely echoes the curve of the gold sprite.

11. Draw an 86 by 30 rectangle of the same color, duplicate it, and then align the duplicate's top corners inside the oval, as shown in Figure 3-14.

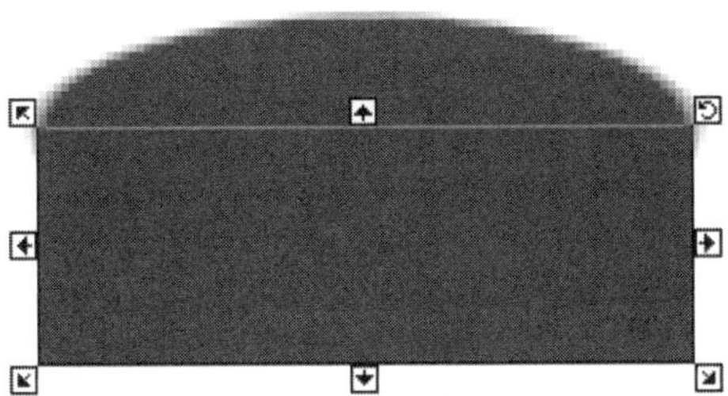

Figure 3-14
Placement of the oval and rectangle sprites.

12. Flatten the two sprites. You should end up with a rectangle that has a curved top.

To create bevels for the button, follow these steps:

1. Make two duplicates of the flattened sprite.
2. Make one duplicate darker (90, 50, 30) and one duplicate lighter (150, 125, 120).
3. Position the lighter duplicate under the brown shape one pixel up and to the left.
4. Position the darker duplicate under the brown shape one pixel down and to the right.
5. Flatten the three sprites and move the newly flattened sprite onto the navigation area, just below the curve at the top.

To create all the rest of the buttons for the navigation area, follow these steps:

1. Select the 86 x 30 rectangle copy you created a few steps earlier and duplicate it two more times.
2. Darken one copy to 90, 50, 30, and lighten the other to 150, 125, 120.
3. As before, place the light copy below the original and move it one pixel up and to the left. Place the dark copy below and move it one pixel down and to the right.
4. Flatten the sprites, duplicate them three times, and position them as shown in Figure 3-15.

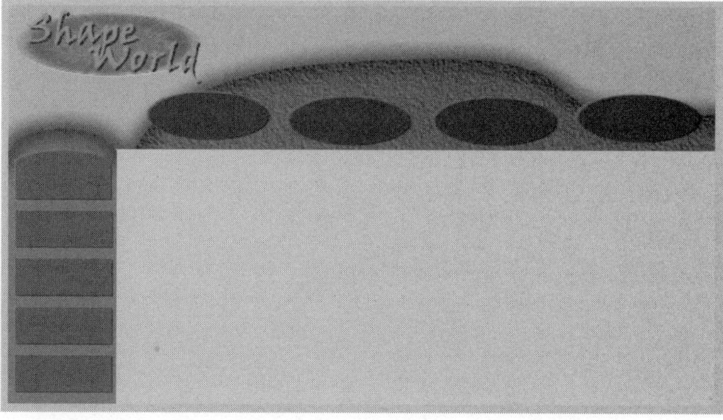

Figure 3-15
The finished shapes for the Web page.

To create a graphics file you can use on a Web page, you could simply save the horizontal and vertical elements you've created with their respective buttons as JPEG files by using the Save As command on the File menu. Before you do, though, you should update the Image Composer MIC file you've been working on all along.

In the next chapter, you will begin to explore working with Photos in Image Composer. You'll learn to do some basic photo retouching as a prelude to sophisticated blending of photos in the chapters that follow.

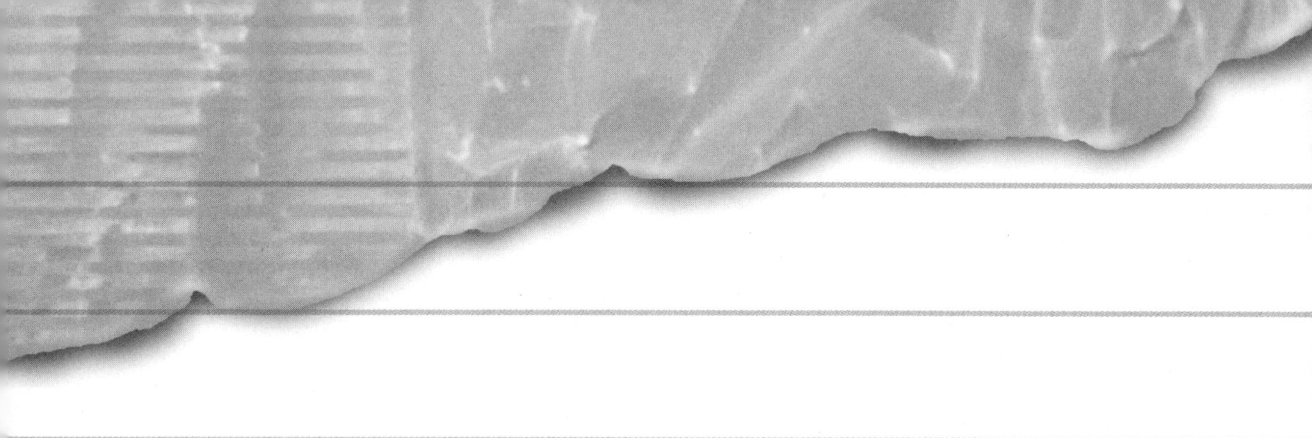

CHAPTER
4

Photo Frenzy: Working with Photographs

You are likely to spend so much time in Image Composer working with photographs that we are devoting an entire chapter to some of the ways you can tailor photos to your designs. In any one project, you're sure to find yourself extracting items from photos, cropping them, retouching flaws, and combining photos seamlessly into primary composition elements or secondary, background elements.

The most abstract, and arguably most difficult, tools to master in any graphics application are those that modify the color qualities of an image, so the projects in this chapter will help to develop your understanding of how Image Composer's color tools work. In later chapters, you will use this knowledge to explore various color tuning techniques in more depth. This introduction will help get you comfortable with the tools you can use to solve basic color tuning problems. Practice what you learn here, and you will develop a feel for how the tools function.

One good way to learn about color tuning tools is to apply them to a collection of images and watch what happens. We've provided an Image Composer file on the CD that contains a number of scans of photos taken by Will Tait that need color tuning. This file is CHAPTER4-1.MIC, in the PROJECTS folder of the CD.

After opening the file, zoom out until you can see all the photos around the Composition Space. These are the original scans; they are similar to what you can expect from scanned photos that were neither shot nor scanned under controlled conditions.

Some of the color tuning changes we suggest make dramatic changes in the images, and some make only subtle, but still important, alterations. We suggest that after trying our color tuning modifications, you apply your own to see the effects of further changes.

Before you begin working on each image, duplicate the image, and move the copy onto the Composition Space, where you can work on it. We'll be starting with the image at the upper left corner and working counterclockwise.

Finding Photos

Image Composer provides all the photo tuning tools you'll want, but where will you get the photos to work with? You can certainly start by browsing the collection of hundreds of photos in ready-to-use sprites that come with the program. You'll also find more than 100 photos taken by Will Tait on the accompanying CD. Then you may need to turn to companies such as PhotoDisc, Time Inc., Corbis, Publisher's Depot, and others. Any of these commercial services would be more than happy to license images to you from their catalogs of millions of thematic and historical images. Although you'll always get a professional-looking photo from an image library, there may be aesthetic modifications you want to make. And don't overlook the images you can produce with your own camera and a few rolls of film. Even an inexpensive camera, local photo processing, and an inexpensive color scanner can give you good quality images. If you recognize deficiencies, you can fix them with Image Composer's photo enhancement features.

A Quick Look at the Color Tuning Controls

You can find all the controls that work with color on the Color Controls tab of the Color Tuning palette. Figure 4-1 shows this tab. The other two tabs, Highlight/Shadows and Dynamic Range, contain controls that allow you to modify the gray levels in images. You'll work with all of these controls in this chapter.

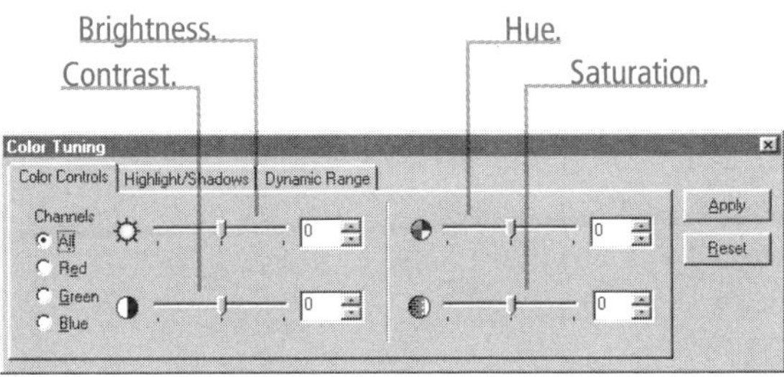

Figure 4-1
The Color Controls tab of the Color Tuning palette.

The Color Tuning palette offers these controls:

- Brightness, the upper left slider, modifies the overall lightness or darkness of all the colors in an image.
- Contrast, the lower left slider, changes the spread between the lightest and darkest values of color in an image.
- Hue, the upper-right slider, moves the pixels of an image around a virtual color wheel.
- Saturation, the lower right slider, controls the purity of a color. Increasing saturation reduces the gray component in the image and makes the colors more intense.

All four controls let you modify all three color channels (Red, Green, and Blue) together, or, by clicking the Red, Green, or Blue button at the left side of the palette, you can change any one channel by itself.

Remember that you must always click Apply after changing a slider to see its effect. Clicking Reset or Undo while color tuning removes all the color tuning changes you have made since your first change, after you opened the Color Tuning palette.

TIP

While a sprite is selected, all the color tuning changes you apply to it are not set in stone until you deselect the sprite or change to a different palette. When you adjust each slider to make a change in the Brightness, Contrast, Hue, or Saturation, Image Composer recalculates the image from scratch each time, so the changes are not cumulative. This gives you plenty of freedom to explore various possibilities without having to undo prior to each adjustment.

Color Tuning the Sample Images

We'll help you analyze each image and come up with the best color tuning fix. But we want you to get a feeling for analyzing images yourself, so we recommend you also explore the tools with some of the images provided on the CD.

Horses at Sunrise

Starting at the upper left corner, the first image is of horses in a sunrise scene in a high mountain meadow. There is frost on the grass and mist rises as the sun warms the ground. Move a copy of this image onto the Composition Space.

Considering the time of day, sunrise, this image appears too light overall. You want to make it darker. Also, with the sun coming up on the right rather than overhead, you might expect to see more contrast between the shadows below the shrubs, in the trees, and in the rest of the image.

Until you become familiar with color tuning, make changes one control at a time. Soon, you will get a feel for it and be able to combine changes by adjusting as many controls as you need, and applying the changes all at once.

1. Select the image and, on the Color Controls tab of the Color Tuning palette, adjust the Brightness slider to –30. Click Apply.
2. Copy the sprite and, with the copy selected, set the contrast slider to 3 and click Apply. Place the two images side by side to see the difference.

   The grass, the horses, and the shrubs become more colorful. Shadows separate from the rest of the image. The mist is more distinct.
3. Save the file, if you'd like, and delete the horse image so that you can move on.

Mountain Lake

Move a copy of the mountain lake image onto the Composition Space. A brief visual analysis tells you that it is too light overall, with the result that there is no detail in the clouds or the snowy regions of the main mountain top. Here's a simple way to get a quick idea of just how light the image is.

1. Use the Pan tool to move the image near the top of your screen.
2. Click the Color Swatch to open the Color Picker, move it away from the image, and activate the Eyedropper.
3. Move the Eyedropper slowly over the upper left corner of the image while observing the RGB numbers on the Color Picker.

   Much of that area registers Red 255, Green 255, and the blue component ranges from a high of 251 down into the 230s. This means that the clouds and snowy parts of the mountain are practically white, or burned out.
4. Now move the Eyedropper to the darkest shadow under the bushes to the left of the lake on the hillside nearest to the viewer. The numbers range in the high 50s to mid 60s. Press Esc to close the Color Picker.

   Lowering the brightness so that there are some black pixels in the shadows would help.
5. On the Color Tuning palette, adjust the Brightness slider to –20, and click Apply.

   The shadows beneath the bushes have turned completely black, but this is bit too dark.
6. Click Undo, change the Brightness slider to –15 and click Apply again.

   That's better. The image has become more colorful and more of its detail appears. The colors could still be stronger, however.
7. Adjust the Saturation slider to 10 and click Apply.

   That's not bad, but the image looks a little out of focus.
8. On the Effects palette, apply the Sharpen Lite effect once.

Now compare the modified image side by side with the original image to see the improvements you have made. Then save the file, if you'd like, or delete the image and move on.

The Cat

Move a copy of the cat image onto the Composition Space. Here's a different method you can use to analyze an image.

1. Open the Color Tuning palette, if it's not already open.
2. With the cat image selected, click the Dynamic Range tab.

   Most of the data in the histogram is clustered just below the mid-point, as shown in Figure 4-2, indicating a lack of light values and little black. We'll explain this further when you correct the next image.

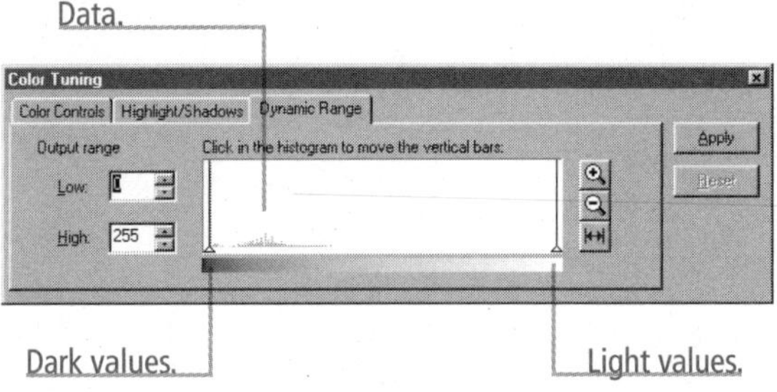

Figure 4-2
Dynamic Range histogram showing data clustered below the mid-point.

3. Click the Auto Fit button, then click Apply.

   The cat looks more vivid, but it still needs more contrast.

4. Click the Color Controls tab and adjust the Contrast slider to 5, and click Apply.

   That's much better. The darks are now truly dark. You can even see the small spot of grease the cat got on its side while climbing under the car during an oil change. But still, the image could be a little sharper.

5. Apply the Sharpen effect twice.

   Here, you have a judgment call. You might like the sharp look, or you might prefer less sharpening. It's up to you. Now delete the image and move on.

The Small Arch

The small arch image next to the cat image will give you another chance to use the Dynamic Range controls.

1. Place a copy of the small arch photo on the Composition Space.
2. Duplicate the copy and then apply the Grayscale effect to it.
3. With the color copy of the arch image selected, open the Dynamic Range tab of the Color Tuning tools. The histogram looks like Figure 4-3.

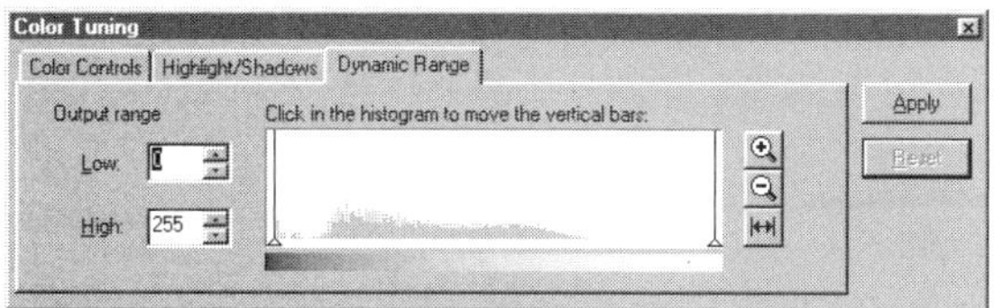

Figure 4-3
The Dynamic Range histogram.

A Dynamic Range histogram represents the number of pixels of each grayscale value in an image. In the histogram, these 256 grayscale values are arranged from black at the left to white at the right.

The histogram for this image shows a wide range of grayscale values, but none at the far right end of the histogram and very few at the far left. This means that most of the pixels in the image are in the dark to mid-level grays.

You can extend the Dynamic Range of the image by dragging the sliders in on either side. This sets black at the darkest grays and it sets white at the lightest grays, so the darkest grays become black and the lightest grays become white.

To try it, follow these steps:

1. Select the grayscale copy of the image, type "128" into the High Output Range field and click Apply. The image becomes darker because the grays in the image extend only from 0 (black) to mid-gray (128). They no longer extend all the way to white (255).

   You didn't move the vertical sliders on the histogram, however, so the distribution of pixels between darkest and lightest remains constant. What you did was to lower the value (lightness) of the pixels represented by the slider at the right side of the histogram.

2. Click Reset.
3. Now type "128" into the Low Output Range field and click Apply. The image becomes much lighter overall. Again, you have not adjusted the distribution. You have made the darkest dark a middle gray.
4. Click Reset.
5. Move the left vertical slider on the Dynamic Range histogram to the right as shown in Figure 4-4, and click Apply.

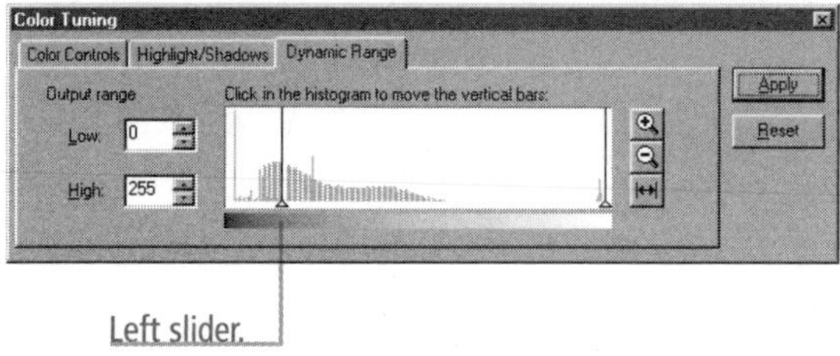

Figure 4-4
Dynamic Range histogram with left slider moved to the right.

This time you have changed the distribution of values. The darkest dark in the image now starts where the slider is positioned, so the image now has more dark pixels.

6. Now select the color image and set the Dynamic Range histogram sliders as shown in Figure 4-5. The left slider is moved slightly to the right.

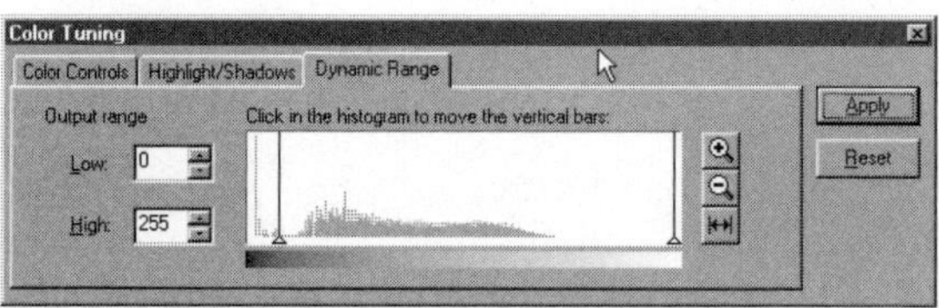

Figure 4-5
Dynamic Range histogram with left slider moved to the right.

When you click Apply, you see that the colors are closer to what they are in nature.

7. Finish adjusting this image by setting the Brightness to –5, and the Saturation to 2. Click Apply. The warmth of the sunlight reflecting into the arch is enhanced.
8. Save the file or delete the two image copies, and move on.

Okeefenokee Swamp Sunrise

The Okeefenokee at sunrise is an awesome display of gradients. The water surface and the sky blend from dark to light in the subtlest colors imaginable. The sliver of sun and the mist rising from the water add yet another dimension to the gradient display. The dark to light contrast could be enhanced.

1. Copy the Okeefenokee Swamp image and place the copy on the Composition Space.
2. Select the image and adjust the Contrast setting to 5. Click Apply.

That's all this image needed, so save the file or delete the copy of the swamp image and move on.

Delicate Arch in Moab, Utah

Awesome is an apt description for this unique sandstone arch, too. This photograph was shot from within a huge natural bowl whose sides rise up to the arch, then drop straight off for hundreds of feet to the desert floor. The intensity of the blazing sun has burned out the sky and the intense oranges and golds of the sandstone.

The color tuning goal for this image is to bring the sandstone alive with color and make the sky look as natural as possible. The rocks are not difficult; a bit more contrast and added saturation is all they need.

You can fix the sky in two ways. You can cut out a sprite with the Curve tool, or use the Select Color Region tool, which looks like a magic wand. If the Select Color Region tool will work, it can produce a cleaner edge than the Curve tool.

On the Workspace, to the right of the delicate arch image, is a grouped image.

1. Copy the grouped image and place it on the Composition Space, to the left.
2. Ungroup the sprites, and then, while they are still selected, set their home positions.
3. Deselect all the sprites, and then drag the dark blue sprite above the Composition Space.

4. Copy the unmodified delicate arch image and move the copy to the right side of the Composition Space. Now you can compare the before (on the right) and the after (on the left).

   Here's how to create the image that you see on the left.

1. Select the unmodified image.
2. Increase the Contrast to 15. This darkens the sandstone colors and lightens the sky.
3. Click the Highlight/Shadows tab and drag the upper right control handle (highlights) to adjust the curve to match the curve shown in Figure 4-6.

   Dragging the highlights control handle on the Highlight/Shadows curve raises the intensity of the brightest areas in the image. Similarly, dragging the shadows control handle at the lower end of the curve lets you adjust the darkest areas in the image. Moving these control handles produces a general effect that is similar to changing the sliders on the Dynamic Range control. But the Highlight/Shadows control also provides a mid-level control handle you can use to raise or lower the intensity of the mid-levels areas in the image. By using this control handle to re-shape the curve toward dark or light, you can raise or lower the mid-levels in an image.

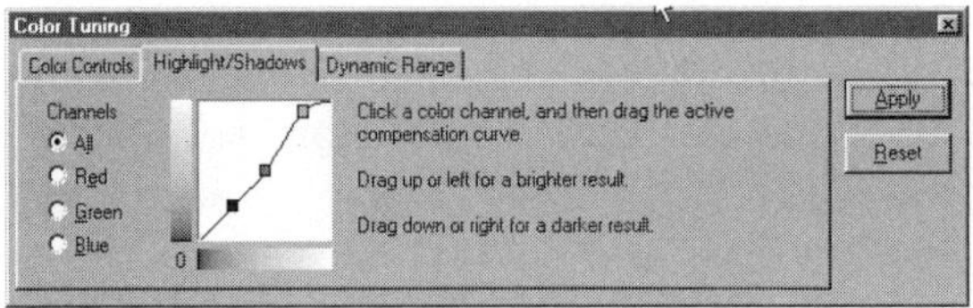
Color Tuning
Color Controls
Highlight/Shadows
Dynamic Range
Channels
All
Red
Green
Blue
0
Click a color channel, and then drag the active compensation curve.
Drag up or left for a brighter result.
Drag down or right for a darker result.
Apply
Reset

Figure 4-6
Highlight/Shadows adjustment. Only the upper right control handle needs to be changed.

4. Increase Saturation to 6. The sandstone really comes to life.
5. On the Cutout palette, click the Select Color Region tab and set the parameters shown at the top of the facing page.

Select Color Region Settings	
Hue	11
Whiteness	90
Blackness	31
Selection	Add
Search mode	Global
Edge	Hard

6. Set the current color to a dark blue so that you can easily see what will happen next. Zoom in so that the sky is large.
7. With the color-tuned image selected, click the Select Color Region button (the wand) on the Select Color Region tab.
8. Click once near the upper right corner of the hole in the arch. Most of the right side of the sky turns blue.
9. Click between the left side of the arch and the left side of the image, a short distance up from the bottom of the sky. An additional amount of sky turns blue.

   Now you have to click several times, here and there in the top left corner area, and near the corner, to get most of the rest of the pixels in the sky to turn blue. Don't worry about the anti-aliased edges around the arch. They can be cleaned up later with the Paint tools. Also, don't bother with the gray line or black outline around the edge of the sky. You can crop the edges of the photo to remove the outline. You should be able to get most of the sky to turn blue, as you can see in the blue sprite you moved above the Composition Space.
10. Click the right mouse button and choose Cut Out from the shortcut menu. A new sprite is created that is the same light color as the original sky.

    If the bounding box of the new sprite extends below the bottom of the sky on the right side of the arch, you probably got some pixels around the edge. Use the Crop tool to crop the new sprite up from the bottom. The bottom of the sprite should be just below the bottom of the sky to the right of the arch, as shown in Figure 4-7, on the next page.

Figure 4-7
Bounding box of the cutout sky sprite.

11. Now, apply the Gradient effect to the sprite you have just cut out using these color settings on the Details tab, and click Apply.

Gradient Effect Colors	
Upper left color	120, 156, 226
Upper right color	109, 188, 231
Lower left color	175, 228, 255
Lower right color	206, 238, 255

12. Select and flatten the sprites, and then crop the edges to get the final image.
13. Move the current sprites off the Composition Space so that you can move on.

Great White Heron on the Chassahowitzka

The last image in the introductory color tuning series is a white heron that has just taken flight in front of some rare wood storks on the Chassahowitzka River, on the Gulf of Mexico side of Florida.

1. Place a copy of the image on the Composition Space. Although the image has an overall gray tone, you can see that there are probably many dark shadows behind the birds and in the water. This image is typical of grayscale or dynamic range problems.
2. With the image selected, click the Dynamic Range tab on the Color Tuning palette.

Most of the bars on the histogram cluster about halfway between the left side and the middle.

3. To check the range of gray levels in the image, click the Auto Fit button. The left and right sliders barely move. This means there are some pixels that are almost white and almost black, but there must be very few, because they are not visible in the histogram unless you click the Zoom In button to the right of the histogram a few times.
4. To lower the grayscale value of the group of pixels in the image, move the left slider to the right, as shown in Figure 4-8, and click Apply.

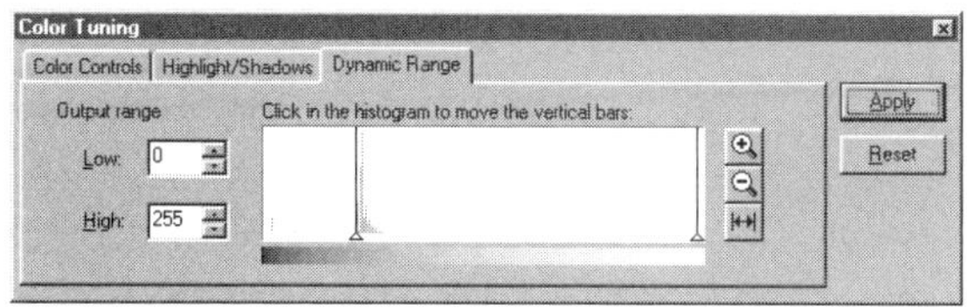

Figure 4-8

Dynamic Range histogram showing left slider adjusted to extend the dark range of values.

The pixels that were formerly a medium-dark gray are now near black, so the image looks much better. As this example shows, sometimes one simple adjustment is all it takes to bring a photograph to life.

Using Color Tuning to Prepare an Image for Effects

So far you have looked at how to use Color Tuning to make images look more natural. There will be times, however, when you want to prepare an image to achieve optimal results with a particular effect.

Color Tuning for Contrast

1. Move aside the sprite that you just modified, make another copy from the original, and place it on the Composition space.

   This time you want the darks to get very dark and the lights to become very light, with very little color showing.

You could use a combination of the Contrast and Brightness controls, but that would intensify the color. To see this, select the sprite and adjust the Contrast slider to 25, then Apply. Now you see too much color information, so click Reset on the Color Tuning tab and try Step 2, instead.

2. Slide the left vertical bar in the Dynamic Range histogram to the position shown in Figure 4-9, and click OK. The left bar should be in the middle of the spike.

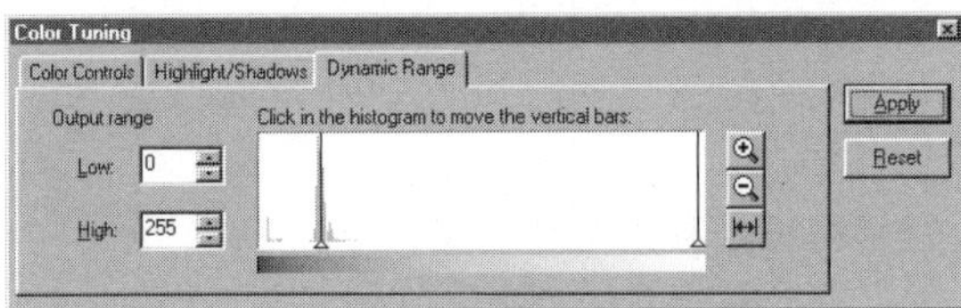
Color Tuning
Color Controls
Highlight/Shadows
Dynamic Range
Output range
Click in the histogram to move the vertical bars:
Low: 0
High: 255
Apply
Reset

Figure 4-9
Dynamic Range histogram. Left slider is farther to the right than it was in the first image.

Now you want to separate the lights and darks further.

3. Adjust the Highlight/Shadows curve to match the curve shown in Figure 4-10, and click Apply.

   The shadows are much darker and the highlights are much brighter, with only a few tree trunks still visible. Very little color information is evident.

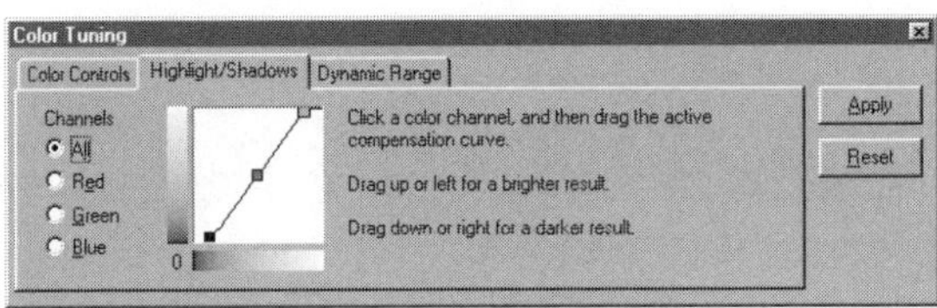
Color Tuning
Color Controls
Highlight/Shadows
Dynamic Range
Channels
All
Red
Green
Blue
0
Click a color channel, and then drag the active compensation curve.
Drag up or left for a brighter result.
Drag down or right for a darker result.
Apply
Reset

Figure 4-10
Highlight/Shadows control. Only the top and bottom control handles have been moved.

Applying the Technical Pen Effect

The Technical Pen effect uses two colors: the Composition Space color and the current color. You want the background to stay black, so you need to change the color of the Composition Space to black.

1. From the File menu, choose Composition Setup, and set the Composition Space color on the Composition Setup dialog box to black.
2. Set the current color to white.
3. Apply the Technical Pen effect to the image using these settings:

Technical Pen Effect	
Stroke length	15
Stroke direction	Left diagonal
Light/dark balance	10 (more dark than light in the final image)
Opacity	20

4. Click Apply.

   Figure 4-11 shows the result.

Figure 4-11
Result of color tuning and Technical Pen effect.

Taking It a Step Farther

Let's say you wanted to use this image as a logo or banner image on a Web site. A solid or lightly textured background would work well. You would like a set of matching buttons and navigation controls.

1. Move the image up off the Composition Space, copy it, and move the copy down.
2. Apply the Technical Pen effect again with these settings:

Technical Pen Effect	
Stroke length	9
Stroke direction	Right diagonal
Light/dark balance	15
Opacity	20

   The image now has a pattern of smaller light colored strokes from the upper right to the lower left.

3. Use the Rectangle tool on the Cutout palette to cut out a 130 by 100-pixel rectangle from the lower left corner of the image, as shown in Figure 4-12.

Figure 4-12
130 x 100-pixel rectangle area in lower left corner.

4. Move the heron sprite aside, place the small sprite you just made in the upper left corner of the Composition Space, copy it and move the copy near the center of the Composition Space.

5. Set the Composition Space color to 90, 90, 90, a dark gray. This will lighten the background in the result.
6. Again, apply the Technical Pen effect with these settings:

Technical Pen Effect	
Stroke length	4
Stroke direction	Horizontal
Light/dark balance	–20
Opacity	25

The resulting sprite would work well with either of the heron images. Colored text with a drop shadow would stand out nicely.

Make another copy of the original cut out rectangle and try this:

1. From the Plug-Ins menu, choose Impressionist. Then choose Impressionist on the Impressionist menu.
2. Use these settings on the Impressionist dialog box and click Apply:

Impressionist Dialog Box Settings	
Style	Natural/Crushed Gum Mosaic
Background	Custom color = 72, 0, 145 (RGB)
Brushsize	100
Coverage	80
Pressure	95

Make a copy of the small rectangle with the dark gray background and horizontal Technical Pen effect, then do this:

1. Set the current color to 164, 102, 64.
2. Apply the Tint effect on the Effects palette, with a setting of 10.

This effect can be applied in a rainbow of colors. Using the same textured surface with different tints can make a good navigation scheme.

Here's one last thing to try:

1. From the tinted rectangle, cut out a 70-pixel circle.
2. Apply the Relief effect to the circle.

Don't be afraid to explore the possibilities. Remember to keep notes as you go. You will make discoveries that are unique and cool, and you will want to know how to reproduce them.

Project: Retouching a Landscape Photo

As part of a project to upgrade telephone service to a rural community, the local utility company is considering burying its telephone lines underground. Managers at the company are preparing a presentation for a meeting with members of the local planning commission. To help smooth the process and justify to the community the temporary disruption the digging will cause, the commission has requested that the utility company put on its Website a representation of how the landscape might look after the change. This would allow a majority of local residents to participate in the process. Your job is to create that photograph by touching up a picture of a local road to show how it would look without telephone poles and wires.

In this short exercise, you will learn two techniques that are central to retouching photos: Using "patches" of an image to cover unwanted objects, and using the Transfer tool to do fine image retouching.

Begin the project by opening a file named CHAPTER4-2.MIC in the PROJECTS folder of the CD-ROM.

The file shows the image before and after the work you are about to do. Move the group of images up onto the Workspace and ungroup it. Duplicate the Before image so you can work on a copy of the original.

Cropping the Image

Now take a look at the Before image. To focus the viewer's attention more on the beauty of the surrounding landscape and less on the road, you will crop the image to remove some of the foreground. You also want to remove the black border surrounding the image.

Crop/Extend button

1. With the image selected, click the Crop/Extend button on the Arrange palette.
2. Drag the control handles at the corners and sides of the image toward the center of the image until the image looks like the After image shown in Figure 4-13.

Figure 4-13
The image after it is cropped.

When the Crop/Extend tool is active, you can adjust the control handles as many times as necessary until you deselect the sprite. Then cropping becomes permanent. You can use Undo, if necessary, until you make another action happen.

Removing Unwanted Objects with the Cutout Tools

You are now ready to use the Cutout tools to begin removing the telephone poles. The Cutout tools allow you to transfer something, like the grass and trees, from another part of the image onto something that you'd like to remove, like the telephone poles.

1. Zoom in to 300 or 400 percent on the tallest telephone pole.
2. Make sure the image sprite is selected.
3. On the Cutout palette, select the Rectangle tool.
4. Draw a tall, narrow rectangle to select a region just to the left of the telephone pole, as shown in Figure 4-14, on the next page.

Rectangle Cutout tool

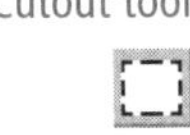

Notice that the shading on the hillside closely matches what is behind the pole. This close correlation is what enables you to use a patch in this instance instead of the more time-consuming transfer procedure. Whenever possible, use this technique as it can save significant amounts of time.

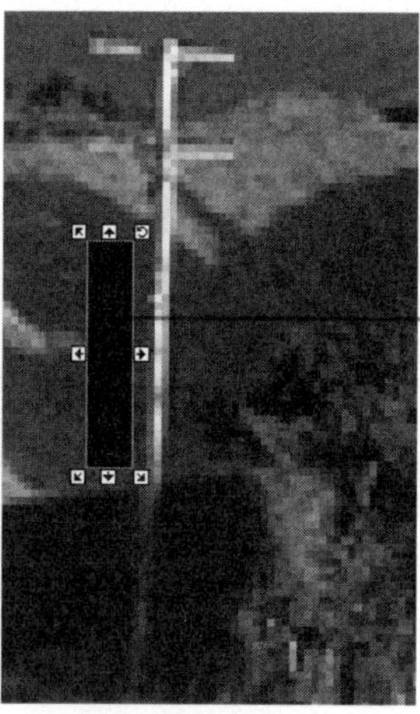

Portion of image that is suitable to be repeated to the right.

Figure 4-14

Select a portion of the image that you want to repeat.

5. Click Cut Out on the Cutout palette and then drag the new sprite just to the right, so it covers the telephone pole.
6. Select the large image sprite and the small sprite and flatten them.

In addition to copying rectangular regions, you can also use the Oval, Curve, and Polygon tools on the Cutout palette to replicate irregular shapes.

Painting Over Objects with the Transfer Tool

Transfer tool

Like the Cutout tools, the Transfer tool on the Paint palette allows you to cover unwanted items in an image, but it does so by allowing you to paint one area of the image with information from another part.

1. Select the image and click the Transfer tool on the Paint palette.

2. Click once on the dark green grass that is about two telephone pole widths to the left of the bottom of the top half of what remains of the large telephone pole, as shown in Figure 4-15.

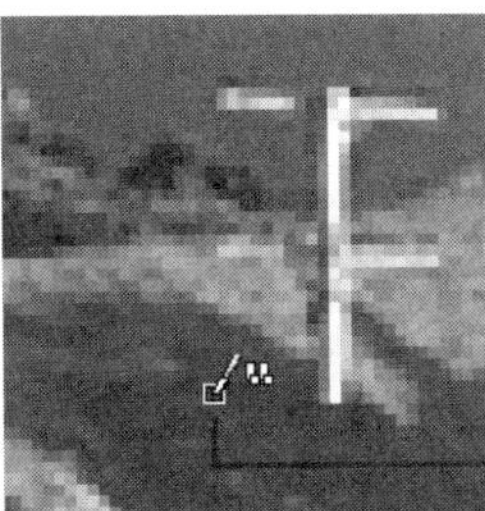
Click here with the Transfer tool.

Figure 4-15
Click to the left of the bottom of the upper portion of the telephone pole.

3. Move the pointer to the right, onto the telephone pole, and click once. The green grass is transferred onto the pole.
4. Now press and hold down the mouse button and drag up the pole starting from where you just clicked. As you drag, you are painting over the pole with information that is two telephone widths to the left.
5. When you get to the portion of the pole that is in front of the sky, click the Transfer tool again and then click a spot on the sky just above the top of the pole. Then you can paint across the top of the pole with the new sky information you just picked up.
6. To remove the portion of the pole in front of the hedge, select an adjacent point on the hedge to transfer over in front of the pole.

You can do the same with the wires, and by carefully choosing the spots from which you pull information, you can paint over the rest of the telephone pole and all the other poles. You will need to frequently reset the Transfer tool by clicking it on the Paint palette and clicking a new spot to pick up and use. Figure 4-16, on the next page, shows the finished photo after the retouching is complete.

Figure 4-16
The photo after retouching.

This technique works fine for removing unwanted portions of low-resolution images destined for Web pages. For high-resolution images, such as those you'll use for printing, you might want to work in more detail by using the Eyedropper on the Color Picker to select individual colors, and then using the Paintbrush or Pencil tool on the Paint palette to paint in pixels one by one. With a fine brush or the pencil point, you'll have all the control you need to remove scratches and other small imperfections.

Project: Preparing a Magazine Cover Photo

In this second project, you'll take photo editing a step further. You will analyze a photograph that you'd like to use for the cover of a sailing magazine, Wind World, and determine its problems. Then you will fix these problems one by one. Finally, you will add some text and a border to create the cover.

Start a new Image Composer file and then insert the finished image WINDWORLD.TIF from the PROJECTS folder of the CD-ROM. This TIF file will show you the completed cover. Next, insert the file HARBOR.TIF from the PROJECTS folder. This original scanned photo shows sailboats on the water in front of a cityscape.

Analyzing the Photo

After examining the harbor photo, you determine that it needs the following adjustments:

- The entire image needs straightening and sharpening.
- A hair in the upper right sky that intruded on the scan needs to be removed.
- You want to remove the dark sailboat from the foreground so the large white sailboat in dry dock can become the focal point.

Figure 4-17 shows the areas that need repair or adjustment.

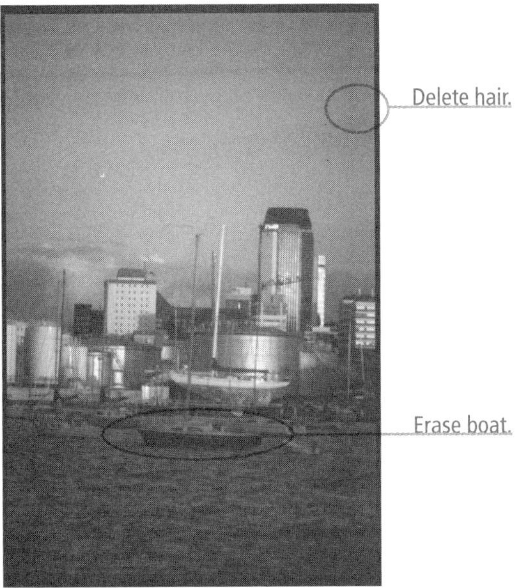

Figure 4-17
The original scan with areas marked for adjustment.

Rotating the Image

To straighten the buildings and boats in the picture you need to rotate it.

1. On the Arrange palette, type "–2" into the Rotation control (you want to rotate the entire sprite minus two degrees).
2. Click the Apply button next to the Rotation control.

Cropping the Image

To prepare the image to fit a magazine cover, you figure out that 8.5 by 11 inches scales down to 510 by 660 pixels. At 300 dpi, 8.5 inches equals 2550 pixels, and 11 inches equals 3300 pixels. You divide these numbers by five to get 510 pixels and 660 pixels, an easily workable size.

Cropping the image will allow you to both remove the slanted sides of the image and choose a 510 by 660-pixel portion to use. The sky would be a good place for the magazine title, so you will remove some of the foreground water.

1. Use the Crop tool to reduce the size of the image to 450 by 600 pixels, which leaves room for a 30-pixel border all round. Refer to Figure 4-18 to see where to crop.

Figure 4-18
Image cropped to 450 by 600.

2. Before going on, choose Composition Setup from the File menu and set the size of the Composition Space to 510 by 660. Set the color of the Composition Space to black.

Align Centers button

3. Select the cropped image and use Align Centers on the Arrange palette with Relative To Composition Space turned on to center the image on the Composition Space.

   The image looks a bit soft, so use Sharpen on the Effects palette to bring it more into focus.

4. Select the image, then apply Sharpen once (not Sharpen Lite, which applies less sharpening).

Retouching the Photo

To remove the hair in the upper right portion of the sky and to remove the black foreground boat, you can use the Transfer tool on the Paint palette.

1. Select the Transfer tool on the Paint palette and click the sky near the hair. You will want to zoom in to do this.
2. Paint across the hair with the Transfer tool.

While you are at it, you can also use the Transfer tool to remove the one or two small, dark spots you will find in the sky.

Continuing to use the Transfer tool, very carefully remove the black sailboat. You'll find that you can pick up an area of water just under the hull of the sailboat and then drag across the hull to remove it. Choose several different areas of the water to transfer over the boat so that it doesn't all look the same. To remove the mast and the rigging that cross the white sailboat in the background, the sky, and the wall in the back, carefully choose a spot just next to the mast as the source to transfer. Take your time and work carefully. Figure 4-19 shows the result of the Transfer procedure.

Figure 4-19
Result of the Transfer procedure.

Adding the Magazine Cover Elements

For the magazine title text, you'd like to use a color from the photo, so zoom in on the brilliant gold colored building next to the tallest building in the photo and use the Eyedropper on the Color Picker to pick up the color. We picked up 255, 218, 66. Make a note of the RGB values of the color you picked up, as you will need to enter these values into the color picker on the Text palette.

To create the text, follow these steps:

1. Zoom out to 100 percent and then open the Text palette by clicking the Text button on the Toolbox.
2. On the Text palette, choose Bees Knees for the font, and 48 points as the size. Enter the RGB values of the yellow color you picked up, and make sure Smoothing is on.
3. Drag a text box as wide as the image and type in "Wind World." Then click to set the text.
4. Select a darker golden color from the same area as before (We chose 190, 120, 0) and select the Edge tool from the Effects palette.
5. On the Details tab of the Effects palette, enter the second color you selected, and set the Thickness to 2 and the Opacity to 100. Then click Apply.

Now add a topic title beneath the Title.

1. Begin by choosing a dark color from the water. We chose 34, 66, 78.
2. Open the Text palette and choose Arial, Regular, 22 points. Be sure Smoothing is turned on, and set the color to the color you chose from the water.
3. Drag a text box and type "Dry Dock."
4. Press Enter and add "When do you need it?" Figure 4-20 shows the placement for this text.

If you were to save the resulting image as a TIF file, the black background of the Composition Space would become a border around the image.

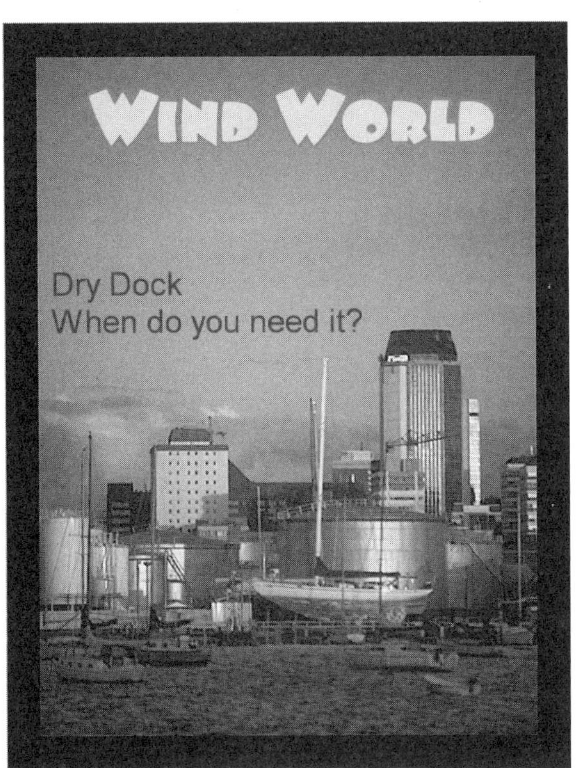

Figure 4-20
The finished piece with text properly placed and aligned.

For now, though, save the file as an Image Composer file and admire your work.

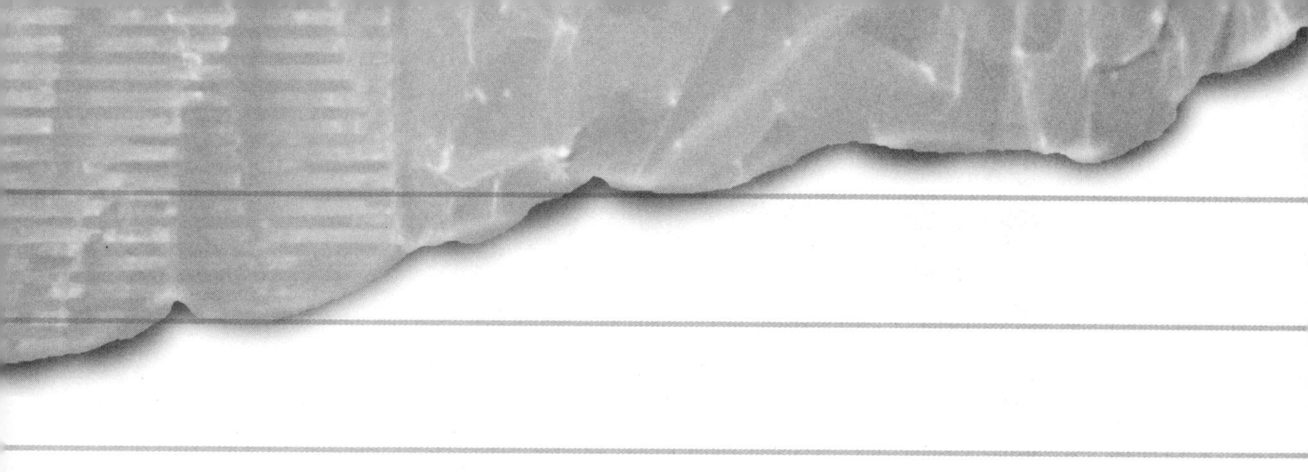

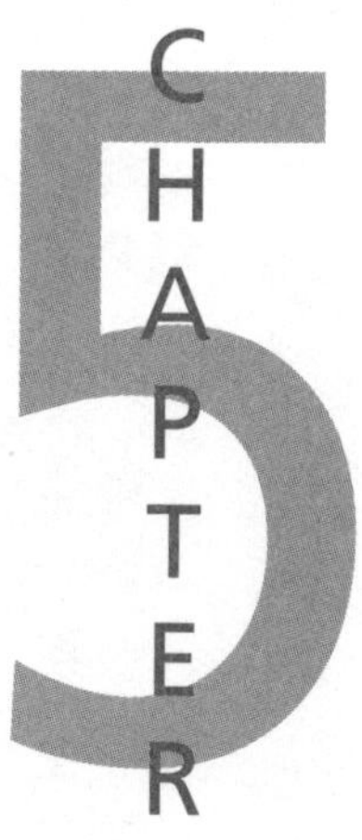

5
CHAPTER

Blendo: Blending Images with Transparency

In the projects so far, you have used a variety of tools and techniques to accomplish some pretty impressive image effects. In this chapter, you'll explore a new subject, transparency. Manipulating the transparency of sprites is a key strength of Image Composer, and it allows you to combine and blend images almost magically.

About the Project: Big Sur Poster

In this project, you will lay out a travel poster for a famous stretch of the northern California coast called Big Sur, one of the most spectacular meetings of land and sea in America. You will represent it by skillfully combining two scanned photos of the coastline into a single scene. Through the magic of Image Composer, you will blend the immediacy of crashing ocean waves with the grandeur of cliffs to create a visual synthesis that embodies the majesty of the Big Sur coast. As you work through this exercise, you will get the chance to learn how to use transparency to combine multiple photos into a single, seamless image.

Examining the Finished Product

For this project, we'd like you to see the finished piece before you begin, along with the elements you'll use. To start the project, open CHAPTER5.MIC, an Image Composer file located in the PROJECTS folder on the accompanying CD-ROM. In the file, you will see that the completed poster rests to the right of the Composition Space, and the two original scanned photos, used as elements for the poster, are to the left.

The upper scanned photo shows the Big Sur coastline at sunrise from a high vantage point. Toward the foreground, a meadow at the top of a rocky cliff climbs the sides of the coastal mountains. The lower scanned photo, taken midday from a boat, shows a close-up of waves rolling in against the rocks.

Using the power of Image Composer's transparency controls, you will combine these photos, taken from two different vantage points at two different times of day, to make a single scene that appears to be authentic. You can see how well the final image will look in the finished poster. Then you'll finish off the poster by adding a border and some laid-back, California-style text.

As you create this poster, you will be working at a very small size. You can see this by clicking the completed poster and examining the status bar. Notice that the poster is only 600 by 855 pixels. If you were to send the poster to a typical laser printer, the resulting printout would be only one inch wide. A typical poster, on the other hand, is obviously much larger. To create a file that you could deliver to a commercial printer for such a poster, you'd have to work with a Composition Space set to be something like 5400 by 7200 pixels in size. That particular combination would create an image that is 18 by 24 inches at 300 dpi. The output file you would then deliver to the printer would be 5400 x 7200 pixels x 3 (for the three RGB colors), which would result in a file size of more than 116 megabytes.

NOTE

Image Composer lets you create images as large as the example above, but working with large elements can be extremely slow, because Image Composer must process millions of pixels. A solution is to do all your experimenting and designing first, working quickly with small elements on a reduced-sized version of the final product. After you've worked out all the details, you can re-create the final project at the correct size.

Positioning the Images

For this example, we've cheated a bit by setting the Composition Space at a size that will help you align the two images properly in relation to one another. We experimented to find a positioning that would work best.

Begin by saving the current file as a new file on your system. Then duplicate each of the scanned photos. To position the duplicates together, follow these steps:

1. Select the duplicate of the upper image and align its upper left corner with the upper left corner of the Composition Space.

Remember, you can use Relative To Composition Space and the Upper-Left Corners Align button on the Arrange palette to align a sprite on the Composition Space.

2. Select the duplicate of the lower image and align its lower left corner with the lower left corner of the Composition Space.
3. Set the home position of each sprite and move the lower sprite back out onto the Workspace.

Preparing the Images

To properly blend the two different photos into a single image, you need to make a few adjustments to them. First, you need to color tune the images, so that they look good individually and they share similar brightness and saturation. Second, you need to add transparency to the lower portion of the upper sprite and to the upper portion of the lower sprite. Because both sprites will be progressively transparent where they overlap, the two images will seem to blend into each other.

To make this blending technique virtually unnoticeable, you can give each image a gradient of transparency that gradually runs from opaque to transparent. The top image will be opaque at the top and become more and more transparent farther down. The bottom image will be exactly the opposite: opaque at the bottom and more and more transparent higher up.

To add a gradient of transparency to a photo, you need to create a second sprite with a standard black to white gradient. Then you can overlay the second sprite on the photo and use Map Transparency to have Image Composer transfer the levels of gray in the gradient to an opaque to transparent gradient on the photo. Where the second sprite is black, the photo will be fully transparent. Where it is white, the photo will be fully opaque. Where the second sprite is gray, the photo will be semi-transparent to a degree that depends on the gray level.

Applying a Transparency Gradient to the Upper Sprite

Before you begin modifying the transparency of either sprite so that you can combine the images, you should color tune them separately while they are still discrete.

Notice that the original sunrise image on the Composition Space is a little dull. To color tune this upper image, try increasing the Saturation setting on the Color Tuning palette to 12. You will see that the greens in the grassy hillsides and the blues and golds in the sky and early morning mist are more vibrant.

Now you can work on the transparency. You want the photo to be fully opaque from its top edge down to the top of the cliffs. This is the part that will not be overlapped by the lower photo. Then you want the transparency to begin and gradually increase, reaching about 85 percent transparency at the bottom of the sprite.

To create this transparency gradient, follow these steps to make a second sprite with a black to white gradient.

1. Draw a 625 by 365-pixel rectangle that starts to the left of the top of the cliffs, as shown in Figure 5-1.

The 625 by 365 rectangle.
Use the area inside the circle to help place the rectangle.

Figure 5-1
Placement of the rectangle sprite.

2. With the new sprite still selected, choose Gradient as the Effect and then, on the Details tab of the Effects palette, choose the preset gradient named Grayscale Up from the Gradient Name drop-down list. Click Apply.

Grayscale Up produces a gradient that washes evenly from dark to light, but it would be better if the image remains more opaque in the upper areas and becomes transparent quickly where the two images overlap. To achieve this, you have to change the gradient on the rectangle so that there's more white area, which maps to opaque, and less black, which maps to transparent.

To modify the gradient on the rectangle, use the Highlight/Shadows control on the Color Tuning palette and set the curve to match Figure 5-2 on the next page. Figure 5-3, also on the next page, shows the rectangle with the gradient after it has been color tuned.

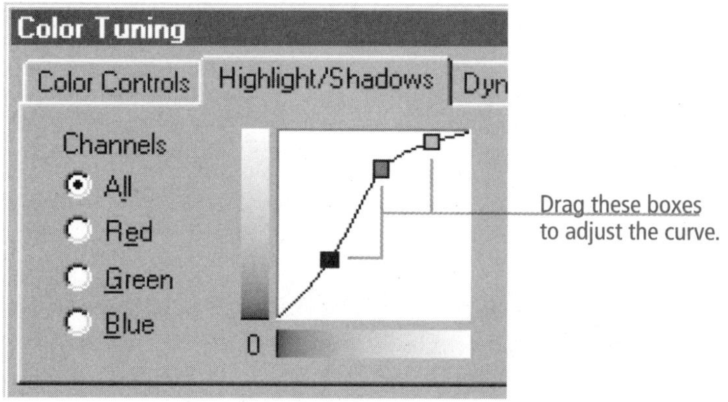
Color Tuning
Color Controls
Highlight/Shadows
Dyn
Channels
All
Red
Green
Blue
0
Drag these boxes to adjust the curve.

Figure 5-2
Adjustment for the grayscale gradient.

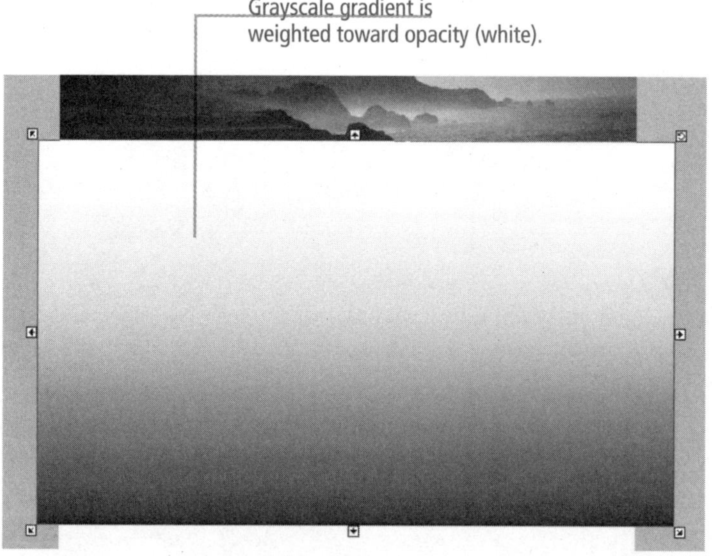
Grayscale gradient is weighted toward opacity (white).

Figure 5-3
The grayscale gradient after color tuning.

1. Move the grayscale gradient to the back so you can see both the photo and the gradient and tell the relationship between the two, and then Shift-click the photo to make sure the gradient is the source sprite. You can tell by looking at the selection handles. The source sprite's handles will be black. If they aren't, click it again.

2. On the Texture Transfer palette, select Map Transparency and click Apply.
3. To see the new transparency gradient on the photo, delete the grayscale gradient.
4. Move the upper sprite out of the way so you can work on the lower photo.

Preparing the Lower Sprite

Your next task is to remove some of the lower sprite to let an important part of the upper sprite show through. You will remove a portion of the rock in the lower sprite with the Cutout tools.

1. Select the lower sprite and send it home so that it is again aligned at the lower left corner of the Composition Space.
2. Zoom in to the upper right corner of the sprite.
3. Use the Curve tool on the Cutout palette with Opacity set to 100 percent and a Hard edge to erase the portion of the rocks shown in Figure 5-4. Make the first and last points you click just outside the edge of the sprite, and, to be sure to the get the entire upper right corner within the curve, also click a point outside the upper right corner of the sprite.

Use the Curve tool on the Cutout palette to select this black area.

Figure 5-4
Erase the black shape from the sprite.

4. Click Erase on the Cutout palette.

Don't rush as you place control points while drawing the curve with the Cutout tool. This kind of work requires time and careful concentration. You'll see the payoff later, when you finish your work and take a look at the final piece.

While you are working on the lower sprite, you should take a moment to extract a second sprite that shows only the foreground ocean area. You will need this sprite later in this chapter to color tune the ocean portion of the image and make it more prominent. Make sure the sprite is selected and use the Curve tool on the Cutout palette again, but this time, after you've drawn the correct shape, click Cut Out rather than Erase on the Cutout palette. Figure 5-5 shows the portion to cut out.

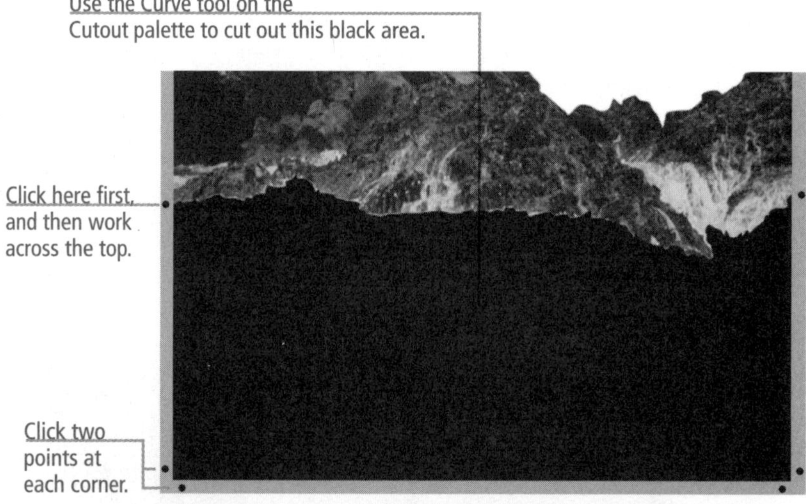
Use the Curve tool on the
Cutout palette to cut out this black area.
Click here first,
and then work
across the top.
Click two
points at
each corner.

Figure 5-5

Cut out the black area from the lower sprite.

While using the Curve tool to cut out a portion of a rectangular sprite, you can click a pair of control points outside each corner of the rectangle instead of clicking a single control point. This helps create a sharp, 90-degree bend in the curve. Sometimes this also produces loops at the corners rather than 90-degree bends, though. Before you click Cut Out to use the shape, use Move Points to pull the control points of the loop apart and straighten it out.

Before you click elsewhere, set the home position of the new sprite while it is selected and move it aside for now.

You are now ready to apply a transparency gradient to the lower sprite. When you are finished, the top of the sprite should be somewhat transparent where the two sprites overlap, and then move rapidly toward being opaque. To accomplish this, follow these steps:

1. Draw a 625 by 390-pixel rectangle and send it to the back so that you can reposition it properly. Figure 5-6 shows the placement of the rectangle.

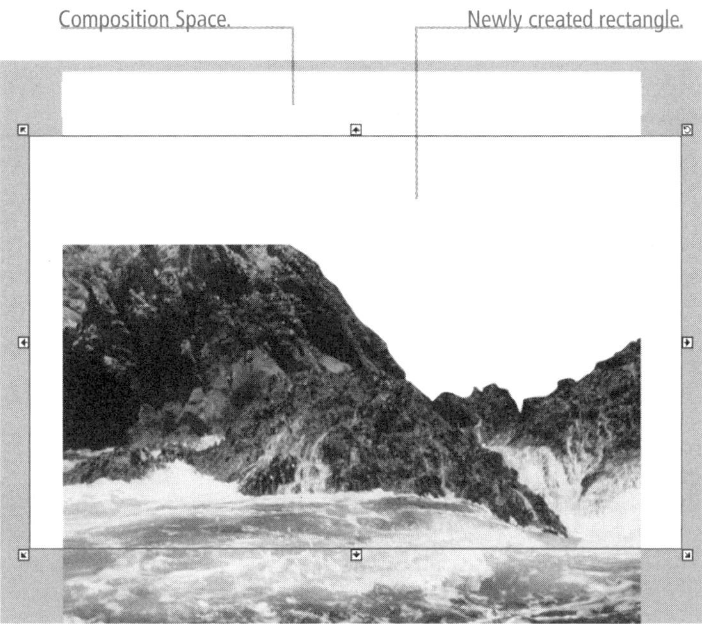

Figure 5-6
Placement of the rectangle for the gradient.

2. On the Effects palette, choose Gradient and apply the gradient named Grayscale Down on the Details tab.
3. Use the Highlight/Shadows control on the Color Tuning palette to adjust the curve as shown in Figure 5-7, on the next page, making the photo transparent primarily at the top of the image.

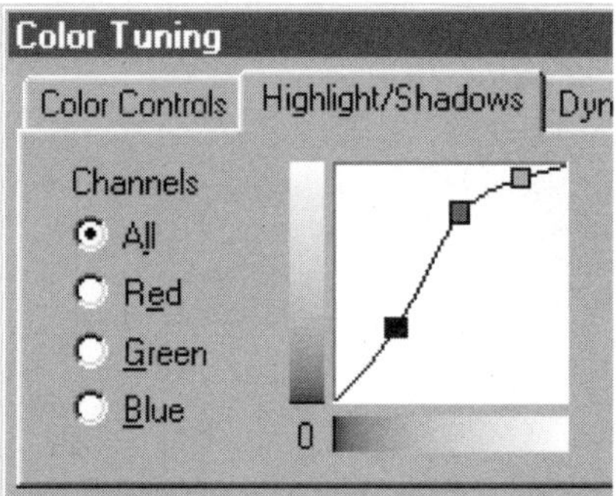

Figure 5-7
The Highlight/Shadows curve for the gradient.

4. Select the lower sprite, make sure the rectangle is the source sprite, and apply Map Transparency on the Texture Transfer palette.
5. Delete the gradient.
6. Finally, zoom out to find the top image sprite and send it home. You will see that the two sprites are overlaid and roughly blended because of the transparency you have added.

Now choose a zoom level that will allow the two sprites to fill most of the screen. Notice that the ocean at the bottom of the upper sprite is somewhat grayed out from the slight transparency it received. You want it brought back to full opacity but you still want to retain the transparency in the cliffs. Notice also that the top edge of the rocks in the lower sprite fits well against the top of the cliffs in the upper sprite, but not perfectly. You need to do a bit more careful blending.

The last thing to notice is that the lower sprite's colors could be a bit more saturated to match the upper sprite. Saturating the colors will also visually move the lower image to the foreground, where it belongs.

Tweaking the Two Photo Sprites

To fix the portion of the upper sprite that has become transparent, simply duplicate the upper sprite and send the duplicate home. But the duplicate now sits on top of the other two sprites and its cliffs block the rocks in the lower sprite. To fix this, follow these steps:

1. Shift-click the lower sprite on the Composition Space and click it again to make it the source sprite.

2. On the Texture Transfer palette, select Snip at 100 percent to cut its shape from the duplicate of the upper sprite.
3. Finally, select the lower ocean and rocks sprite and bring it to the front. Now you can draw a selection box around the two upper sprites and flatten them.

As you look at the current composition, you may see that the color intensity of the lower sprite does not quite match the intensity of the upper sprite. To fix this, you increase its Saturation by 10 and then use Sharpen Lite on the Effects palette, which has the effect of bringing the foreground more into focus.

Blending the Sprites by Hand

Zoom in closely to where the top of the rocks on the left side of the lower sprite meet the meadow of the upper sprite. Look carefully and you will see that the ledge of the meadow in the upper sprite shows through the semi-transparent rocks in the lower sprite. Figure 5-8 shows the area you should examine. You need to work on this area to make the top of the rocks blend at the top of the cliff to meet the meadow ledge. You can accomplish this by using the Eraser tool on the Paint palette with a soft brush and low opacity. With these settings, you will be painting on transparency to the top of the rocks. This transparency will create the smooth blending.

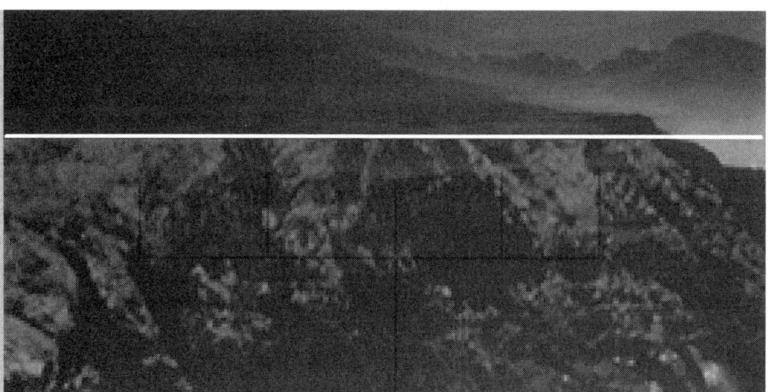

Use the Eraser to blend the area between the white line and the top of the ledge showing through the semi-transparent rocks.

Figure 5-8

The two sprites need blending at the area shown.

To paint on the transparency, follow these steps:

1. Lock the position of both sprites, to make sure you don't move them inadvertently.
2. On the Paint palette, click the Eraser tool and choose the third brush from the left in the top row of the grid of brush styles. This brush has a width of nine pixels.
3. Set the Opacity to 20.
4. Select the lower sprite and then work along its top edge, using sideways strokes that swing downward a bit over the top edge of the rocks where they cover the forward ledge of the meadow.

NOTE As you use the Eraser tool, you can easily click outside the boundaries of the sprite you are working on, which ends up selecting a different sprite. If this happens, re-select the sprite you want to work on and then select the Eraser tool again and continue working.

You may have to go over the area a few times before you're satisfied with the consistent blended look you've achieved. For reference, you may want to look at the finished image in the poster. Don't worry if you can't achieve a perfect blending. You'll soon use another technique to improve the blending.

The meadow at the top of the cliffs might look a lot better with a bit stronger color. To increase the color saturation of just that portion of the image, you can make a separate cutout sprite to overlay the existing meadow.

1. Use the Curve tool on the Cutout palette again to cut out a meadow sprite from the top sprite. The black shape in Figure 5-9 shows the shape of this sprite.
2. With the new cutout sprite selected, increase the Saturation to 25 on the Color Tuning palette.
3. Using the Eraser with the same settings as before, blend the rocks into the meadow. This time, however, erase up from the bottom of the meadow sprite to let the rocks show through a bit. You should lock the position of the meadow sprite so that it doesn't move as you work.

Figure 5-9
The shape of the cutout for the meadow sprite.

Adding the Ocean Foreground Sprite

Now is the time to work with the ocean sprite that you extracted from the lower image. Select the ocean sprite, bring it to the front, and send it home. This places it neatly on top of all the other sprites.

To add more saturation to its main color so that it tends to move forward visually, increase the saturation of only the blues in the sprite by following these steps:

1. Make sure the sprite is selected.
2. On the Color Controls tab of the Color Tuning palette, click the button labeled Blue to limit your modifications to the Blue color channel.
3. Increase the Saturation to 15 and click Apply.

You have now made all the modifications necessary to the sprites in the image, so select them all, group them, copy the group and put the copy aside, and then return to the original and flatten the grouped sprites into a single sprite on the Composition Space.

Adding the Border and Aligning the Image

For the poster, you'll want to add a border around the image and an area on which you can place text. To add this space and align the image within it, follow these steps:

1. From the File menu, choose Composition Setup.
2. Set the Composition Space to 600 by 855 pixels and click OK.
3. Select the image sprite and, on the Arrange palette, make sure Relative To Composition Space is turned on and click the Align Centers button. The image moves to the center of the Composition Space.
5. Draw a rectangle that is 16 pixels high and a little wider than the Composition Space.
6. With Relative To Composition Space still turned on, make sure the rectangle is selected and click Align Tops to move the rectangle to the top of the Composition Space.
7. Click Relative To Composition Space on the Arrange palette to clear it and select both the rectangle and the image.
8. Make sure the rectangle is the source and click the Touch Edges button on the Arrange palette. This moves the image to the bottom of the rectangle, 16 pixels from the top of the Composition Space.
9. Set the home position of the image and delete the rectangle.
10. Finally, set the current color to black and draw a rectangle that is 600 by 855 pixels, the same size as the Composition Space. Align the rectangle on the Composition Space using the Align controls with Relative To Composition Space turned on. Then send the rectangle to the back.

Creating the Title

For the poster title, you'll want to choose text in keeping with the feel of the subject. Because Big Sur is a casual place, you might want to try a casual font, like Tempus Sans ITC.

To add the text, follow these steps:

1. Set the zoom level to 100 percent so that you can work with the Text tool.
2. On the Text palette, set the current color to 0, 215, 225, choose Tempus Sans ITC from the font list on the Text palette, and enter 100 as the size.
3. Click the black space below the Big Sur image and, in keeping with the casual feeling, type "big" in all lower case characters.
4. Click the Text button again and type "sur" in lower case characters.
5. Click the Text button once again, change the Size to 50 on the Text palette, and create a "california" sprite. Remember, while you are typing, you can stretch the right edge of a text sprite to fit all the text you need to enter.
6. Position the text sprites as shown in Figure 5-10, select all three, and set their home positions.

Text sprites in place.

Figure 5-10
Text sprites in place.

To add a 3D effect to the title, you will build up several layers of text, so create three duplicates each of the "big" and "sur" sprites. Then set them aside for the moment.

1. Select the "big" sprite that is still on the title area.
2. Choose the Edge Only effect and, on the Details tab, set the color to 21, 90, 115, and set the thickness to 8 pixels.
3. To soften this sprite, apply the Blur effect with Horizontal and Vertical on the Details tab set to 2 pixels. This creates the background glow.

4. Select one of the "big" copies and send it home. Then bring it to the front.
5. Send another "big" copy home and bring it to the front. With it still selected, apply the Edge Only effect with a color of 92, 0, 139, and a Thickness of 6.
6. Select the last "big" copy, send it home and bring it to the front. Then apply Edge Only with a color of 68, 0, 197, and a Thickness of 2. This puts a thin, dark blue outline around the light blue text. Leave the sprite selected.
7. Duplicate the currently selected sprite and send the duplicate home.
8. Apply a Blur effect with a setting of 2 pixels.
9. Duplicate this sprite and send it home.
10. Finally, repeat the same procedure with the "sur" sprite.

A Note about Transparency and the Alpha Channel

Although we have not explicitly named it in this chapter, the transparency you have been manipulating is called alpha channel information. Here's a way to think about the alpha channel: each pixel in an image has four channels of information. The Red, Green, and Blue channels determine the level of red, green, and blue in the pixel. The alpha channel determines the degree of transparency in the pixel. Any one pixel has a level from 0 to 255 of red, green, blue, and alpha.

Because the alpha of each pixel in a sprite is maintained by Image Composer with the rest of the information about the sprite, you can use this alpha information to achieve sophisticated transparency effects like those you've seen in this chapter.

Some Things to Note

To clean up the Image Composer window before saving the file, zoom out and inspect the Workspace. Delete any leftover sprites (but leave the two original images), and then select the sprites on the Composition Space and group and duplicate them. Move the duplicates aside and flatten the original group. Now you can save a neat and clean Image Composer file.

That's it, a completed Big Sur poster.

A More Advanced Exercise

To explore further possibilities with transparency, try the following short exercise.

You'd like the sunrise image to be fully opaque near the center and gradually become transparent toward the edges. To achieve this, you can create a circular area of transparency mapped to the sunrise image. Follow these steps:

1. Duplicate the sunrise image that was left behind on the Workspace.
2. Move it to an open space, set its home position, and use the Pan tool to center it on your screen.
3. Set the current color to white.
4. Draw a circle 775 pixels in diameter. This will become your transparency map.
5. Send the circle to the back and center it around the sunrise image, as shown in Figure 5-11.

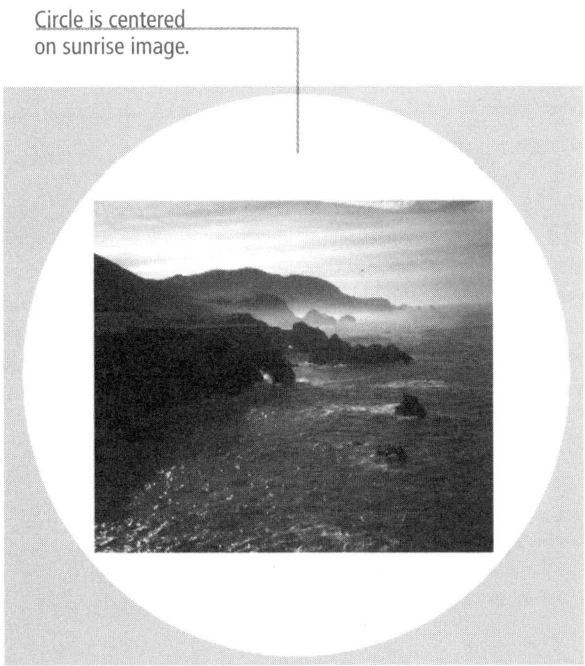
Circle is centered
on sunrise image.

Figure 5-11
Circle centered around sunrise image.

6. Select the circle sprite and apply a Gradient effect, choosing the gradient named Grayscale Left on the Details tab. The circle will have a gradient that is white at the left and black at the right.
7. Apply the Radial Sweep effect with the Angle on the Details tab set to 0. The black to white gradient now becomes the edge of the circle to the center.

To make sure the central area of the image is fully opaque, you can adjust the level of white in the gradient circle.

1. Set the Highlight/Shadows curve on the Color Tuning palette to match Figure 5-12. This extends the midrange of the gradient, so you end up with a higher concentration of light in the center and dark at the outside.

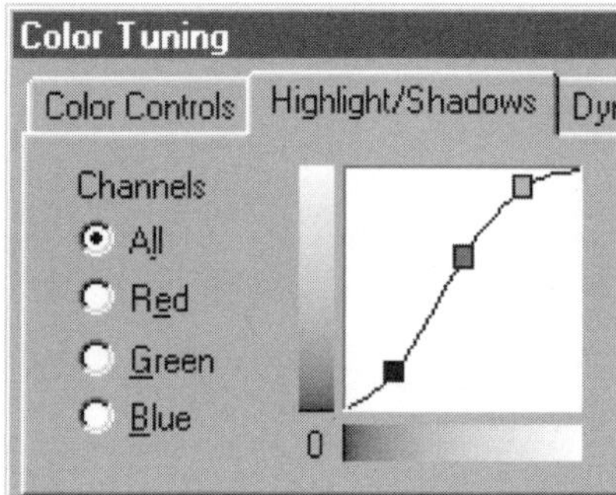

Figure 5-12
The Highlight/Shadows setting on the Color Tuning palette.

2. Bring the circle to the front and then adjust the Dynamic Range settings on the Color Tuning palette to match Figure 5-13. This widens the central area of pure white so that more of the center of the photo will be opaque after you apply a Transparency Map.

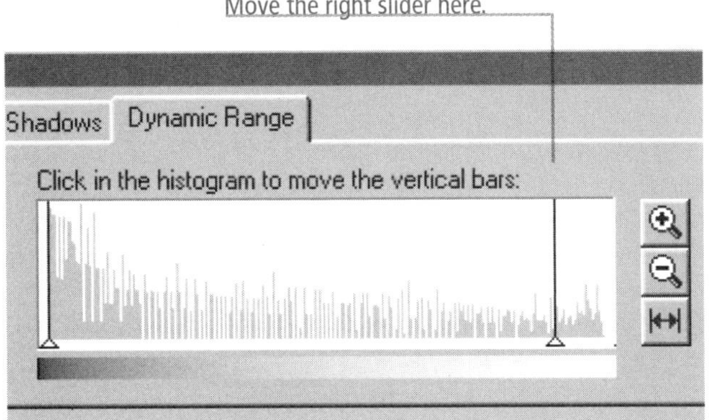

Figure 5-13
The Dynamic Range setting on the Color Tuning palette.

3. Send the circle to the back, Shift-click the sunrise image to make it the source, and then apply Map Transparency on the Texture Transfer palette.
4. Move the circle away.

To enlarge the central opaque area of the photo further, duplicate the image and then send the duplicate home. You can repeat this as many times as you'd like. When you are satisfied, flatten the sprites into a single image.

Here's another interesting possibility to try: convert a scanned image to a grayscale image using the Grayscale effect. Then use it as a transparency map for another sprite. You'll find that you can create a see-through area in the shape of another object.

In this chapter, you've had the chance to practice using transparency to blend images, one of the key features of Image Composer. In the next chapter, you will learn how to prepare tiled backgrounds for your graphics and Web pages.

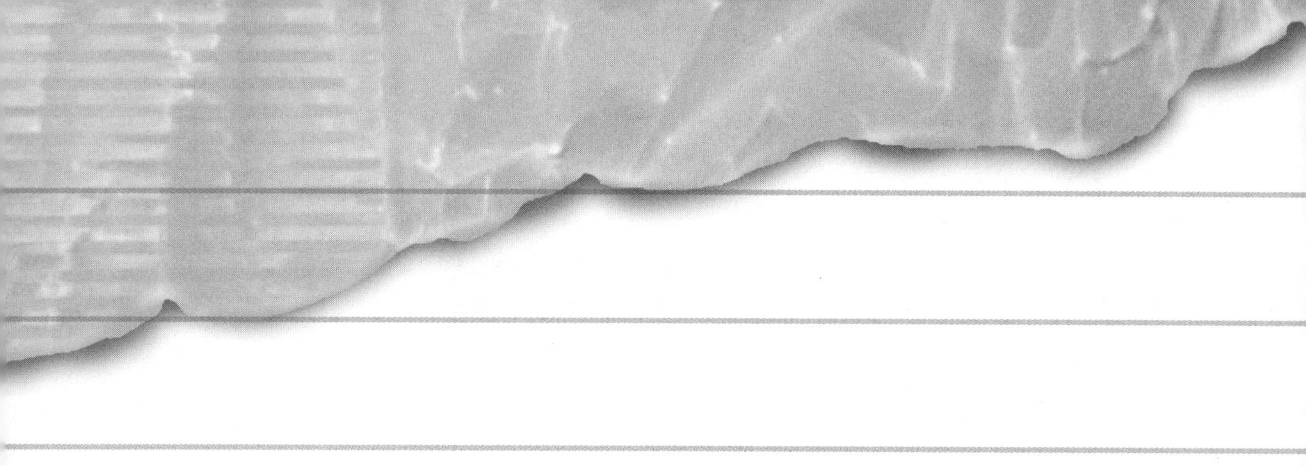

Behind the Scenes: Making Backgrounds

Although you can easily use one simple HTML command to give a Web page a solid color background, supplying a small tile for the browser to repeat across a Web page background can add eye appeal to the page. In this chapter, you learn to create two different types of tiles, simple and seamless.

Simple tiled backgrounds produce a repeating pattern that fills a space. These tiles are like kitchen tiles in that the individual patterns of the tiles fit together to form a larger pattern. With tiles such as these, it's possible to follow the pattern and determine where one tile ends and the next starts.

Seamless tiles, on the other hand, produce a continuous texture rather than a repeating pattern. If a seamless tile is properly made, no one can tell where one tile ends and the next begins.

The style of tile you choose to create depends on the use to which you'll put it. Repeating tiles can produce an interesting border for electronic presentation slides that you create in a program like Microsoft PowerPoint. Seamless tiles can produce an attractive texture for the background of a Web page.

Creating Tiled Backgrounds with a Repeating Pattern

To create a tile that will repeat perfectly, you follow a particular scheme. First, you create only one quarter of the tile and apply any pattern to its surface that you care to create. When that quarter is ready, you duplicate it and flip the copy so that the copy faces in the opposite direction. Then you join the two pieces side by side to produce one half of the final tile. With the first half complete, you duplicate it, flip the duplicate, and then join those two pieces together to form a single, repeatable pattern. Easy, right? Yes, but don't tell anyone. Let's not reveal this secret, used by tile and textile designers for thousands of years.

To try creating a repeatable tile, follow these steps:

1. Set the current color to 220, 210, 220, a pale gray-pink.
2. Draw a 40 by 40-pixel square.
3. Change the current color to 133, 214, 188, a pale green, and zoom in to make the square fairly large on your screen. You will use this new color to add a painted element on the tile.
4. With the sprite selected, open the Paint palette and choose the Airbrush tool. Use a 24-pixel soft brush in the top row and set Opacity to 100. To find the 24-pixel brush, you need to scroll over to the right within the display of brush styles.
5. Point the Airbrush pointer directly at the extreme lower-left corner of the sprite and click three times without moving the pointer. Figure 6-1 shows the result you should get.

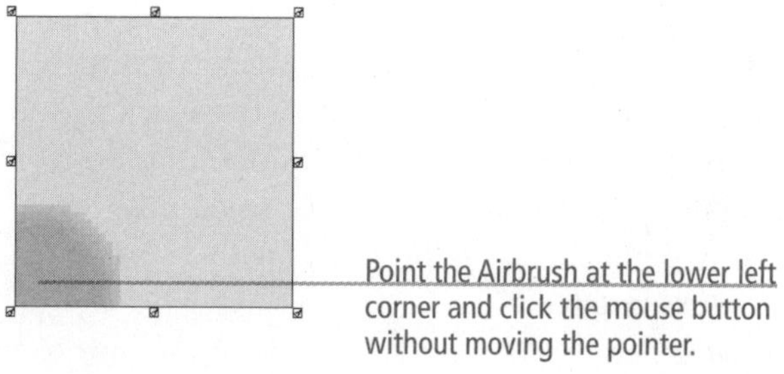

Point the Airbrush at the lower left corner and click the mouse button without moving the pointer.

Figure 6-1
Place the airbrush pointer at the corner and click three times.

6. Change the current color to 149, 64, 225, a medium purple.
7. Use the Paintbrush tool on the Paint palette with a 3-pixel brush from the bottom row to paint a shape similar to that shown in Figure 6-2.

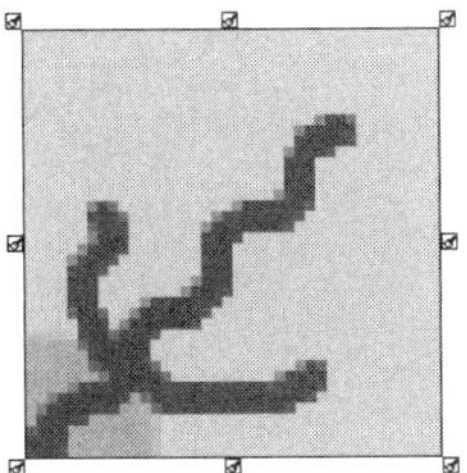

Figure 6-2
Rectangle sprite with the purple shape added.

Now you have created the basic quarter tile. You will use the Duplicate, Flip, and Align tools to produce the full tile.

1. Set the home position of the sprite and duplicate the sprite.
2. Flip the duplicate horizontally by using the Flip Horizontally control on the Arrange palette.
3. Move the duplicate to the right of the original, nearly touching it.
4. Use Align Tops on the Arrange palette to align the tops of the sprites and then use Touch Edges to bring them together.
5. Select both sprites and flatten them into a single sprite, as shown in Figure 6-3.

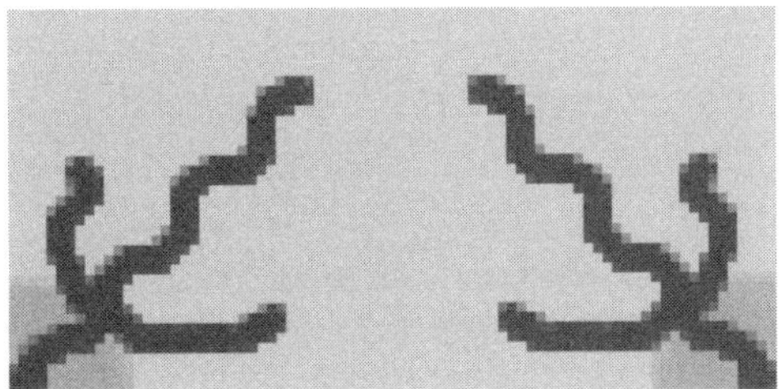

Figure 6-3
Sprite after the first copy, flip, align, and flatten.

6. Copy this sprite and flip it again, but this time flip it vertically.

7. Move the copy above the original and use the Align tools to align the left sides of the sprites, and then touch their edges and flatten the two sprites.
8. You should now have an 80 by 80-pixel pinkish-gray square sprite with green spots at each corner and a purple squiggly design.

To use this sprite to fill a 640 by 480 space, set the Composition Space to 640 by 480 by using Composition Setup on the File menu. Now duplicate the sprite, align the tops of the two sprites, and touch their edges. Flatten these two sprites to make a sprite twice as wide as the original. Fill the top of the Composition Space with a row of duplicates of this sprite and then flatten them. Now duplicate the resulting sprite to produce copies you can place below the original until you have filled the entire space, as shown below in Figure 6-4.

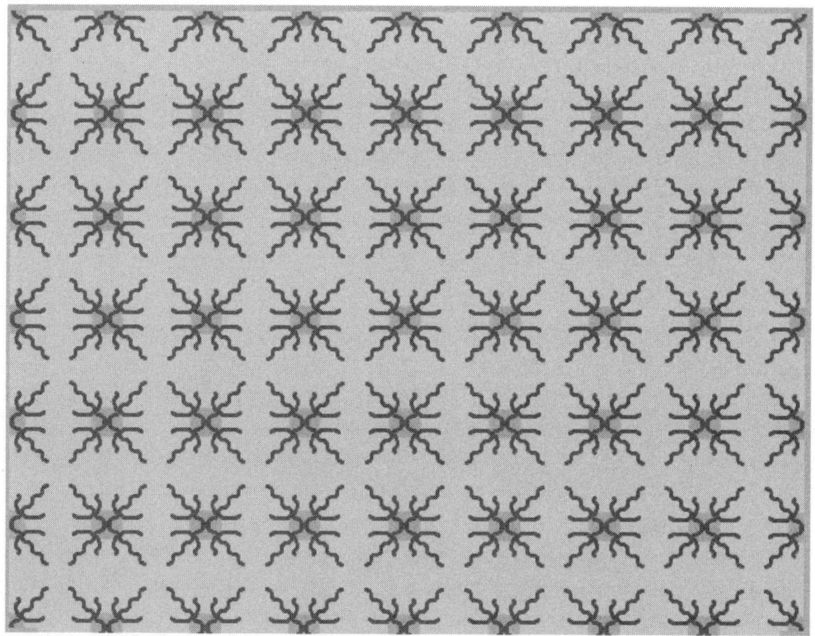

Figure 6-4
Pattern made by repeating the tile to fill a 640 x 480 space.

Don't worry about saving the file, because you will not need it for a later project.

Creating Seamless Tiles

Seamless tiles, unlike the tiles you made above, join together to produce a smooth, unbroken pattern or a patternless texture. This effect is achieved when tiles exhibit color similarities and low contrast.

To try creating a seamless tile, follow these steps:

1. Set the current color to 230, 243, 245, a very pale blue.
2. Draw a rectangle sprite that is 160 by 80 pixels. (160 pixels wide and 80 pixels high).
3. Duplicate the sprite and make sure the duplicate is selected.
4. From the Plug-Ins menu, select Impressionist. Then select Impressionist again on the secondary menu to open the Impressionist dialog box.

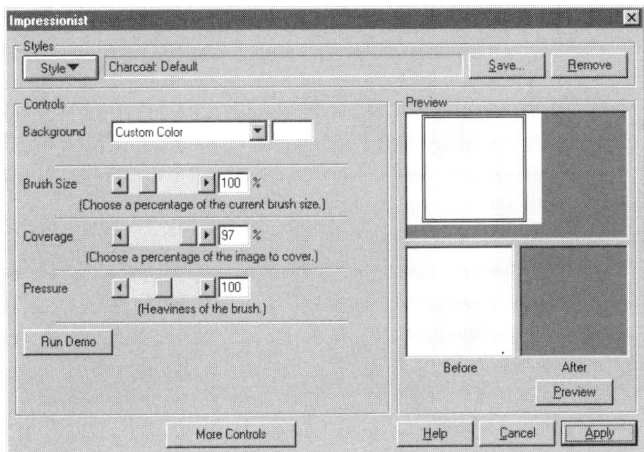

Figure 6-5
The Impressionist dialog box.

5. On the Impressionist dialog box, set the Style to Pencil Sketch and choose Soft Light from the secondary menu.
6. Set Background to Custom Color and, with the adjacent color swatch, choose 191, 193, 215 for the RGB settings. Make sure you use the Red, Green, Blue settings. not the Hue, Sat, Lum (Hue, Saturation, and Luminance) settings.
7. Set Brush Size to 345, Coverage to 50, and Pressure to 81.

8. Click the Preview button on the Impressionist dialog box to see the effect you've just chosen. Then click Apply to apply the effect.

You now have a pale blue sprite with light purple diagonal strokes across its surface.

Making the Tile Seamless

To make a sprite ready for seamless tiling, you need to divide the sprite into quarters with the Cutout tools and then rearrange the quarters. Try it by following these steps:

1. Set the current color to black and zoom in to make the sprite large on your screen.
2. Using the Rectangle tool on the Shapes palette, make an 80 by 40 rectangle and duplicate it three times. You will use Texture Transfer and the Transfer Shape option to make these into quarter-tile sprites. Place the black sprites just outside the four corners of the textured sprite.
3. Select the textured sprite and Shift-click the upper-left black sprite.
4. On the Arrange palette, make sure Relative To Composition Space is unchecked and click the Align Upper-Left Corners button. The black sprite lines up with the upper-left corner of the textured sprite.
5. To texture the black sprite, use Transfer Shape on the Texture Transfer palette at 100 percent with the textured sprite as source and the black sprite as receiver.

NOTE

If you find that the texture does not seem to transfer fully to the black sprite, you've hit an intermittent bug in Image Composer's Transfer tools. The solution is to use Undo, move the Opacity slider away from 100 percent, put it back at 100%, and then click Apply again. The second time, it should work.

6. Deselect all the sprites and move the small, newly textured sprite outside the upper-left corner of the source textured sprite.

7. Repeat this procedure with the three remaining black sprites, lining them up with the lower-left, lower-right, and upper-right corners of the source sprite before using Transfer Shape.
8. As you make the sprites, place them outside their respective corners.

You should now have four 80 by 40-pixel sprites placed near the corners from which they were made. You need to switch their positions diagonally, align and flatten them, and then do a bit of fine-tuning.

1. Move the original sprite out of the way.
2. By dragging them, switch the positions of the upper-left and lower-right sprites, and then switch the upper-right and lower-left sprites.
3. Select the two left sprites, align their left sides, touch their edges, and then flatten them. Do the same with the two right sprites.
4. Align the two resulting sprites and flatten them to make one sprite, as shown in Figure 6-6.

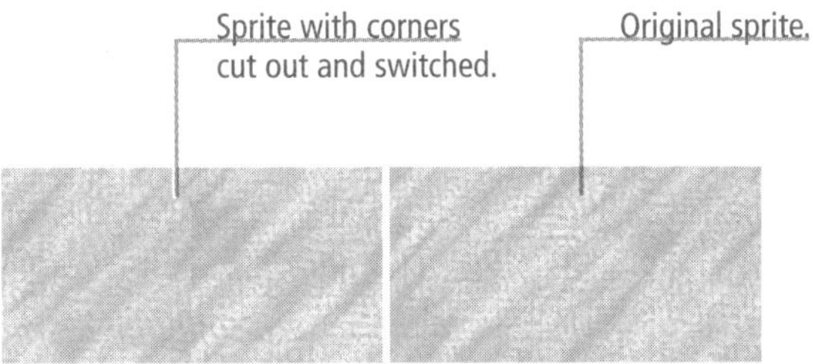

Figure 6-6
Four cut-out sprites combined to make one.

Blending the Join Marks

Notice that a break in the pattern at the boundaries of the four smaller sprites makes it possible to distinguish where the sprites were joined. To fix this break, you can blend the boundaries with the Transfer tool to eliminate the vertical and horizontal lines that are apparent within the sprite without altering its outside edges.

1. On the Paint palette, select the Transfer tool and choose a soft, 9-pixel brush style at 100 percent.
2. Select the sprite and look for places within it where the seam is obvious. Click once near one of those spots to set the origin point of the transfer.
3. With the mouse button held down, drag over the adjacent seam in the diagonal direction of the pattern. The image from the origin point is transferred to the place you drag across.

NOTE

Each time you want to transfer a new area, you must re-click the Transfer tool on the Paint palette and then click another origin point on the sprite.

4. Repeat this procedure until you are satisifed that the seams have been properly blended.
5. Duplicate the sprite twice and set aside one of the copies. Move the other copy next to the original.
6. Align the tops of both sprites and touch their edges, and then flatten the sprites into one.
7. Duplicate the result and repeat the align-flatten procedure to fill the top of the Composition Space with a row of sprites. Then duplicate the row and repeat until you have filled the entire Composition Space with the duplicates.

Figure 6-7 shows the final result on the right. The left half of the figure shows how the original sprite would have looked if you had not switched corners and blended the seams before tiling.

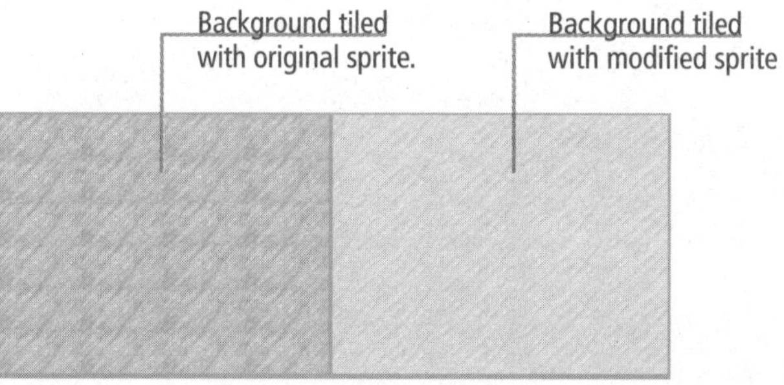

Figure 6-7

Tiled background before and after the sprite is modified.

Now that you know the mechanics of producing seamless tiles, you will explore using Image Composer to create some interesting, additional textures.

Creating Textures for Tiles

In this section, you will create subtle textures for tiles that will not compete with the foreground elements on Web pages. To accomplish this, you will combine several effects to obtain backgrounds that are distinct without being busy.

Prepare for this exercise by deleting all the current sprites and setting the current color to 237, 237, 237, a light gray. Now follow these steps:

1. Draw a 240 by 240-pixel square sprite and make three copies.
2. Move the copies out onto the Workspace for now.
3. Draw a 160 by 80-pixel rectangle sprite and use the Color Swatch and the Color Fill buttons on the toolbar to fill the sprite with black. You will use this black sprite to cut out tiles from the larger sprites you are about to make.

To apply a burlap texture, follow these steps:

1. With the original 240 by 240-pixel sprite selected, select Rough Texture from the Effects palette.
2. On the Details tab of the Effects palette, click the Texture Controls button and choose the settings below and then click OK.

Texture Controls Dialog Box

Type	Burlap
Light position	Bottom right
Scaling	200
Relief	2

3. Make sure the Invert Texture check box on the Details tab is checked, leave Opacity at 100%, and click Apply.

The surface of the sprite now has a soft, open burlap texture that is not too prominent. Next try the Grain effect by following these steps:

1. Put the burlap sprite aside and drag another plain gray sprite onto the Composition Space.
2. On the Effects palette, select Grain and, on the Details tab, use these settings:

Grain Effect Details	
Graininess	32
Type	Enlarged
Contrast	22
Opacity	100

3. Click Apply to see the effect.

   The sprite now has a soft, subtle pattern of color. You may want to zoom in a few times to see it closely. Drag this sprite off the Composition Space and drag another plain sprite on.
4. Choose the Grain effect again, but on the Details tab, choose these settings:

Grain Effect Details	
Graininess	11
Type	Regular
Contrast	10
Opacity	100

   This sprite is much darker. The texture is still there, but it's barely noticeable.
5. With the same sprite selected, choose the Watercolor effect and choose these settings on the Details tab of the Effects palette:

Watercolor Effect Details	
Brush detail	13
Shadow intensity	0
Texture	2
Opacity	100

The sprite turns a middle gray with a lighter, textured pattern. Move this sprite off the Composition Space. Now copy the burlap sprite and move the copy onto the Composition Space.

1. On the Color Controls tab of the Color Tuning palette, click the Blue channel button and set Brightness to 10, and click Apply. The sprite picks up a bluish tint.

   Finally, try a Chalk and Charcoal effect on another copy of the burlap sprite by applying these changes:

2. On the Effects palette, choose Chalk and Charcoal, and then choose these settings on the Details tab:

Chalk and Charcoal Effect Details	
Charcoal area	1
Chalk area	6
Stroke pressure	1
Opacity	42

When you apply this effect, the sprite gets an irregular texture with a diagonal feel that runs from upper right to lower left. For people who read from upper left to lower right, the current pattern would produce a visual tension and call attention to itself, which is exactly the opposite of what you want. To make the pattern less conspicuous, reverse it by flipping the sprite horizontally.

Clean up your Composition Space and save the file to your hard disk where you can find it.

Using the Surface of a Sprite for a Tile

You have made four large, textured sprites with various effects and different ranges of lightness. This is the smallest tip of the proverbial iceberg. The combinations and permutations of effects you can achieve with the Paint tools and the Impressionist plug-in, in particular, are endless. Here, you'll try out some basic effects to prepare for some of the wilder stuff you'll come across later in the book.

Begin by following these steps:

1. Move the first sprite, the sprite with the burlap texture, to the middle of the Composition Space.

2. Select the 160 by 80-pixel black sprite you made earlier, copy it, and move the copy onto the burlap sprite, as shown in Figure 6-8. Now zoom in so that the Composition Space nearly fills the screen.

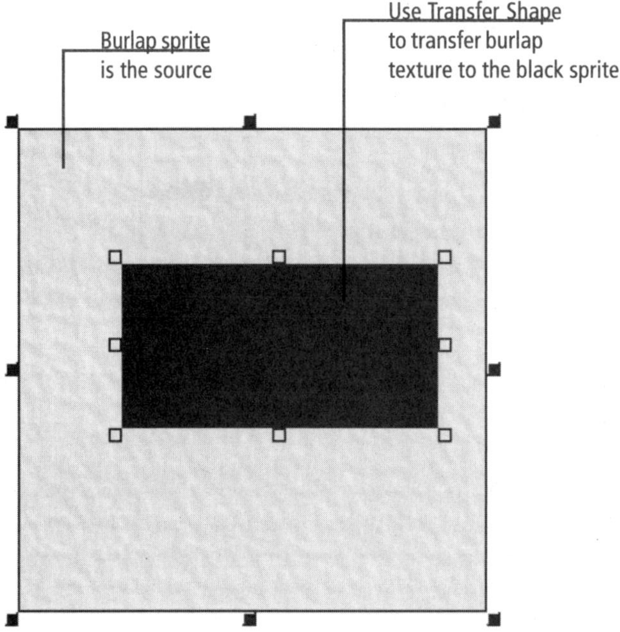

Figure 6-8
Black sprite ready for Texture Transfer.

3. Use Transfer Shape on the Texture Transfer palette at 100 percent to transfer the burlap texture to the black sprite. Remember to select both sprites and make the burlap textured sprite the source sprite.
4. Zoom out, deselect all the sprites, and move the larger sprite off the Composition Space, leaving the new sprite with the burlap texture.
5. Use the technique you learned earlier in the chapter, cutting out four quarters of the sprite and repositioning them, to make the sprite ready for seamless tiling.
6. For additional practice, transfer the textures from the other

sprites to the small black rectangle sprite and make them ready for seamless tiling too.

Making Tiles with a Staggered Logo

As you browse the Web, you'll often see pages that have a logo staggered across a tiled background. Here's an easy way to obtain that effect.

First, copy the black 160 by 80-pixel sprite and use Texture Transfer to transfer the burlap texture from the large burlap sprite. When you finish, you will have a 160 by 80-pixel burlap sprite. Move the larger burlap sprite away and position the smaller one on the Composition Space.

Now create a sample logo by following these steps:

1. Click the 100% button on the Toolbar so that you can add text.
2. Click the Text button on the Toolbox and, on the Text palette, choose Snap ITC, Bold, 18 points, and black.
3. Make the letters "I" and "C" and position them together like any one of the logos shown in Figure 6-9. Then flatten them into a single sprite.

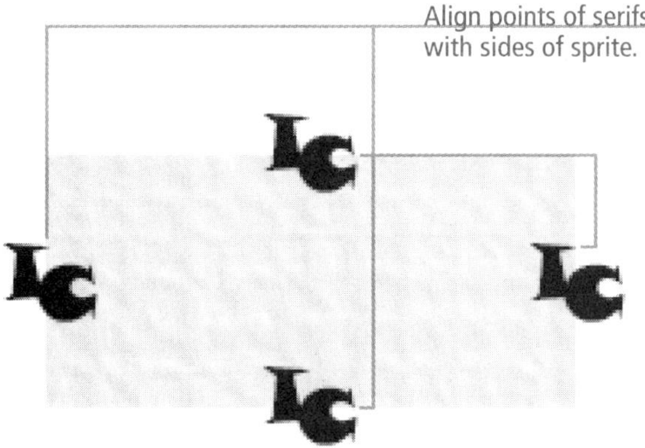
Align points of serifs with sides of sprite.
IC
IC
IC
IC

Figure 6-9
Layout of text/logo for staggered display.

Next you will position the logo sprites on the rectangle sprite so that you can transfer to the sprite the parts of the logo sprites that overlap.

1. Make three duplicates of the logo sprite and position the duplicates roughly centered on each side of the rectangle sprite, as shown in Figure 6-9 above.

2. To position one of the logo sprites on the side edges of the rectangle, select the rectangle sprite and the logo sprite, make sure the rectangle sprite is the source, and then use Align Centers Horizontally to align the sprite on the edges. Do the same for the sprite on the opposite side of the rectangle. Figure 6-10 shows the effect of Align Centers Horizontally and Align Centers Vertically.
3. To align the sprites on the top and bottom edges of the rectangle, use Align Centers Vertically, instead.

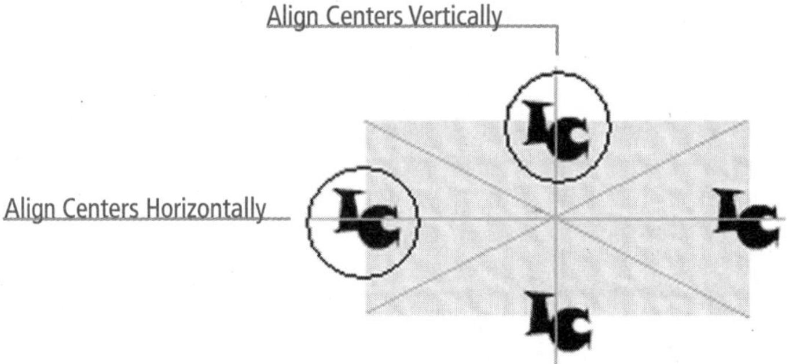

Figure 6-10
Using Align Centers Vertically and Align Centers Horizontally.

TIP

To fine-tune the positions of the sprites, look at the sprite at the opposite side of the rectangle and use the Arrow keys on the keyboard to move the sprite so that it overlaps the edge in the exact same way.

4. Select a logo and then Shift-click the rectangle sprite. The logo is the source sprite.
5. Use Transfer Shape on the Texture Transfer palette at 30 percent to transfer a light gray text logo to the rectangle, as shown in Figure 6-11.
6. Repeat for each of the other logos and then delete the logos, leaving only the rectangle sprite.

Figure 6-11.
Result of Texture Transfer.

Now you can use the remaining rectangle as a tile that will repeat the logo across a Web page background. Figure 6-12 shows how this tiled surface will look.

Figure 6-12
Tiled sprite with staggered logo.

NOTE

The distance between the staggered logos is determined by the size of the rectangle sprite. You could double the size of the rectangle tile and the logos would then be twice as far apart.

In the next chapter, you will put to good use many of the techniques you've learned in the past few chapters by making a Web site menu map for WalkRight, Inc., an outdoor equipment company.

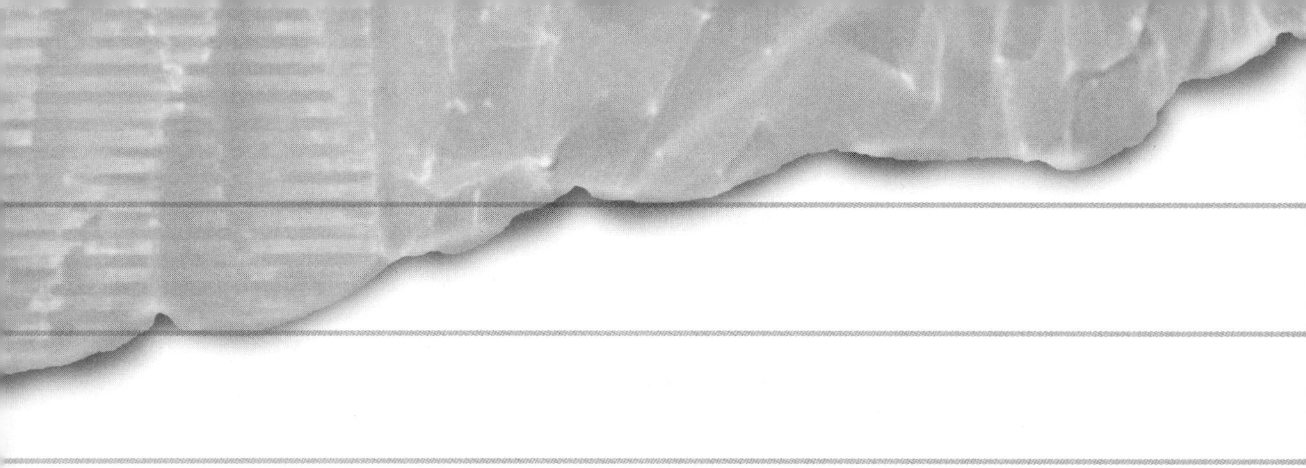

CHAPTER 7

WalkRight Adventure Gear: Web Page Elements

The WalkRight Adventure Gear company just doesn't do things like other companies. That's why their equipment is so wildly sought after. Despite the overwhelming demand for their products, WalkRight still wants a Web site that will be easy for new customers to use.

To make its Web site readily navigable, WalkRight has hired you to create a graphical navigation system so users can easily move through the Web site, get their bearings, and find their way back home without confusion.

You decide to make the opening page one large, graphical menu map so users can click an icon and head off in the right direction instantly. To make a graphical menu map, you also plan to use scans of photos you took on an adventure walk of your own.

For this project, you'll create a background tile and a banner area. You'll also make all the menu map elements you need to create a clear and clean navigational aid. In this project, you will make a tile seamlessly repeatable and create foreground elements with interesting visual effects, using a combination of choices on the Effects palette. When you're done, you'll get the chance to save the sprites you've created as Web-ready GIF files using Image Composer's Save for the Web wizard.

Begin the WalkRight project by opening the file CHAPTER7.MIC. It's in the PROJECTS folder of the accompanying CD. Above the Composition Space, you'll find several scanned photographs that have a natural affinity because they were all taken on a single hike. Below the Composition Space, you'll also find a bitmap image of the completed composition to use as a reference while you work.

Preparing the Background

Although we know you've just been through an entire chapter on backgrounds, we'd like you to get the chance to prepare a background as part of the natural sequence of tasks in designing a Web site. In fact, when the background you plan is a tiled pattern, getting the background made should be the first step in any project you undertake, because it gives you a reference against which you can create fitting foreground elements. For this project, you'll create a background from an extracted portion of one of the images you've collected for the project.

If, however, you've had enough background practice for now, you can use the ready-made background that we have provided on the accompanying CD. Use Insert From File to insert a file called CHAPTER7 BACKGROUND.TIF in the PROJECTS folder of the CD-ROM. If you'll be using the ready-made background, place the TIF file on the Workspace, align it with the center of the Composition Space and lock its position. Leave room around the Composition Space for placing working sprites and then skip to the next section, "Making the Banner Area."

Calculating the Background Tile Size

As always, when you create a tile for a Web page background, you want a file that is small enough to transmit very quickly, but you also want a tile that is large enough to have enough pixels to work with. Because the Composition Space is 605 by 330 pixels, the default size you set in Chapter 2, you must divide the length and width of the Composition Space by some number that will produce the correct tile size. Dividing 605 and 303 by 5 produces 121 by 66 pixels, a perfectly good size for a tile.

Cutting Out the Tile Sprite

The large gray thistle—the spiky, gray flower—has plenty of neutral gray areas and subtle textures that would serve well as the beginnings of a background tile. To cut out a suitable portion of the thistle, follow these steps:

1. Drag the thistle sprite onto the Composition Space.
2. Use the Rectangle tool on the Cutout palette to draw a 121 by 66-pixel rectangle at the spot shown in Figure 7-1.

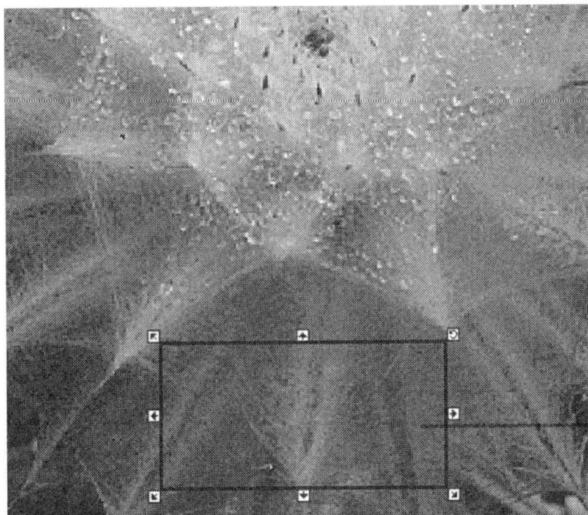

Draw a rectangle at this location.

Figure 7-1
Cut out a sprite from the area indicated by the black rectangle.

3. Click Cut Out on the Cutout palette to extract the sprite portion.
4. Move the thistle sprite back out onto the Workspace and leave the cutout sprite on the Composition Space, where you can work on it in detail. Select the cutout sprite.

   To make the pattern within the sprite less distinct, and thus make the sprite better suited for use on the background, you need to reduce the contrast within the sprite and make its colors more neutral.

5. Click the Dynamic Range tab on the Color Tuning palette, click Auto Fit, and click Apply, which brightens the sprite somewhat.

6. To lighten the sprite and reduce its contrast more, click the Highlight/Shadows tab, leave Channels set to All, and adjust the curve to match the one shown in Figure 7-2.

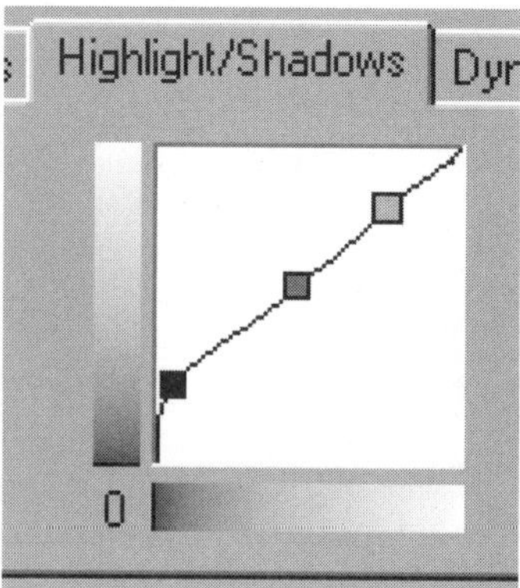

Figure 7-2
Highlight/Shadows adjustment.

For a final touch, you can blur the sprite to remove any remaining obvious pattern.

1. Before you blur the sprite, set aside a copy of it to use after the blurring.

   You need a copy of the sprite because blurring a sprite not only blurs the surface, but it also anti-aliases the sprite edges, which increases the size of the sprite and takes away the hard edge needed for the tiles to fit together properly. To fix this problem, you can use the copy of the original sprite to return the blurred sprite to its original size, with hard edges.

2. Select the sprite and apply the Blur effect with a blur setting of 3 pixels Horizontal and 2 pixels Vertical.

   To regain the hard edges of the sprite and correct the sprite's size, you will now use the spare copy you set aside earlier.

3. Select the spare copy of the sprite you put aside.
4. Move the copy near the blurred sprite and select them both.
5. Select the blurred sprite first, then the original sprite, to make sure the blurred sprite is the source sprite, and then

open the Arrange palette. Ensure that Relative To Composition Space is unchecked and click the Align Centers button to align the two sprites perfectly.

6. With the blurred sprite still set as the source sprite, use Transfer Shape on the Texture Transfer palette at 100% Opacity.

   This gives you a hard-edged sprite with the soft surface quality that you want. Now move the soft-edged sprite off the Composition Space.

Fine-Tuning the Background Color

Shifting the color of the background a little would increase the contrast between the background and the foreground elements. One possibility for shifting the background color is to apply the Negative effect on the Effects palette to the tile you are making. Go ahead and try it. You'll see that the colors of the tile change from neutral greens to neutral lavenders.

A final touch would be to brighten the sprite and reduce its contrast. On the Color Tuning palette, set Brightness to 30 and Contrast to –50.

Applying a Texture to the Background Tile

Adding some texture to the surface of the tile sprite would break up the pattern somewhat, and you can certainly create plenty of textures with Image Composer.

1. From the Effects palette, choose the Rough Texture effect and, on the Details tab, click the Texture Controls button.
2. On the Texture Controls dialog box, enter these settings:

Rough Texture Effect Details

Type	Sandstone
Light position	Top
Scaling	200
Relief	4
Invert Texture	on

3. Click OK, set the Opacity slider to 60, and click Apply. The sprite takes on a mild 3D surface texture.

Making the Tile Seamlessly Repeatable

To make the sprite ready for seamless tiling, you need to divide the sprite into quarters with the Cutout tools. Zoom in so that the sprite is large on your monitor and select it.

NOTE If necessary, refer to "Creating Seamless Tiles" in Chapter 6 for review.

Using the Rectangle tool on the Cutout palette at 100 percent Opacity and a hard edge, cut out a sprite from each quarter of the original source sprite. As you cut out the sprites, place them outside their respective corners.

NOTE For this project, as in many real world situations, the tile you will create is not zdivisible by two. This means the four small sprites you cut out from the 121 by 66-pixel sprite will not be identical.

Make the two left sprites 60 by 33 pixels, and the two right sprites 61 by 33 pixels. When put back together, they will add up to 121 by 66 pixels. Figure 7-3 shows the sprite after quartering, realigning and flattening.

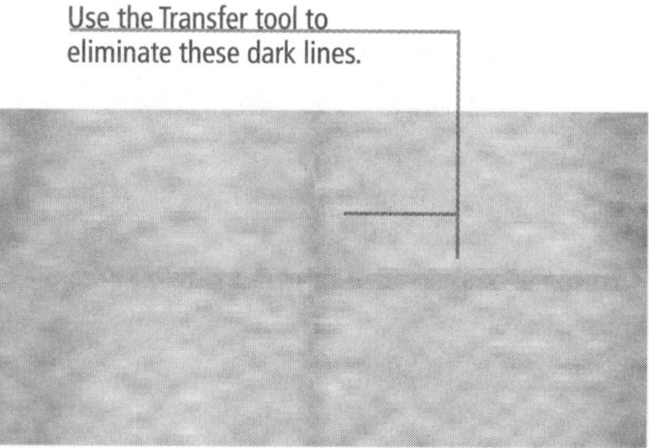
Use the Transfer tool to
eliminate these dark lines.

Figure 7-3
Sprite after quartering, re-aligning and flattening.

Use the Transfer tool on the Paint palette to transfer lighter material to the dark lines and edges at the seams between the tiles. Use a small (9-pixel or so) soft brush. Transfer only what you need to replace the darkest areas.

If you want to do an exceptional job with this tile, quarter, re-align, and flatten one more time. Then use the transfer tool one more time to produce a well-blended texture.

Tiling the Composition Space

Before you tile the sprite on Composition Space, so you can work on the background as it will appear on a Web page, place one duplicate of the tile out on the Workspace. This is the sprite that you will save as a Web graphics file later.

Place the original tile on the upper left corner of the Composition Space and copy and align a complete row. Then flatten the row and duplicate the resulting sprite as many times as necessary to fill the rest of the Composition Space.

After you've arranged the background sprites, select them, flatten them, and then set the flattened sprite's home position. Lock this sprite's position so it won't move accidentally while you are working over it. This is how the background will look like when tiled on the Web.

Now clear up the Composition Space and delete any unneeded sprites. Move the others well away from the Composition Space.

Making the Banner Area

You should begin by creating the graphic at the upper left corner of the Web page. Copy the scanned photo of a trail going up a mountain, and using the leftmost X, Y indicator on the Status bar, position it near the upper left corner of the background, about twenty pixels in.

Notice that the image does not "read" well against the light background. To make foreground images stand out more, you can darken the background by lowering its contrast.

1. Select the background.
2. On the Color Tuning palette, set Brightness and Contrast to –25 and then click Apply.

That's better—the background feels more like it is behind the image, just as you'd like.

Framing the Image

To further enhance the appearance of the image on the background, you can create a frame that will surround the image and create a transition between the image and the background.

1. Zoom in on the image and open the Color Picker.
2. Use the Eyedropper in the Color Picker to select a dark green from the image, as shown in Figure 7-4. The dark green you want is 46, 43, 34, and it's prominent in the lower right corner of the image. If you can't find this exact green with the Eyedropper tool, go ahead and enter the RGB numbers in the Color Picker.

Figure 7-4
Use the Eyedropper to find a pixel close to 46, 43, 34.

3. Draw a 203 by 122-pixel rectangle. That's 8 pixels above and below and 10 pixels on each side larger than the trail image.
4. While the rectangle is selected, Shift-click the background to select both.
5. Click the background once again to make it the source, and then click the Before button on the Arrange palette.

Before button

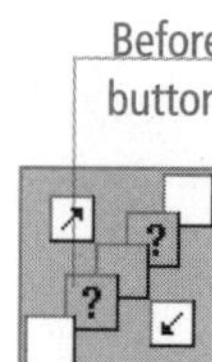

6. Position the green rectangle by selecting it and the trail image. The background should no longer be selected.
7. Make sure the trail image is the source sprite and make sure Relative To Composition Space is unchecked. Then click the Align Centers button on the Arrange palette.
8. Set the home position for the two sprites.

Now the image is surrounded by a dark green rectangle, but the rectangle needs to be softened to make a more gradual transition from the image to the background.

1. Select only the green rectangle and apply the Transparent effect at 85 percent Opacity.

2. Blur the rectangle using a setting of 5 pixels both Horizontally and Vertically.
3. Apply the Recess effect to the blurred sprite.
4. Use the background as a source and apply Transfer Shape on the Texture Transfer palette with an opacity of 20. This brings some of the pixels from the background into the frame to help blend it with the background.

NOTE

We have found that using Transfer Shape with an opacity of less than 100 percent sometimes produces a Transfer Shape at full 100 percent opacity. If this happens to you, undo the texture transfer and move the Opacity slider away from the setting you've just tried. Then return the slider back to the opacity you want and try again. The second time's a charm.

The green rectangle now acts as a frame, as shown in Figure 7-5. Zoom out a bit and you'll see that it now feels so real that you could walk right into the scene and start hiking up the trail.

Figure 7-5
The frame separates the image nicely.

To prepare the trail and frame sprites for saving for the Web, select the image and frame sprites, flatten the selection into a single sprite, and save the sprite's home position. To make room to work, move any sprites away from the top and right side of the Composition Space now.

Adding the Banner Area Text

The Banner area of the Web page requires two sprites: a large heading and a smaller sprite. The large heading sprite will have a thick, soft, recessed sprite behind the text, and the small sprite will have a soft background too. Figure 7-6 shows how these sprites will look when finished.

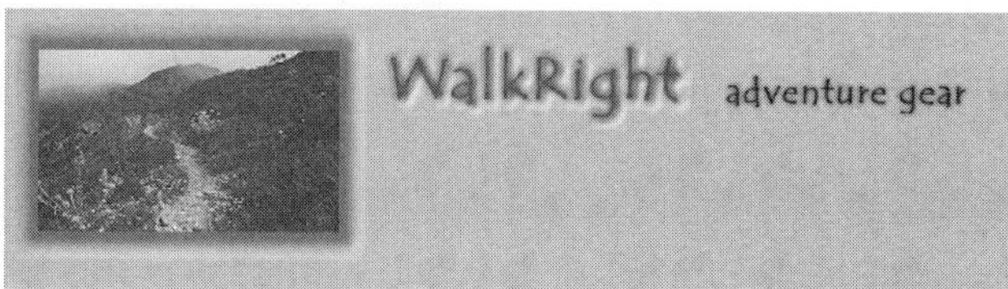

Figure 7-6
The finished text sprites.

Creating the WalkRight Text Sprite

The WalkRight text element consists of red text on a thick, recessed background element. The red color, like all the colors for this site, came from one of the scanned elements; in this case, the flowering thistle.

1. Select the Text tool and drag a text editing box large enough to contain the word WalkRight. The settings on the Text palette should be Tempus Sans ITC for the font, Bold, 28 points, Smoothing checkbox checked, Opacity 100, and local text color 157, 74, 85.
2. Type "WalkRight" and click outside the text editing box to set the text.
3. Zoom in twice, keeping a small part of the Workspace showing at the top of the Composition Space. Position the text as shown in Figure 7-6 above, and set its home position.
4. Duplicate the current sprite and put aside the copy. You will use it after making the recessed element.
5. Change the current color to black and use Color Fill to apply black to the original sprite that is still in position.
6. Duplicate and send home the sprite twice so there are three sprites on top of each other. This thickens the strokes of the letters and makes the anti-aliasing less transparent.

7. To avoid selecting the background sprite, start a selection box outside the top of the Composition Space and enclose all three sprites. Flatten them and set the home position of the resulting sprite. See Figure 7-7 for the starting point for the selection box.

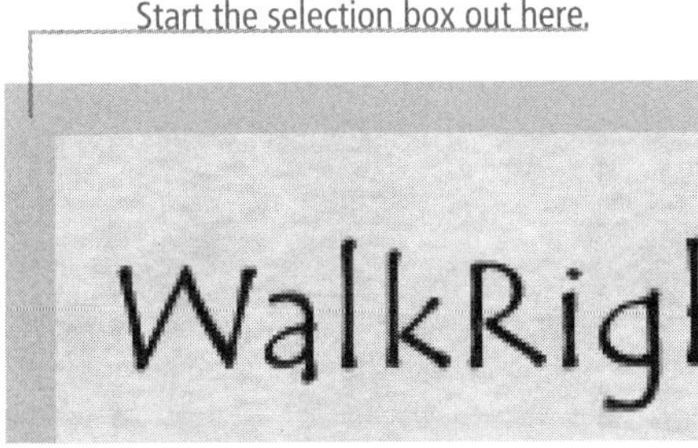
Start the selection box out here.
WalkRig

Figure 7-7
Start drawing a selection box outside the Composition Space.

To make the recess area thick and soft, you need to thicken the black text sprite's strokes.

8. Apply the Edge effect with a Thickness of 1 pixel, black as the color, and 100% Opacity.
9. Applying the Edge effect thickens the edges but produces a lot of anti-aliasing. To fix this, copy the sprite and send the copy home. Repeat, and then select all three sprites, flatten them, and set the home position of the resulting sprite.
10. To soften the sprite, apply the Blur effect at 3 pixels both Horizontal and Vertical.
11. Apply the Recess effect, and then set the resulting sprite's home position.

Recessing the sprite has moved it slightly so that the original red text sprite will no longer align properly if you just send it home. Instead, follow these steps:

1. Select the red text sprite that you set aside a while ago and bring it to the front.
2. Select the recessed sprite and then Shift-click the red text sprite so that the recessed sprite is the source.

3. On the Arrange palette, make sure that Relative To Composition Space is unchecked and then click the Align Centers button. The red sprite centers itself over the recessed sprite.

This looks good when you zoom out, except that the dark parts of the recessed sprite seem to be fighting with the red text, making it less readable than it could be. To harmonize the recessed sprite with the overall look and to make the red text more prominent, you can transfer some of the background texture to the recessed sprite with the Transfer Shape technique.

1. Select the background sprite and Shift-click the recessed sprite.
2. Apply the Transfer Shape effect on the Texture Transfer palette at 15 percent Opacity. This transfers some of the background texture to the recessed sprite so that it blends better with the background.
3. As a final tweak to bring the red text a little more into the foreground, use the Saturation control on the Color Tuning palette to apply 30 percent more saturation to it.

When sprites overlap, it can be hard to tell which sprite you have selected. To find out, click the right mouse button and choose Properties from the shortcut menu. The Properties dialog box shows the currently selected sprite.

4. Move the red text sprite 2 pixels left and 1 pixel up. Figure 7-8 shows the final positioning of the sprites relative to each other.
5. Flatten the text and recessed sprites so they are ready for saving for the Web and set their home position.

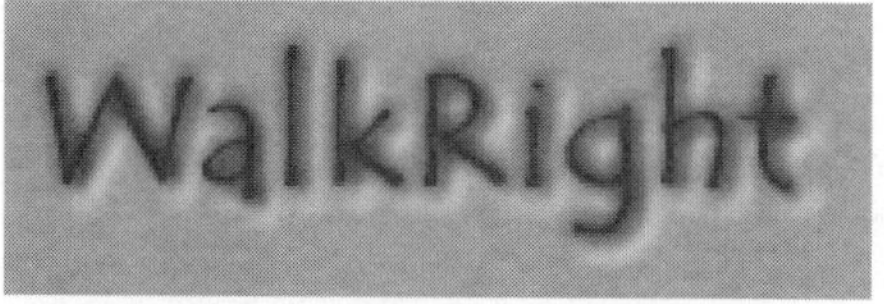

Figure 7-8
The final, flattened text sprite.

Making the Adventure Gear Text Sprite

The "adventure gear" text sprite consists of two elements, a black text sprite and an underlying soft red background. To create the sprite and its background, follow these steps:

1. Select the Text tool and choose the Tempus Sans ITC font on the Text palette. Also select 16 points, Bold, 100% Opacity. Make sure that Smoothing is turned on and the local text color is set to black.
2. Drag out a text editing box to the right of WalkRight and type in "adventure gear." Then click away from the text box to set the text as a sprite.
3. Set the sprite's home position. Duplicate it, send the copy home, select both sprites and flatten them. Finally, set the home position of the resulting sprite.
4. Copy the flattened sprite and set the copy aside to use after you make the red background.
5. Set the current color to 157, 74, 85 and apply it to the original "adventure gear" sprite.
6. Apply Blur at 2 pixels to the sprite. Set its home position, copy it and send the copy home. Select and flatten the two sprites.
7. Select the black "adventure gear" sprite you put aside. Send it home and then to the front.
8. Select the soft, red background and black text sprites and then flatten them. Set the home position of the resulting sprite.

The banner is now complete, so you can turn your attention to the navigation graphics and text.

Creating the Navigation Graphics and Text

To help users navigate easily through the WalkRight Web site, you can use two graphic devices: a site map page that leads to the main areas of the site and a graphic on each page that leads back to the main site map.

In keeping with your desire to use elements from the photos, you decide to use the pink, flowering thistle as the basis for the main site map page. You'll also use a miniature version of the thistle as an icon that users can click to return to the site map.

Extracting the Graphics

To create the large thistle sprite, you need to extract the shape of the flowering thistle from the scanned photo. To help you, we have created a template you can follow to extract the thistle from the background.

1. Copy the pink, flowering thistle image and move the copy onto the Composition Space. Set its home position before continuing.
2. Copy the black template, which looks like the silhouette of the flowering thistle, and move it onto the thistle sprite so it fits, as shown in Figure 7-9.

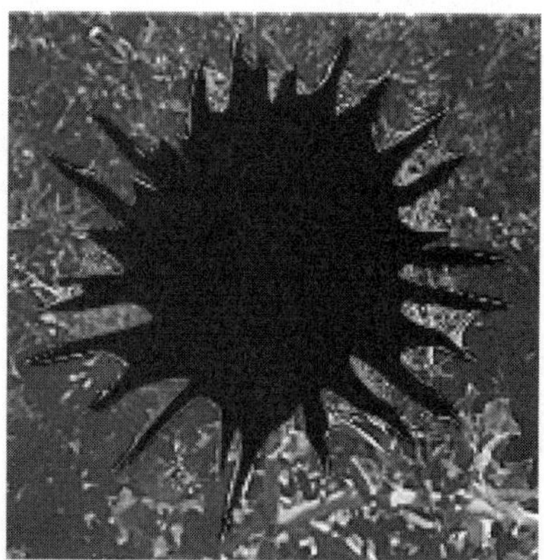

Figure 7-9
Template laid on the thistle image.

3. Lock the positions of the thistle image and the template so that you don't select and move them inadvertently while working with the Cutout tool.
4. Select the thistle image (deselect the template) and then open the Cutout palette and select the Curve tool.
5. Zoom in so that the thistle is large.
6. Slowly work your way around the template, placing control points with the Curve tool.

7. When you're done, click Cut Out on the Cutout palette. You have a beautiful cutout thistle.

While you are using the Cutout tools, go ahead and make the sprites for the navigation buttons. For these, cut out the flower from the scanned photo of a California poppy by following these steps:

1. Set aside the cutout thistle sprite for the moment.
2. Unlock and move the thistle source and the template off the Composition Space.
3. Copy the poppy image and drag the copy onto the Composition Space.
4. Lock the image's position and cut out the poppy. You're on your own this time, without a template.

When you have a poppy sprite cut out, put it aside. Unlock the source image and move it off the Composition Space. You will need four poppy sprites, so make three copies now and leave them where they are.

Positioning the Thistle

Begin creating the final composition by moving the cutout thistle sprite into its approximate position as shown in the finished version of the composition. This thistle sprite could use something to help it stand out from the background a bit. Continuing the look you've established, you can create a recessed sprite beneath the thistle.

1. Use the Scale controls on the Arrange palette to scale the thistle down to 100 pixels in width, while maintaining its aspect ratio. Place it at its final position and set the home position.
2. Copy the thistle sprite and send it home.
3. Set the current color to 51, 46, 90, a color that will work well with the sprites and the background.
4. Apply the current color to the copy of the thistle using the Color Fill button.
5. As before, blur the dark blue thistle sprite at 3 pixels both horizontal and vertical, and then apply the Recess effect. Send the recessed sprite behind the flowering thistle sprite. An easy way to do that is by clicking the Send Backward button on the Arrange palette.
6. Select the flowering thistle sprite and increase Saturation to 12 percent to brighten the colors and make the sprite stand out.

7. Select the thistle and the recessed sprite and flatten them for saving for the Web later. Set the flattened sprite's home position.

Placing the Poppy Sprites

Before composing the poppy sprites, you need to change their color. This adds the element of color as a navigation guide. Each colored poppy can relate to specific products. To apply color to the sprites, you will use Map Color on the Texture Transfer palette. Map Color transfers the color from one sprite to another without altering the destination sprite's grayscale values. The result is that it looks like the original in all respects, except for the new color.

1. Set the current color to 217, 46, 212, a cerise, and then make a 65-pixel square sprite.
2. Select a poppy, bring it to the front, and move it on top of the cerise square.
3. Select both sprites and make sure the square is the source sprite.
4. On the Texture Transfer palette, select Map Color and set the Threshold to 80. Click Apply. This will maintain the value range of the original. Lower threshold values produce lighter results, and higher threshold values produce darker results.
5. Using the same source square, repeat this procedure on two more poppy sprites, changing the color of the square to 46, 203, 213 (a blue), and 46, 158, 87 (a green).
6. As with the thistle, place the sprites, set their home positions, make copies, fill them with the color 51, 46, 90, and blur and then recess them. Send the recessed sprites behind the poppy sprites. As you finish each set of poppy and recessed sprite, select the pair, flatten them, and set their home positions so you can save them to the Web later.

Drawing the Connecting Lines

To make the lines that connect the large thistle to the smaller poppies, you can create an open polygon.

1. Open the Shapes palette and ensure the Close checkbox is turned off (unchecked). This enables you to draw lines.

2. Use the Polygon tool with an Opacity of 100, a slightly soft Edge (about a tenth of the way to the right of Hard), and a Line Width of 4.
3. Click once over the thistle and then click once over a poppy. Right click and choose create. Refer to the finished composition for placement. Do this for each poppy.
4. To place the lines under the thistle and the poppies, select all four lines and the background sprite. Click the background sprite again to make it the source sprite.
5. On the Arrange palette, click the Before button to send the thistle sprites in front of all the line sprites.

Adding the Navigation Text Sprites

Add the final text sprites shown in the finished composition. The font is Tempus Sans ITC at 16 points, Bold, black, and 100 percent Opacity. Remember that each text element consists of two sprites flattened to strengthen the text. Align the three sprites on the right side using the Align tools.

Saving the Sprites for the Web

To use the set of sprites you've created on a real Web page, you'll need to save them as individual GIF files that you can refer to in HTML. Image Composer helps prepare sprites for use on the Web with its Save For The Web wizard. You used this wizard in Chapter 2 to save some buttons, but this time you'll choose a background color for the sprites and make other choices that are different from the defaults.

Before you use the wizard, you need to take some preparatory steps. Before the text can be used, each text sprite must be made into a GIF file. The lines, poppies, thistle, and trail image sprites must also be saved as GIF files. First however, make sure each sprite that has a recessed element under it has been flattened with that element. Also, select all the sprites and click Set Home Position. Now would also be a good time to record the X,Y position of each sprite as it is displayed on the status bar. These numbers will help you position the graphics when you create the Web page.

In this project, you have used blur and recess techniques that use sophisticated transparency and color blending. To get the best result when saving for the Web, you must choose settings that are different from the defaults. The following settings work best for the sprites in this project. For your own projects, you may need to do some experimentation by trying some of the things we'll point out.

1. Open the Color Picker and click the Custom Palette tab. From the Color Palette drop-down list, select Web (Dithered). This displays your graphics with the same color palette that a Web browser will use, dithering any colors in the 24-bit images that are not in the browser's palette.
2. Select the flattened trail image sprite.
3. From the File menu, choose Save For The Web.
4. On the first screen, choose The Selected Sprite Or Group and then click Next.
5. On the next page, select Let The Web Page Background Show Through and then click Next.
6. On the next page, select My Web Page's Background Is The Following Solid Color. Click the color button to open the Color Picker.
7. On the Custom Palette tab of the Color Picker, click Import, choose WIN95.PAL on the Import Color Palette dialog box, and then click Open.
8. On the bottom line of the color grid, select the sixth gray to the right of the red, as shown in Figure 7-10. Click OK and then click Next.

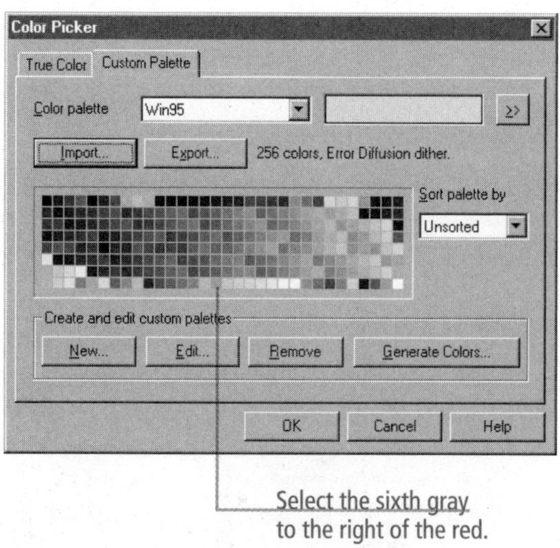

Figure 7-10

Click the sixth gray to the right of red on the last row of the Win95 color palette.

9. On the last page of the wizard, click Save.
10. On the Saves The Current Selection dialog box, choose COMPUSERVE GIF (*.GIF) as the file type and select a folder and name for the file.
11. From the Color Format drop-down list, choose Web (Dithered).
12. Leave the Transparent Color at its default.
13. Set the Threshold slider to 30. This setting produces an 8-bit result closest to the look of the sprite in Image Composer while working in 24-bit color.

How did we arrive at a threshold of 30? Simply by experimenting with different settings until we found the one we liked. The lower the threshold, the lower the transparency level in the image that will be transparent in the GIF file.

Repeat this exact same procedure for the other sprites on the Composition Space. To see how these GIFs look, you can use Insert From File to bring them back into Image Composer.

To create the button you can use on other Web pages to enable users to return to the site map, you can scale down the thistle sprite and save it a second time. Similarly, the poppy sprites could be useful on other Web pages as graphic navigation icons people can click to move directly to particular areas of the Web site, without having to return to the site map.

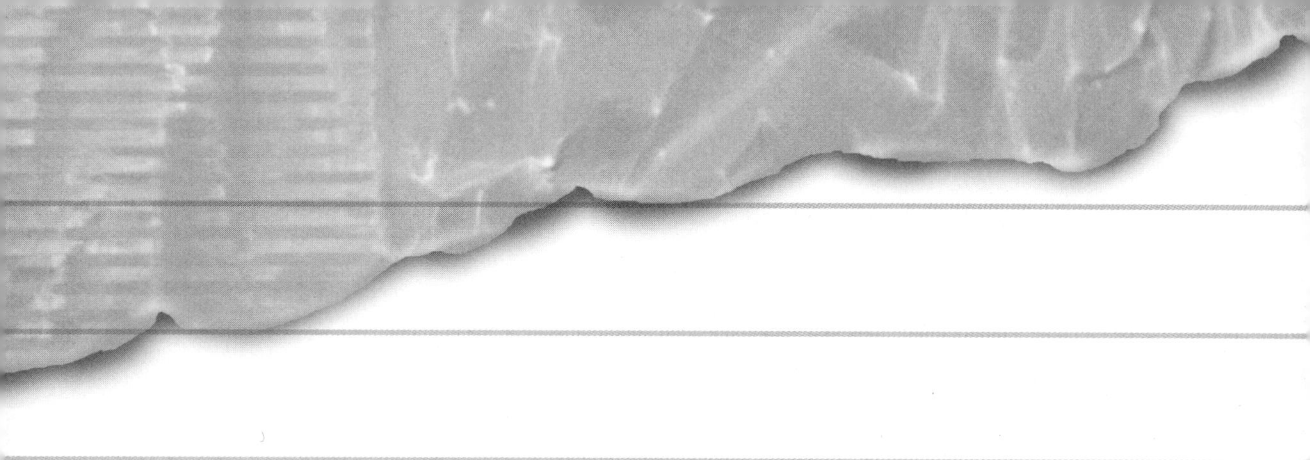

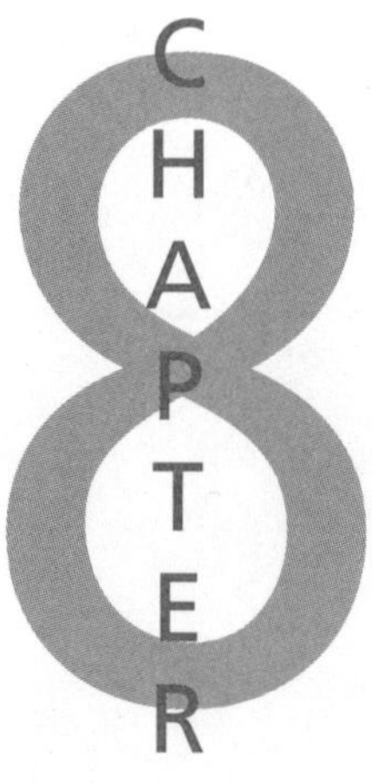
CHAPTER

Tropical Fantasy Web Site

In this chapter, you will create an entire Web page design from a collection of stock photographs provided by a company called PhotoDisc. In the process, you will analyze the concept for the site so that you can choose images that will work well.

To blend the images into a montage, you will tightly integrate the use of the Cutout, color tuning, transparency, and Transfer tools, creating a major graphic element with topical bullets that reflect the theme for the site, "Tropical Fantasy."

Selecting the Images

Your client is a travel agency catering to young singles in the computer and entertainment industries. Singles have plenty of disposable income but little time, so they are ready to pay a premium for an all-fun, no-hassle holiday. Your client has tailored for this market some vacation packages to lush tropical islands where relaxation and water sports mix to create a romantic ambiance. The Web page should stimulate a desire to check out the company's vacation options.

Initial Concept Decisions

As creative director, you have done your homework. Your research indicates that the three activities most enjoyed by potential purchasers of these travel packages are scuba diving, sailing, and relaxing on the beach with a good book. These activities guide your selection of images with which to build the home page banner.

Another common denominator among potential customers is access to the Internet with high-speed connections and high-end color displays on the desktop. In fact, you plan to design the site for a very narrow target audience by using 24-bit color graphics on the site and JPEG images rather than GIF files. JPEG files can be 24-bit, color graphics files with 16.7 million colors. GIF files are limited to 256 colors.

In keeping with your belief that the target audience will access the site with high-speed Internet connections, you decide to create a design with a relatively large central graphic, composed from several smaller images. The luxurious central graphic will help the page create an attractive first impression.

To begin your search for suitable images, you put together the following short list of image topics:

- Tropical
- Underwater sports
- Sailing
- Relaxing on the beach

With this list in mind, you dig out catalogs of stock images. A few hours of looking reward you with a dozen or so possibilities. Using the small images on the CDs that accompany the catalogs, you decide on four that work well together in terms of color, composing possibilities, and subject.

The first image, a scuba diver swimming from left to right, has an uncluttered right side that would be conducive to blending with other images. With the exception of the diver's red outfit, which stands out nicely, the blues are the dominant colors. The second photo is a dynamic image of a sailboat coming out of a golden sunset directly at the camera. Timeless relaxation emanates from the third image, that of a young woman reading a book, silhouetted against a blazing sunset. For Web site buttons, you decide to use a pineapple in a photograph of tropical fruit.

The Design Layout

After some time considering "what if" possibilities with the images, a strong design emerges. You develop a composition with a strong left to right movement that will draw people into the main image. You accomplish this with the image of the diver swimming in from the left side. At the right side of the composition, you'll place the woman reading a book, with the result that the shape of the outline dynamically guides the users' attention back into the main image. The sailboat between the two framing images adds a strong element of action directed at the viewer that will surely get his or her attention. Additional copies of the sailboat, scaled down and placed behind the original, add a sense of real space, a feeling that "you are here."

To see the final composition, open the file CHAPTER8.MIC. On the Composition Space, a TIF file shows the completed Web page. The sprites we made as we created the composition are arranged from top to bottom to the left of the Composition Space, so that you can use them as a reference while you work.

Preparing the Images

To begin, set the Composition Space color to white in the Composition Setup dialog box. Although the background will be black in the final piece, you'll find it easier to work on a white background for now so that you can see the dark silhouette clearly. Move the TIF image just below the Composition Space so you can refer to it from time to time.

Use From File on the Insert menu to add the raw image files to your Workspace. The images you need are DIVER.TIF, FRUIT.TIF, SAILBOAT.TIF, and READER.TIF from the PROJECTS folder of the CD-ROM.

You will begin with the image of the reader, so place a copy of it on the Composition Space.

Now that you are getting into more time-consuming, multi-step tasks, you should be careful to make copies of every sprite you work on as you go along. Without copies, you won't be able to retrace your steps if changes you make don't work out as well as you thought.

Preparing the Reader Sprite

Zoom in so that the Composition Space fills the screen and look carefully at the image of the reader. What appeared to be a black silhouette when you were zoomed out now shows a considerable amount of color bleed from the sunset. This is common in photographs of dark objects shot against bright, colorful backgrounds. You will use the Color Tuning tools to fix the color bleed and cut out a clean silhouette. Even so, you may still need to use the Eraser tool on the Paint palette to remove any stray pixels of color.

Color Tuning the Image

Before acting, analyze the image to get a feel for what is necessary. The goal is to totally separate the silhouette from the sunset. You will use the Dynamic Range histogram for this analysis, because it graphically depicts the distribution of light and dark values in an image. With the image selected, open the Color Tuning palette and click the Dynamic Range tab. Refer to Figure 8-1.

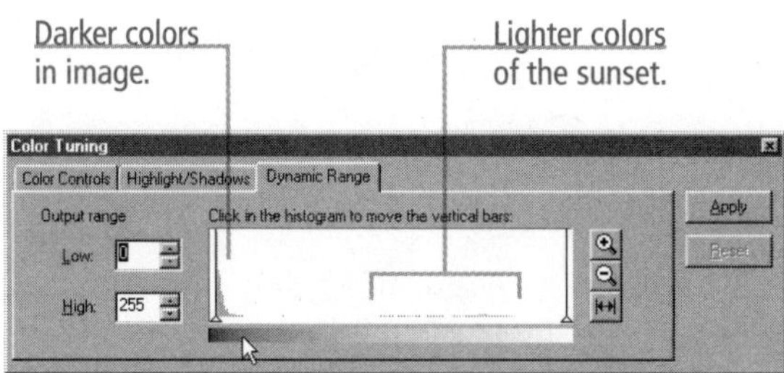

Figure 8-1
The Dynamic Range histogram shows two separate areas of colors.

Notice that the histogram shows two areas of data. The gray bars at the left end of the scale represent the darker colors in the image, the black and spillover colors in the silhouette. The second set of very small bars, along the middle of the scale, represent the lighter colors of the sunset.

The wide separation between the two sets of bars means you can modify the darks with little effect on the sunset colors. That's exactly what you need to do.

When the Output Range settings on the Dynamic Range control are set to their defaults, 0 and 255, moving the left vertical slider to the right makes more of the dark colors turn black. In effect, you are using the control to instruct the program that black should begin to the right of the darker colors in the image. In this case, that would turn most, if not all, of the silhouette black.

1. Set the left slider as shown in Figure 8-2 (don't worry about the right slider yet) and and click Apply. The spill colors on the silhouette disappear and the silhouette becomes uniformly black.

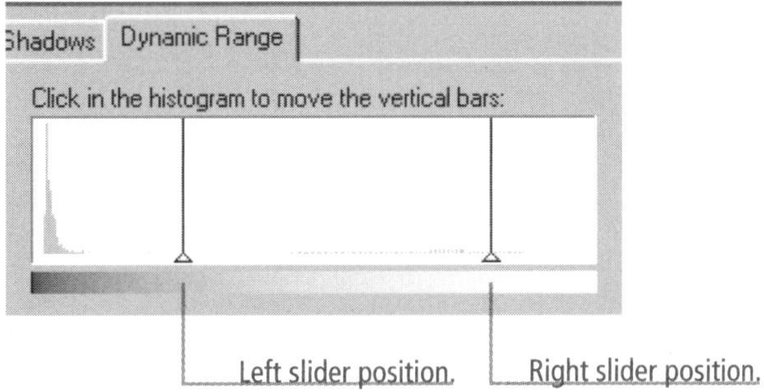

Figure 8-2
Dynamic Range histogram with sliders set to darken the darks and compensate for darkening of the lights.

Now examine the image. You'll see that a secondary result of changing the Dynamic Range is that the sunset is now a little darker. You'd like to maintain a good light to dark contrast in the image, so you can drag the right vertical slider to the left a bit to brighten the brightest colors.

2. Drag the right slider to the position shown in Figure 8-2 and click Apply again. The sunset lightens up again.

Image composer recalculates the Dynamic Range changes from scratch with each change until you deselect the sprite, so you can make as many adjustments as you'd like until you're satisfied.

Cutting Out the Silhouette

Now that the silhouette is a uniform, dark color, you are ready to cut it out of the image. Follow these steps:

1. Set the current color to 143, 0, 235, a purple that will stand out distinctly from the other colors in the image.
2. Make a copy of the color-tuned sprite and set it aside.
3. Select the original, and then open the Cutout palette and click the Select Color Region tab.
4. To select only black, drag the Blackness slider on the Select Color Region tab to 100, and drag the Hue and Whiteness sliders to 0. Figure 8-3 shows these settings.

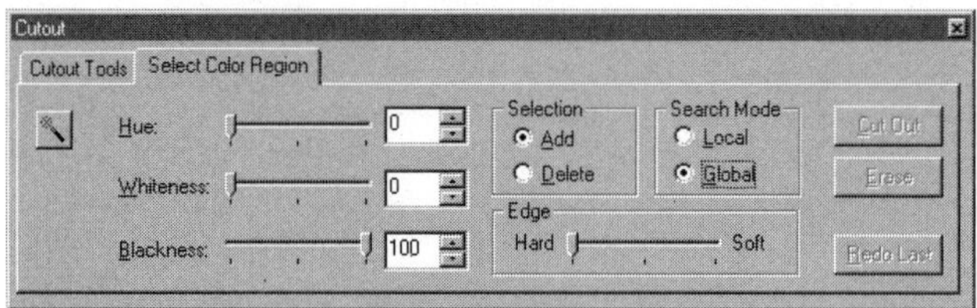

Figure 8-3
Settings on the Select Color Region tab.

5. Make sure Selection is set to Add so that the black pixels found are added to the selection, and make sure Search Mode is set to Global, so the control will search the entire image for black pixels.
6. Make sure the Edge slider is set to Hard so that the cutout sprite you are about to make does not have an anti-aliased edge.
7. Click the Select Color Region wand button near the left end of the palette and then click once on the black silhouette. Purple floods the selected black pixels to show you what the cutout will look like.
8. Compare the area selected with the sample. If any part of your image is not included, click the area to add it to the selection.
9. Click Cut Out on the Cutout palette. Everything turns black again as the new sprite is created.
10. Deselect both sprites and then drag the new cutout sprite aside. Figure 8-4 shows the new cutout. You'll also find

Gallery of Projects

The pieces that follow are completed images for projects in this book.

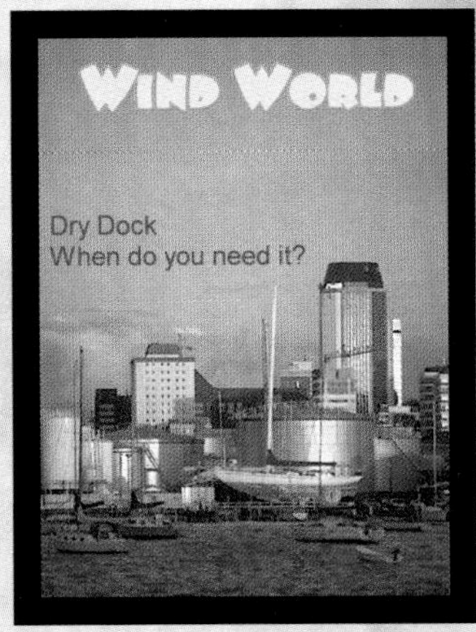

From Chapter 4,
Wind World magazine cover

From Chapter 8,
Tropical Fantasy Web page

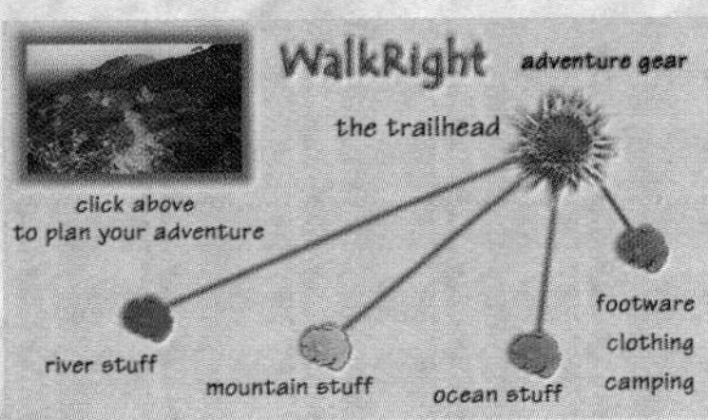

From Chapter 7,
WalkRight Web page

From Chapter 5, Big Sur poster

From Chapter 9,
Global Business poster

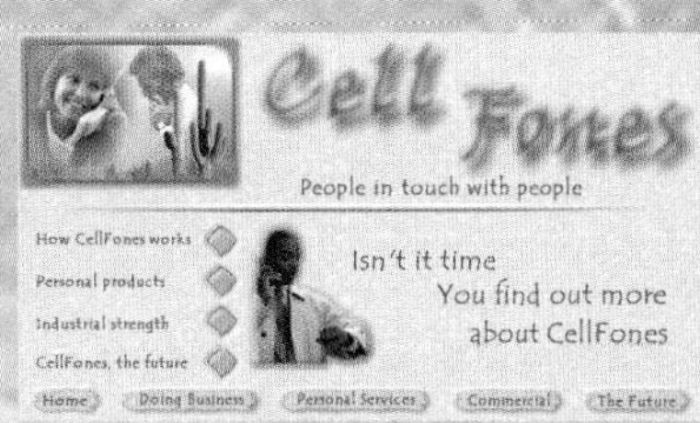

From Chapter 11,
Cell Fones Web page

From Chapter 10,
Channel Graphics mailer

Gallery of Art by Will Tait

The titled images on this and the next four pages were created entirely in Image Composer by Will Tait using the techniques taught in this book.

Enigma 1 © *1997 Will Tait*

Mind Mirror 1 © *1997 Will Tait*

Wave © *1997 Will Tait*

Make Art © *1997 Will Tait*

Gator © *1997 Will Tait*

our version of this sprite above and to the left of the Composition Space, so you can compare your sprite with the one we created.

Figure 8-4
The silhouette after cutting out.

11. Finally, move the cutout sprite off the Composition Space for use later.
12. Delete the original sprite from which the cutout was made. It worked well for making the cutout but the sunset is too dark for your next task.
13. Save the file to your hard disk with a suitable name.

Preparing the Sailboat Sprite

Now consider the sailboat image you inserted. It is oriented vertically rather than horizontally, and for the final composition you want a wide image with the sailboat on the left. Also note that the sky in the image is warm, but somewhat uninteresting compared to the wide expanse of ocean and the beautiful sunset you'd rather have.

Look at the sprites that came with the project file. Below the silhouette sprite are three sprites: a wide sprite with a sailboat on the left, a wide expanse of ocean and a nice sunset on the right, a sprite that is all sunset, and a sprite that is all ocean. Your next task is to make your own versions of the sprites that are all sunset and ocean and then compose them with the sailboat to create the image you need.

First make the sunset image. You'll need another copy of the original reader image, so make one now and place it on the Composition Space.

Creating a Sunset Sprite with the Transfer Tool

To create the sunset sprite, you will use the Transfer tool on the Paint palette to pick up portions of the sunset that are visible in the background behind the reading woman, and use them to paint over the silhouette of the woman. When you are done, the silhouette will be entirely obscured by repeated portions of the sunset.

Begin by zooming in on the Composition Space so the image fills your screen (you will need to work in detail). Then follow these steps:

1. Select the image and then click the Transfer tool on the Paint palette and choose a 21-pixel wide, soft brush from the grid of brush styles. Set the Opacity slider to 20.
2. Click the spot shown in Figure 8-5, just to the right of the woman's chest, as the source location.

Figure 8-5
First source location and area transferred to.

3. Drag the brush back and forth horizontally across the area where the book and hand meet the sky. The sunrise colors will be painted onto the silhouette, as you can see in the Figure above.
4. Now click the Transfer tool again and select a spot to the right of the book as the source and paint back into the area where you just worked. This keeps a blend happening.
5. Keep working back and forth, picking up pieces from one place and painting them into others, until you have a whole sprite of sunset. An especially interesting area for a source is the sky above the woman's head. Don't overdo it though. Varying the source keeps it from looking all the same.

Remember, after setting a source point for the Transfer tool, the duplicate you transfer over radiates out from the destination spot you click. You will need to stop and set new source points frequently at first, and less as you go along. Sometimes you will be able to make only a stroke or two before selecting a new source. Don't worry, once you get started, it doesn't take long to do the whole image. Look at the sprite we've provided as a guide, but don't try to make yours exactly the same—an impossible task. But do take the time to complete the entire image, because the practice will help you gain control of the tool.

6. When you have finished the sprite, put it aside for now and save the file.

Joining the Sailboat and Sunset Sprites

Now you can join the sunset sprite with the sailboat sprite.

1. Make a copy of the sailboat sprite and move it onto the Composition Space a little to the left of center.
2. Copy the sunset sprite and move it onto the Composition Space next to the sailboat sprite.
3. Align the tops of the two sprites and touch their edges with the Align controls, as shown in Figure 8-6. Remember, Relative To Composition Space should be turned off on the Arrange palette.
4. Flatten the two sprites.

Figure 8-6

The sunset and sailboat sprites aligned for flattening.

Creating the Ocean Sprite

To extend the ocean, you need to make a rectangle to fill the space below the sunset sprite.

1. Use the Rectangle tool on the Shapes palette to draw a rectangle that is a little larger than the space under the sunset portion of the newly flattened sailboat-sunset sprite.
2. Send the rectangle to the back, deselect it, select it again and use the arrow keys to fine-tune its position so it fits the space neatly, as shown in Figure 8-7.

Rectangle fills the space neatly.

Figure 8-7
Rectangle filling the space where the ocean will be transferred.

3. Flatten the two sprites into one.

Now use the Transfer tool again to transfer ocean from the sailboat image over onto the rectangle. Also use it to transfer sky from the sunset image onto the sky near the sailboat. While working on the ocean, keep in mind that, as you look further toward the horizon, the waves appear smaller and have less contrast. To make the new ocean look real, you want to transfer horizontally from the sailboat image to maintain this look. Try experimenting with a harder, larger brush, too. To blend the two different kinds of sky into one, use the Transfer tool with a very low opacity to make the transfer gradual.

After completely covering the sunset and rectangle sprites with ocean, you can transfer areas from various places to break up the pattern a bit. Look at the sprite we've provided as a reference.

Congratulations. You have a sailboat sprite.

Adding Two More Sailboats

While the sailboat sprite is still on the Composition Space, you can use the Cutout tools to make a sprite of the sailboat by itself. Follow these steps:

1. Zoom in on the sailboat image so it is quite large.
2. Select the sprite and open the Cutout palette.
3. Use the curve tool to click control points around the outside of the sailboat, and then click Cut Out to create the new sprite. Figure 8-8 shows the shape of the cutout.

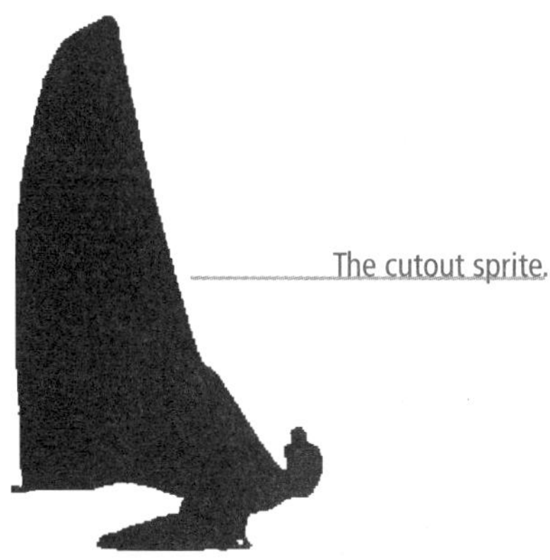

Figure 8-8
Shape of the cutout sailboat.

To make the additional sailboats, duplicate the cutout sailboat sprite twice. On the Arrange palette, change the Units to Percent, and then use the Scale control to scale one duplicate to 70 percent and another to 35 percent. Leave the original cutout sprite at 100 percent. Make sure Keep Aspect Ratio is checked so that the sprites remain the same shape.

Set the duplicate sailboat sprites aside on the Workspace for now. You'll need them later.

Joining the Diver and Sailboat Sprites

Now that you've prepared all the sprites you'll need, you can begin combining them into a composition. First you'll join the diver and sailboat sprites into one flattened sprite.

Clear the space immediately around the Composition Space because the composition will extend beyond the edges of the Composition Space for now. Then place a copy of the diver and sailboat sprites next to each other, as shown in Figure 8-9.

Figure 8-9
Placement of diver and sailboat sprites.

Positioning the Sprites

When you have the two sprites adjacent, you notice that the diver sprite is shorter than the sailboat sprite. Rather than scale the sailboat sprite down, you choose to scale up the diver sprite because you want the final composition large enough to cross the entire Composition Space.

1. Select the sailboat sprite.
2. Look at the status bar for the size of the sprite. The sailboat sprite is 461 pixels wide by 275 pixels high.
3. Select the diver sprite and enter the height of the sailboat sprite into the Height control on the Arrange palette, and then click Apply. As long as Keep Aspect Ratio is checked, the scale command will scale up the diver proportionately to the same height as the sailboat sprite.
4. Use the alignment tools to align the tops of the sprites, and then touch their edges.

The scaling operation has made the edge of the underwater sprite anti-aliased. Don't worry about that; you will use the cropping tool later to clean up the edges of the final image. Before you go on, though, be sure to set the home positions of the two sprites. For this procedure, having the home positions of the sprites set will really count. Finally, before you proceed, save the file to update it.

Blending the Sprites

As in the Big Sur poster project of Chapter 5, you need to blend two images together using a transparency gradient, but this time your goal is different. Rather than trying to make the two images look believable as a single scene, you want to flow the two images together to create a montage of related images.

1. Using the Rectangle tool on the Cutout palette, make the cutout sprite shown in Figure 8-10, and set its home position.

Figure 8-10
Sprite cut out from sailboat sprite.

2. Move the large sailboat sprite aside and make two copies of the new sprite.
3. Move one of the copies aside to keep as a backup. Then, with the remaining new sprite selected, open the Effects palette and select the Gradient effect. On the Details tab, choose Grayscale Right and click Apply.
4. You need to have access to the gradient sprite, so turn off Keep Aspect Ratio on the Arrange palette, and scale the sprite vertically to 300 pixels. Now you can put it behind other sprites and still reach it.

You want a smooth blend between the underwater and sailboat scenes, which is all the more difficult because they have such dissimilar colors. To achieve this blend, follow these steps:

1. Move the grayscale sprite aside, and then send the sailboat sprite behind the diver sprite.
2. Use the left arrow key to move the sailboat sprite horizontally underneath the diver sprite to the position shown in Figure 8-11. You want the right edge of the diver sprite about even with the person sailing the sailboat.

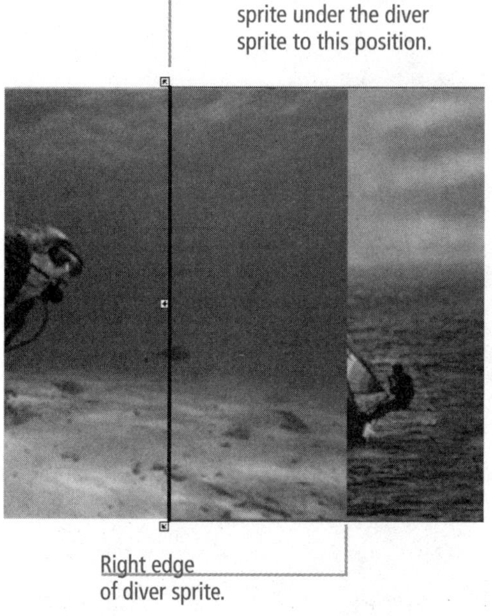
Slide the sailboat sprite under the diver sprite to this position.
Right edge of diver sprite.

Figure 8-11
Sprites overlapped.

3. Bring the sailboat sprite to the front and set its home position.
4. Move the grayscale sprite onto the sailboat sprite so its left edge is 1 pixel farther to the left than the sailboat sprite. The grayscale sprite should be in the back. If it's not, send it there.

You're now ready to map the transparency from the gradient sprite to the sailboat sprite. You want the left edge of the sailboat sprite to be completely transparent with a fast transition to fully opaque before the middle of the grayscale gradient. To achieve this effect, you need to adjust the Highlight/Shadows setting of the grayscale gradient on the Color Tuning palette. The precise adjustment for the curve on the Highlight/Shadows tab is a little difficult to convey, so we have provided a grayscale sprite pre-adjusted to which you can refer. This sprite is to the left of the Workspace with the other supplied sprites, but if you want to try adjusting your own grayscale gradient, follow these steps:

1. Select the grayscale gradient sprite.
2. Open the Color Tuning palette and click the Highlight/Shadows tab.
3. Adjust the control handles of the curve to match those shown in Figure 8-12, and click Apply.

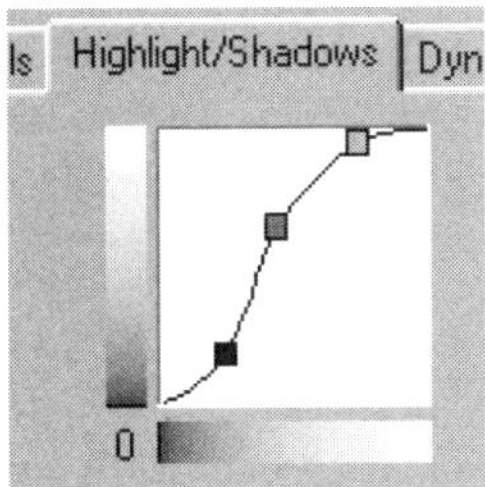

Figure 8-12

Move the control points to match the figure.

Refer to the pre-adjusted grayscale sprite to see how close your adjusted grayscale sprite is. Don't worry if it is not perfect. It takes practice to understand the relationship of the grayscale gradient to the transparency mapping. Practice and you will get it.

With the gradient prepared, you are ready to transfer its grayscale gradient values to the sprite as transparency levels.

1. With the grayscale gradient selected, Shift-click the sailboat sprite. The gradient is the source sprite.
2. Open the Texture Transfer palette, select Map Transparency, and click Apply. The small sailboat sprite becomes transparent on the left, moving toward opacity on the right. Move the gradient sprite aside.

3. Lock the position of the small sailboat sprite. You are going to move the large sailboat sprite under it and align the upper left corners.
4. Move the large sailboat sprite near the sprite you just transparency mapped.
5. Shift-click the small sailboat sprite, click it again to make it the source and then align the upper left corners of the sprites. Deselect all and send the large sprite to the back.

Too much blue is showing through the transparent gradient sailboat sprite. That's OK, just duplicate the transparent sailboat sprite and send the copy home. That's better. It's time to save your file.

Adding the Sailboat Cutouts

A while ago, you cut out, duplicated and scaled several sailboat sprites. To set their front-to-back order (Z-order) properly, start with the smallest sailboat. Duplicate it and move it onto the water. Repeat this with the middle size boat. Then repeat once more with the full-size boat sprite, which is positioned right on the boat in the composition.

Use the arrow keys to adjust the placement of the boats, comparing your image with the finished image that was on the Composition Space when you opened the Image Composer file.

Select the underwater sprite and all the sailboat sprites that currently make up your composition. Group them and make a copy of the group. Put the copy aside, select the original group and flatten it in preparation for the next step.

That's it for this part of the project, so save the file once again. Figure 8-13 shows the current state of the composition.

Figure 8-13
The current state of the composition.

Adding the Reader Sprite

Your composition is now ready for the addition of the silhouette you created earlier. Before you start, there are a few things to consider, though. The silhouette needs to be flipped horizontally because you made the earlier decision to use the silhouette as a design element that directs the viewer's attention back into the page. Besides, if left as is, it would cover the diver.

You also want the silhouette to have a somewhat dreamy quality. In contrast to diving and sailing, which are active sports, reading a book under palm trees is relaxing and soothing. A small amount of blur will soften the hard edges of the image and help it blend smoothly with the background and provide the dreaminess you want.

Once again you will apply a transparency gradient, but this time, instead of starting with a wide band of total transparency at one side of the image, you will make a transition from only partial transparency to full opacity. This will help to maintain a certain amount of visual separation from the background and help the sprite to maintain an identity that balances out the softness produced by the blur.

Before proceeding, move the current composition that includes the diver and the sailboat sprites off the Composition Space and move onto the Composition Space a copy of the silhouette you made earlier.

Scaling and Softening the Sprite

To change the direction the sprite is facing, use Flip Horizontally on the Arrange palette. Also, while you are working on this sprite, you might want to use the Eraser to clean up the random black pixels that appear behind the middle of the woman's back.

To make this sprite fit the overall composition, you need to scale it up, just as you did the diver sprite. In this case, you want to make sure the entire silhouette is included in the final composition, so add 60 pixels to the height using the Scale control on the Arrange palette. Of course, make sure Keep Aspect Ratio is checked.

Now you can give the sprite a blur that will impart to it a warm softness. But in the process, you also want to retain the integrity of the open, lacy quality of the palm fronds. To blur the overall sprite, but still keep the palm fronds clear and distinct, you will create two sprites, one with a single-pixel blur, and one with no blur. Combined, they will produce the effect you want. Follow these steps:

1. Set the sprite's home position and make a copy. Move the copy aside.

2. Select the original sprite and apply the Blur effect at 1 pixel both horizontally and vertically. The original sprite will be the back sprite in the Z-order, so it's the one that gets the blur.
3. Select both sprites and align their centers, making sure Relative To Composition Space is unchecked.
4. Flatten the two sprites, set the home position of the resulting sprite, and save the file.

Aligning and Cropping the Sprite

Now you want to align the reader with the main composition and crop it to fit properly.

1. Move the main composition under the reader sprite so that the reader is centered vertically and both right sides are close to matching. Figure 8-14 shows how this will look.

Figure 8-14
Silhouette and main composition sprites aligned properly.

The blurred edges of the silhouette should be slightly outside the top, bottom, and right edges of the main composition sprite. You will crop these in a minute.

Before going on, zoom out and look at the finished image that was on the Composition Space when you opened the original file. The most transparent part of the palm fronds starts just to the right of the second sailboat. That opens the space around the sailboats and breaks the composition into three distinct visual areas. To achieve this, you must crop the left side of the reader sprite.

2. Zoom back in on the Composition Space and crop the reader sprite as shown in Figure 8-15.

Crop the reader
sprite to here.

Figure 8-15
Silhouette cropped so that the sailboats have visual space.

Now use the Crop tool to crop the top, bottom, and right sides of the silhouette so they are even with the sprite below it. Set its home position.

Creating the Transparency Gradient

The transparency gradient for the silhouette needs to move from a single pixel of total transparency, quickly into a long mid range, with a single pixel of complete opacity at the right. However, you want the entire silhouette to be somewhat transparent. To do this you make the transparency gradient wider than the distance to be mapped.

1. Make a rectangle, send it to the back, and apply the Grayscale Right gradient to it. See Figure 8-16, on the next page, for the size of the grayscale rectangle relative to the reader sprite. Notice that it extends beyond the right side of the silhouette.

   Again, you need to adjust the Highlight/Shadows of the grayscale gradient. Figure 8-17, on the next page, shows the adjustment to the curve.

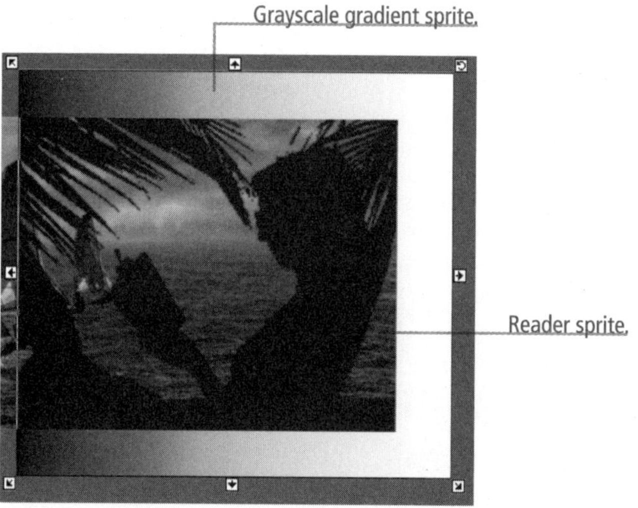

Figure 8-16
Size of grayscale gradient behind the silhouette.

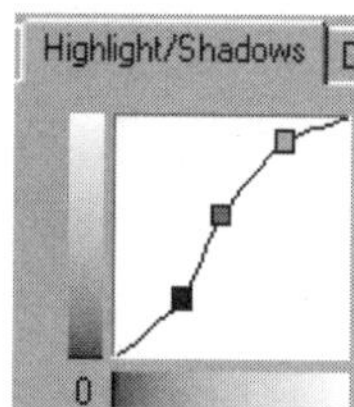

Figure 8-17
Control point settings for the grayscale gradient.

NOTE You will find our version of the color-tuned gradient underneath the silhouette near the bottom of the collection of pre-made sprites in the MIC file.

2. Make sure the left edge of the grayscale gradient is even with the left edge of the silhouette, and then apply Map Transparency to the silhouette.
3. The silhouette could be a bit more opaque. Make sure its home position is set, duplicate it, and send the copy home.

Don't worry that the silhouette sprite extends a little farther to the right than the ocean sprite behind it. You'll fix that when you crop the overall sprite.

4. Select the silhouette and the diver/sailboat sprite, group them, make and move aside a copy, and then flatten the original.

You are now ready to crop the edges and scale the image to fit the final composition. Before you do, though, save your file.

Fine-Tuning the Composition

Zoom in on the flattened composition and look at its edges. Use the Crop tool, where necessary, to crop any edges that need it. You'll also want to crop off the portion of the reader sprite that extends to the right beyond the ocean sprite in the background. All edges should be hard and straight.

To size the overall composition, consider how you'd like the final Web page to look. The size you've been assuming all along is 605 pixels wide (the width of the Composition Space). In addition, you'll want a border around the image, so plan to leave 30 pixels on either side. The final width of the image, therefore, should be 545 pixels (605 minus 60), so set the width to 555. That leaves an extra 10 pixels, so you can crop off the anti-aliasing that will occur when you reduce the size of the sprite. After scaling the image, crop all the sides by 5 pixels to clean up the anti-aliasing and regain the hard edges.

Using the Align tools with Relative To Composition Space turned on, align the flattened composition first with Centers Vertically, and then Tops. The flattened sprite will be centered at the top of the Composition Space.

Creating Navigation Buttons

It would be a good idea to make the navigation buttons next to get a sense of the overall feeling of the composition before you add the title text. That way everything will end up with a more integrated look and feel. The image for the buttons will be cut out from the fruit image. First, however, set the Composition Space color to black in the Composition Setup dialog box.

Creating the Pineapple Buttons

Take a look at the pineapples in the finished image, and then look at the picture of tropical fruit you inserted in the file. You won't find a single pineapple that's exactly like the one we used for the button. That's because none of the pineapples in the photo was complete. They were all obscured somewhat by other items in the image. To make a complete pineapple, we used the Transfer tool to transfer bits and pieces from other pineapples to complete the left front pineapple.

Go ahead and move a copy of the fruit image onto the Composition Space and then, using the Transfer tool on the Paint palette, fill out the left front pineapple. When you finish the pineapple, use the Curve tool on the Cutout palette to cut out the pineapple image. Then set aside a copy and scale down the original to 100 pixels high.

To enhance the final piece, you can create a glow around the pineapple by following these steps:

1. Set the home position of the pineapple.
2. Make a copy and then set the current color to black.
3. Use Color Fill to fill the copy with black.
4. Apply the Edge effect to the black copy with a Thickness of 1 pixel, and a color of 178, 0, 202.
5. Apply the Blur effect at 1 pixel both Horizontal and Vertical and then set the home position of the sprite.
6. Copy the sprite, send the copy home, select both sprites, and flatten them.
7. Bring the original scaled-down pineapple to the front and position it on the black sprite with the purple border. Select and flatten both sprites.
8. Scale a copy of the flattened sprite to 80 pixels high. This size makes the image large enough to recognize, but still leaves plenty of space for text below the buttons.

The scaling has taken from the pineapple some of its color intensity. You can restore it by using color tuning and increasing the Saturation by 5.

The overall composition has strong diagonal elements. You can enhance the buttons and make them feel part of the whole by rotating them.

1. Copy the small pineapple sprite.
2. Rotate one of the two sprites counter-clockwise 45 degrees by dragging the rotate handle at the upper right corner of the sprite's bounding box. The status bar tells you the exact rotation angle.
3. Rotate the other sprite clockwise 45 degrees.
4. Now make a copy of each sprite so that you have four sprites in total and position them roughly, using the completed composition on the Workspace as a reference.

Accurately Positioning the Buttons

To position the buttons perfectly, set the current color to any light color that will contrast with the black background. Then follow these steps:

1. Make a rectangle 10 pixels high and wide enough to extend beyond both sides of the main composition image. Position it so the top is touching the bottom of the main image.
2. Select the rectangle and then select each of the buttons. The rectangle should be the source.
3. Apply Align Touch Edges with Relative To Composition Space turned off. The tops of the buttons align with the bottom of the rectangle.
4. Delete the rectangle and then select and set the home positions of the buttons.
5. Make another rectangle 120 pixels wide by 120 pixels high. With the rectangle selected and Relative To Composition Space turned on, use Align Bottoms, and then Align Centers Vertically to position the rectangle at the bottom center of the Composition Space, as shown in Figure 8-18.
6. Turn off Relative To Composition Space and set the rectangle's home position.
7. Select the rectangle, and then select the pineapple closest to the left side of the rectangle and click Touch Edges. Repeat with the pineapple closest to the right side of the rectangle.

Rectangle centered at bottom of Composition Space.

Figure 8-18
Placement of the second rectangle.

8. Delete the rectangle.

9. Select the main image, and select the pineapple farthest to the left and click Align Left Sides. Repeat with the right side using Align Right Sides. Refer to the finished image to see how the arrangement should look.
10. Set the home positions of all the pineapples again, to guard against moving them inadvertently.

Adding the Text Elements

Text elements will be the final touches to the Tropical Fantasy Web page. For this project, the graphics need to convey strong sensory appeal. The text also needs to be strong, but it cannot interfere with the imagery.

You must also bear in mind that you plan to save the final composition as a Web-ready, 24-bit JPEG file. Because a JPEG file uses lossy compression (a small bit of image quality is lost when the image is compressed into JPEG format), you must take special care to create text that will maintain its integrity when compressed. Ordinarily, you'd want to create text with a hard edge in a complementary color. The hard edge helps the text to stand out when superimposed over a graphic background. But a hard edge of a complementary color will compress poorly. The resulting image will have a high number of compression artifacts, little blotches of unwanted color surrounding the text.

The solution to creating text that will compress well in a JPEG image is to mix the text colors with the colors of the main graphic underneath it by making the text somewhat transparent. You can still add a darker border to help define the words, but you must soften the edges.

To begin adding the text, you'll start with the text for the main image, "Tropical Fantasy."

1. Center your view on the Composition Space and zoom to 100 percent.

To quickly center your view on the Composition Space, press the Home key on the keyboard.

2. Open the Text palette and select Snap ITC, 22 points Regular, Smoothing on, Opacity at 80, and the color on the Text palette set to 241, 160, 21. This is a gold that works well against the blue and harmonizes with the golden tones of the sunset.

Notice that this is not a highly saturated gold. It has some blue in it already to start the blending process.

3. Drag a text box above the diver (refer to the finished image for placement,) and type "Tropical". Click to set the text, and move it into place.
4. Apply the Edge effect with 1 pixel Thickness, and the color set to 123, 0, 21.
5. Apply the Blur effect set to 2 pixels.
6. Apply Transfer Shape with a 10 percent Opacity on the Texture Transfer palette, with the main graphic as the source sprite.
7. Repeat with the word "Fantasy" using 26-point text instead. Place as shown in the finished image.

   Positioning the "Fantasy" sprite in the lower left corner leaves the dynamic center open, like a visual passageway inviting people in for their own fantasies.
8. Select the main graphic and the two text elements. Flatten them and use Fit Bounding Box on the Arrange palette to bring the bounding box in tight around the graphic. Then set the sprite's home position.

The button text elements are also Tempus Sans ITC, but at 12 points. All other settings are the same, except Opacity is a full 100 percent. The blue is 0, 225, 241, and the red is 255, 0, 39. Notice that in our final version, we have moved the position of the button for "season special." Placing it out of the pattern lends emphasis, acting as a visual magnet along with the red text.

If you are curious about what would have happened had you not used slight transparency, blurred the text, and transferred some of the background graphic into the text, try the same text, but make it opaque and use a hard edge. After you save the image as a JPEG file, insert it back into an Image Composer composition and zoom in to the text areas.

Saving for the Web

To save the completed composition for the Web, select the main graphic and choose Save For The Web from the File menu. On the first screen of the Save For The Web wizard, shown in Figure 8-19, choose Selected Sprite Or Group.

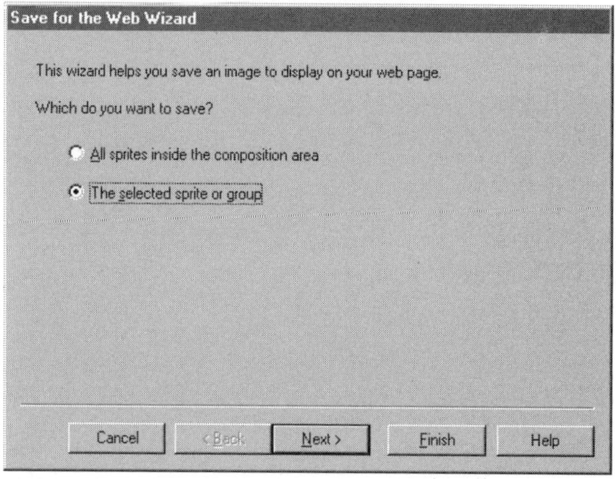

Figure 8-19

The first screen of the Save For The Web wizard.

On the next screen, shown in Figure 8-20, choose Fill Them With The Background Color for the transparent areas.

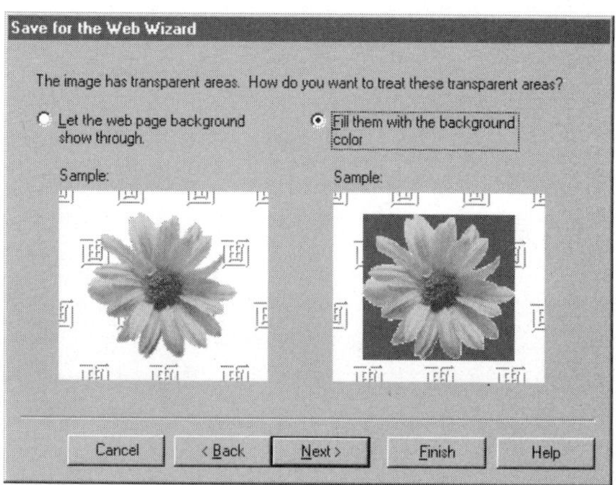

Figure 8-20

The second screen of the Save For The Web wizard.

Click Next, and then choose Black as the background color. Click Next and choose 56K Single ISDN, on the next wizard screen, shown in Figure 8-21. The images to the right show the file size and download time for the image. For this image, click the JPEG (Best Quality) version of the image, and click Next to move to the next page of the wizard. On this page, you can review your choices before clicking Save to save the file.

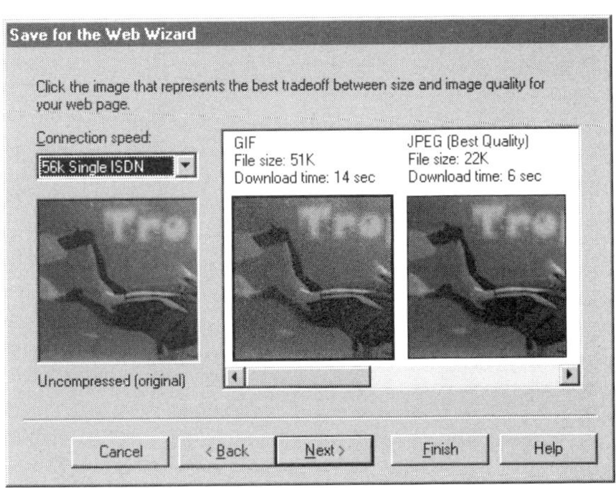

Figure 8-21
The image preview screen of the Save For The Web wizard.

The buttons and their text could be saved together in a separate file, if you'd like. However, saving each button and its associated text as a separate file will allow more flexibility when you place them on the Web page.

That's it, an attractive, highly graphical home page. Clicking any of the buttons would show the highlights of the particular area of interest, then an offer to take the plunge and purchase a Tropical Fantasy, with the convenience of taking care of all the details without leaving the site.

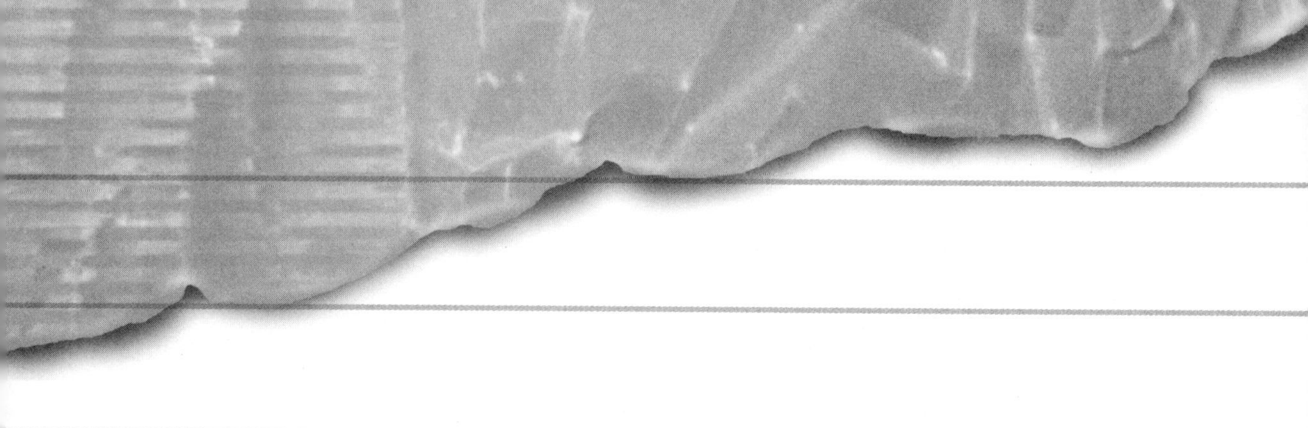

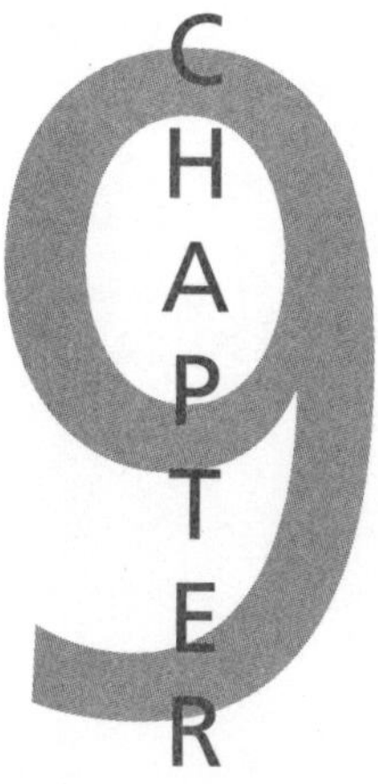
CHAPTER
9

Global Business: A Bridge to the Future

You're getting good at this stuff, and people are starting to see your work around town. One morning a call comes in from the local Chamber of Commerce. San Francisco will be host to Pacific Rim Expo '98, the annual global business trade show. Top level representatives from throughout the Pacific Rim will be sponsoring booths, and the show will be an opportunity for small businesses in the area to make those all-so-important face-to-face contacts with potential trading partners.

The president of the Chamber of Commerce, who recently took a Tropical Fantasy vacation, knows that many of the Chamber's members ride the local rapid transit system every day. Your Web site graphics got his attention before, and now he wants you to design a transit poster to get people thinking about attending the trade show. In fact, he likes your work so much that he offers you the opportunity to submit a paid-for concept piece. If the art committee likes it, you're in.

You have two days to submit a budget for the concept art, and three additional days to have a digital proof printed. The final delivery date is seven days from today, when the committee meets to decide if you're the one.

Because of the potential for so much exposure, you agree to the onerous schedule and conditions. But now you must come up with a hook to get the attention of those executives who ride the rapid transit. You learn that the theme for the show will be global business, right in line with the president of the Chamber's campaign motto that the "the bridge to the future is global business." Aha, you know exactly what to do.

Suddenly, though, in a blinding flash of reality you realize that you have never done a transit poster before. Of course you remember seeing them when you've ridden the rapid transit, but you have no idea who makes them or how big they are. It's time to do some homework.

The Research

Who makes transit posters, you wonder? It must be billboard companies. Quickly, you look up billboards in the yellow pages index. Sure enough, you find billboards under Outdoor Advertising, page 14. A quick call, and moments later you are connected to the graphics department of just the company you need. The person you talk with turns out to be enthusiastic and wants to tell you all about outdoor advertising. OK, you might as well learn something while you're at it. Maybe there is more work out there doing this type of thing.

As you listen, you learn that there are several types of outdoor display. The most frequently seen is the freeway billboard, which is fourteen feet high by forty-eight feet wide. The billboards you see when driving around town are called thirty sheet billboards in the trade. They are ten feet five inches by twenty-two feet eight inches. Not wanting to get off on a tangent, you wisely decide not to ask how that odd size came about. Then there are the twenty by forty-foot monster boards, and a few larger sizes above that. It turns out that the one you want to know about really is called a transit poster, and it is four feet wide by six feet high.

Typically printed on Duratrans or some other weather-resistant material, these posters are created either on an offset press or with a Cactus printer or similar device that produces a color print in a single pass. Offset printing would be cheaper per poster for more than 2,000 posters, but the fewer you print below 2,000, the higher the cost per poster, and the cost goes up quickly. On the other hand, single pass digital printing is relatively expensive, with very little economy of scale, because it takes the same amount of time to print the fiftieth or hundredth poster as it does the first. However, you can print ten or twenty posters for the same cost per poster, so digital printing might cost less for the overall job if you need to print only a few copies.

Because you know the eventual poster size will be four by six feet, you plan your proof of concept around a 1:1.5 ratio so that your piece is an accurate representation of how the poster will look when printed full scale.

If you were to work at full size, you'd be working with a massive file. At four by six feet by 300 pixels per inch, working at full resolution with red, green, blue and alpha channels, the file you'd get would be more than 1.2 gigabytes. That's 48 inches by 72 inches by 300 dpi by 4 channels (R, G, B and Alpha). The mathematical calculation is: [(48 x 300) x (72 x 300)] x 4 = 1,244,160,000 pixels. To find a workable size, you'd need to figure out a number that would divide evenly into both length and height.

An easier alternative is to use the ratio you've determined to create a version at any workable size, making sure the length and width of the size you choose has the same ratio as the original.

The Golden Mean

The ratio of the transit poster, 1:1.5, is very close to the Golden Mean, a mathematical ratio of 1:1.6 that exists in many natural objects. Striking examples are the double spiral patterns found in cactuses, succulents, and many other plants. Starfish and many shellfish also exhibit this ratio, or one of its harmonics, in the growth patterns of their shells. The Golden Mean has been used as a design principle throughout history. The ancient Greeks applied it to their architecture and sculpture. Modern advertising applies it to ad layout. Other examples abound. To learn more about this important principle of design, you might want to study Dynamic Symmetry based on the Golden Mean. We'd recommend your reading *The Elements of Dynamic Symmetry*, by Jay Hambidge, an excellent introduction to the subject. It's published by Dover in paperback. ISBN number: 0–486–21776–0.

Determining the Composition Size

In the tutorial directory, open the file CHAPTER9.MIC. In this Image Composer file, you'll find a TIF version of the completed composition on the Composition Space. To the right and left of the Composition Space are stock photographs, one of the Golden Gate Bridge in San Francisco and one of a landing jet. At the left are the project's individual sprites grouped into a single object. If you want, you can ungroup them for reference while you work on the project.

To determine the composition size, you should consider two important issues: the use of images in the poster, and how large you must make a version to really impress the Chamber of Commerce and convincingly convey your concept.

The target audience for the poster will be executives on their way to and from work, so you need to keep it simple so that the important information gets across quickly. But you also want to get people's attention with high-impact visuals. The Golden Gate photo seems exceptionally suitable for two reasons. First, the wave breaking in the foreground of the photo is a striking visual element. Second, the image of a bridge is a fitting welcoming symbol for overseas visitors, and it can be visually modified to grab people's attention.

To create an image large enough to wow the Chamber and fit the images with enough detail, you decide to create a 12 by 18-inch proof of concept using a state-of-the-art Iris print. A Composition Space size of 600 pixels wide by 900 pixels high would be the correct ratio of width to height, and it would be large enough to allow you to compose the stock images and text elements, but small enough to allow you to work quickly within Image Composer. From this image, you will be able to make the 12 by 18-inch hard copy printout you need.

For this project, we have already set the size of the Composition Space to 600 by 900 pixels.

Resizing the Main Image

To begin your work, move the finished TIF file off the Composition Space and out of the way. Now make a copy of the small bridge image that you can scale up to fit the Composition Space.

NOTE To view the whole image while working on this project, you will need to zoom out at times to 50 percent or even 25 percent. This is typical when you work on large images.

1. Select the bridge image and use the Scale control on the Arrange palette to increase the width of the image to 610 pixels. Make sure Keep Aspect Ratio is turned on and click Apply.

   The image is now 610 by 910 pixels with a fringe of anti-aliased pixels around all the edges. When you save the file for printing to a bitmap image, such as a TIF file, the anti-aliased pixels that extend beyond the edge of the Composition Space will be cut off.

2. With Relative To Composition Space turned on, use Align Centers on the Arrange palette to center the image on the Composition Space, and then set its home position and lock its position.

Soon you will have two additional bridge sprites. By setting the home position of the initial sprite now, you will be able to properly align the additional bridge sprites later.

TIP Now that the original bridge sprite is enlarged, you can easily compare it with the final version to see the effects of the upcoming modifications.

Creating the Wave and Bridge Sprites

To make the imagery within the poster more vivid, you can apply special effects to the breaking wave in the foreground and to the bridge. But to apply these effects, you need to cut out as separate sprites those two portions of the image: the bridge with all its cables and the surf.

Cutting Out the Wave Sprite

Cutting out the wave sprite will be easy. Just as you did during the Big Sur project, zoom in and use the Curve tool on the Cutout palette to cut out a sprite of just the wave at 100 percent Opacity. Figure 9-1 shows the shape of this sprite.

Cut out the shape of the wave.

Figure 9-1
The shape of the cut out wave sprite.

After you finish cutting out the wave sprite, set its home position and move it out onto the Workspace.

Now would be a good time to save your work.

Creating the Bridge Sprite

Cutting out the bridge sprite will be more of a challenge. You need to cut out the bridge and its cables, but you don't want to include the background showing through between the cables and open areas of the bridge, so you need to come up with a strategy.

The Select Color Region capability on the Cutout palette won't work because the colors in the image are too intermingled. Cutting out all the spaces between the cables would be far too tedious. The solution you come up with is to create new sprites that look like the cables and combine them with a cut out sprite of the main bridge structure. This takes the least time and produces the best result.

Making the Cables

To make the cables, you can use the Polygon tool on the Shapes palette to create a line.

1. On the Shapes palette, for the Curve and Polygon options, make sure Close is turned off (unchecked). This lets you make a line with the Curve or Polygon tools.
2. Set the current color to 59, 21, 34, a color selected from the bridge with the Eyedropper in the Color Picker.

   Note that this is not the color of the cables on the image. They are so thin that they got mixed with a lot of blue during the scaling process. The selected color for the cables

came from a middle value area of the bridge that is not too light and not too dark.

3. Zoom in on the upper left corner of the image. Figure 9-2 shows the area on which to work first. This area includes all the cables to the left of the main tower. You will make the cables that are on the opposite side of the bridge first.

The first polygon cable.

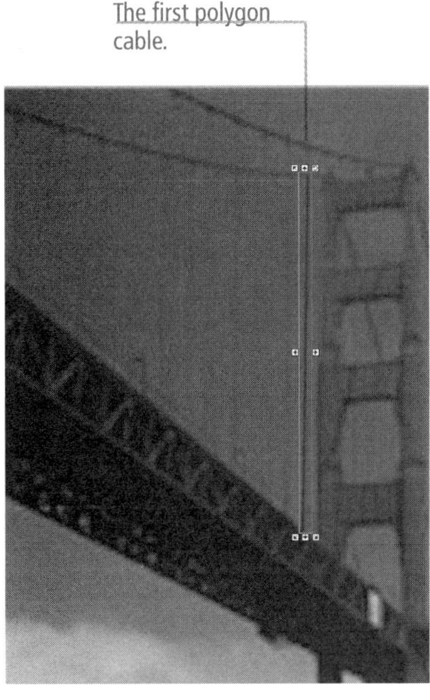

Figure 9-2
The first area of the bridge to work on and the location of the first cable you'll make.

4. On the Shapes palette, set the Line Width to 2 pixels, leave Edge at Hard, and set Opacity to 90 (the cables farther away appear less saturated than those closer).
5. Click the Polygon tool on the Shapes palette and then click once at the top of the cable just to the left of the tower and click again at the bottom of the cable.
6. Right click and use Move Points, if necessary, and then click Create to place the line.

7. Continue making the back row of cables by duplicating the first cable and using the arrow keys to move the copies into place, aligning the top of each duplicate with the suspension cable.

   As you make duplicate cables and move them to the left, the duplicates will extend farther and farther below the horizontal span of the bridge. Don't worry, you will erase this portion of the cables later. Figure 9-3 shows how the first row of cables looks before erasing. The white triangle indicates the area to be erased.

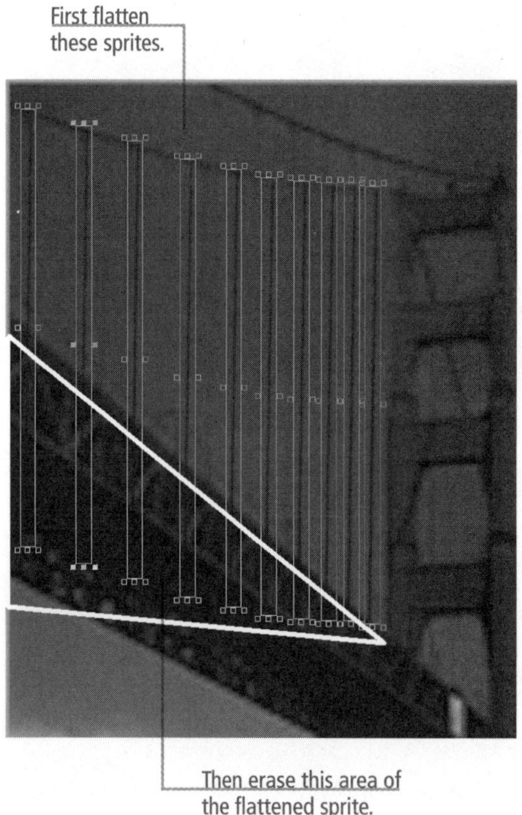
First flatten these sprites.
Then erase this area of the flattened sprite.

Figure 9-3

First row of cables selected. The area within the white triangle will be erased.

8. Select all the cables you've made and flatten them into a single sprite.
9. Use the Polygon Cutout tool to erase the portions of the cables below the railing of the main span, but let the cables hang a little below the railing. The main part of the bridge sprite you will make will cover them. Use Erase on the Cutout palette rather than Cut Out after you draw the Polygon.
10. Set the home position of the final sprite.

Next make the section of suspension cable that the vertical cables you've just made hang from.

1. Use the Curve tool on the Shapes palette to click points along the suspension cable. Make this cable 3 pixels wide, but leave all other settings the same as before. Figure 9-4 shows the suspension cable sprite.

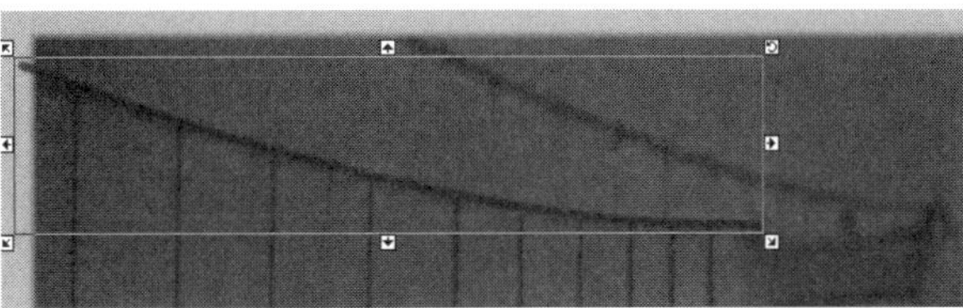

Figure 9-4
The first section of suspension cable.

2. Select the section of suspension cable and the vertical cables sprite and flatten them.
3. If any of the suspension cable is outside the Composition Space, use the Rectangle Cutout tool to erase it.
4. While the cable sprite is still selected, click Fit Bounding Box on the Arrange palette. Be sure to set the home position of the sprite again.
5. Move this sprite aside so you can make the next set of cables.
6. Save the file again.

Repeat the procedure you used to make the first row of cables and the suspension cable to create the cables on the near side of the bridge.

This time, though, set Opacity on the Shapes palette to 100 percent. Figure 9-5 shows the second set of vertical cables, the suspension cable, and the area to be erased.

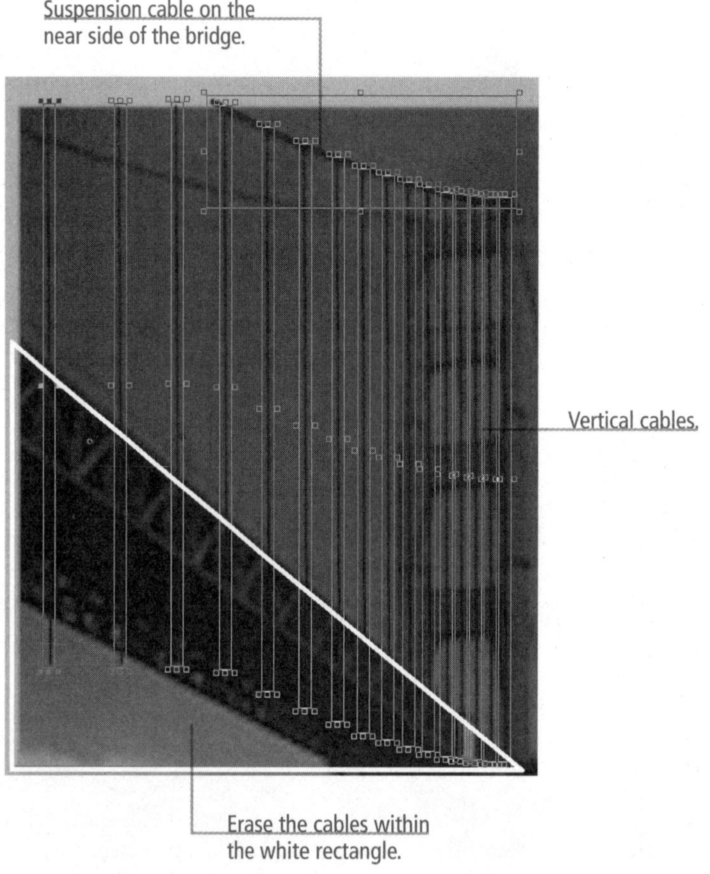

Figure 9-5
Vertical and suspension cables on the near side of the bridge. Erase the area inside the white triangle.

After flattening these cables into one sprite and erasing the necessary pieces at the bottom, set the sprite's home position so it will align accurately on the bridge sprite later, and then set it aside.

Now repeat the cable-drawing procedure again for the section of the bridge to the right of the main tower, but make all the vertical cables and the two suspension cables into a single sprite. Use all the same settings as before to draw the cables, but this time use an Opacity of 85, because the cables that are far away should look less distinct. Don't worry about the vertical cables that overlap portions of the bridge tower—we'll fix that later. Figure 9-6 shows the appearance of this second sprite after a copy has been moved to the right for clarity.

Suspension cables and vertical cables.

Figure 9-6

The cables to the right of the main tower. A copy has been moved to the right of the bridge for clarity.

Move the cable sprites off the Composition Space and save the file again. That wasn't too bad, was it?

Cutting Out the Main Bridge Structure

The main structure of the bridge is relatively simple to make, compared to the cables. Again, you will use the Cutout tools to create one complete bridge without cables, apart from the background.

1. Select and duplicate the bridge image that is on the Composition Space so that the copy has the same home position.
2. Use the Align tools to align the duplicate with the center of the Composition Space and set its home position so that you can align the cut out bridge sprite with the main image.

3. Move the duplicate out onto the Workspace. You may have to zoom out to find a clear space for it.
4. Zoom in so that the bridge takes up much of the screen.
5. Use the Curve tool on the Cutout palette to cut out the bridge structure.
6. Use the Curve and Polygon tools on the Cutout palette to erase any cables that remain. You should end up with only the bridge structure, as shown in Figure 9-7.

Usually, at this point we would ask you to click the Fit Bounding Box button and set the home position of the sprite. In this case, though, you don't want to do either because the current sprite has the same home position as the main image on the Composition Space.

Figure 9-7
Bridge structure by itself.

Now is a good time to check the alignment of the two bridge sprites you have.

1. Select the sprite that shows only the bridge structure currently and send it home. It should fit precisely on top of the bridge image that is on the Composition Space.
2. Unlock the position of the main (complete) image and move it off the Composition Space. The cutout bridge structure should now be the only sprite on the Composition Space.

3. Select and send home the cable sprites you made earlier. They should fit on the bridge structure. If for any reason they don't go to their proper places, move them into position now.
4. When the bridge structure and cable sprites are all in position, select and flatten them all. Set the home position of the resulting sprite and lock its position. Refer to Figure 9-8 to see how that looks.

Figure 9-8
The flattened bridge structure with cables in place.

5. Select and send home the main image. It fits under the new bridge sprite.
6. Save your file once again.

Applying an Effect to the Bridge

While making the bridge stand out, you don't want to lose the structure entirely. The settings in the following effect have been chosen with that in mind.

1. Select and duplicate the new bridge sprite.
2. Move the duplicate off the Composition Space for now. You will apply the effect to the copy still on the Composition Space. Select it now.
3. From the Effects palette choose Glowing Accents. Use the Details tab settings shown on the facing page.

Glowing Accents Details	
Edge width	3
Edge brightness	20
Smoothness	10
Opacity	100

Applying an Effect to the Wave

The effect you've given to the bridge is strong, so you need another strong major element in the composition to balance it. You'll make the wave an equally strong element.

1. Select the copy of the wave you made earlier, and send it home.

   The copy should now be on top of the main image, precisely aligned with the original.
2. Apply Glowing Accents to the sprite with these settings:

Glowing Accents Details	
Edge width	3
Edge brightness	20
Smoothness	10
Opacity	33

3. Duplicate the sprite you've just made, set the copy aside, and leave the original on the Composition Space.
4. Select the large, main image and then the wave sprite. The main image is the source sprite.
5. Apply Transfer Shape on the Texture Transfer palette at 50 percent opacity.

NOTE

On some computers, especially those running Windows NT, you may find that applying Texture Transfer at a setting other than 100 percent still applies the effect at a full 100 percent. If this occurs, click the Undo button and then drag the Texture Transfer Opacity slider to zero. Then move the mouse pointer away, and drag the slider back to the setting you'd like and click Apply. You should now get the correct amount of texture transfer.

Some of the original image is now mixed with the Glowing Accents pattern.

Color Tuning the Wave Sprite

To push the wave toward the foreground and enhance the sense of depth in the image, you can color tune the wave sprite to shift its colors more toward purple. This separates the wave's color balance from the predominantly green hue of the water and causes it to stand out.

Open the Color Tuning palette and set the Hue and Saturation sliders to 10. Click Apply.

Now that the major design elements are in place, select the sprites on the Composition Space, set their home positions, and then lock their positions. Now you will make the smaller elements.

Creating the Airplane Elements

Now you can turn your attention to the airplane sprite at the upper right corner of the poster. As you can see in the finished product, an oval shape surrounding the airplane has been cut out from its peach-colored background.

To create this effect, you'll use an oval to make a stencil. The stencil will be the opposite of the oval (an oval hollowed out from a filled rectangle). You can then use this stencil to cut away everything but an oval shape around the airplane. You'll see what we mean when you try it.

Creating the Oval and the Stencil

1. Draw an oval of any color that is 245 pixels wide by 105 pixels high.
2. Place the oval sprite on top of the airplane image so it is approximately centered on the plane, and leave it selected.
3. On the Arrange palette, use the Crop/Extend tool to extend the bounding box of the oval sprite so that it is wider and taller than the airplane photograph. Figure 9-9, on the next page, shows the the alignment of the oval over the airplane image and the bounding box of the extended oval sprite. The oval sprite is now approximately 410 pixels wide by 270 pixels high.
4. Open the Cutout palette and click the Stencil button at the far right side. The bounding box fills with the current color.

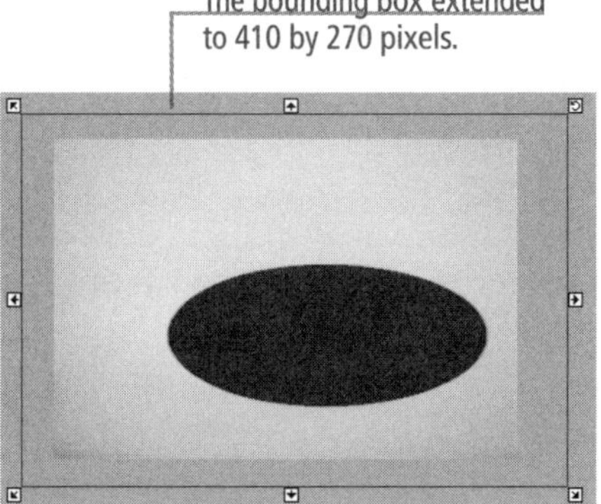

Figure 9-9

The oval positioned over the airplane. The bounding box of the oval has been extended with Crop/Extend.

5. Deselect all the sprites, and then click exactly on the original oval and move it away. A rectangle with a hollow oval in it remains, positioned over the airplane image. This is the stencil.
6. If necessary, use the arrow keys to center the airplane inside the oval shape. See Figure 9-10.

Figure 9-10

Airplane centered inside the oval shape of the stencil sprite.

7. Select the stencil and then the airplane. Use Snip on the Texture Transfer palette at 100 percent to remove everything but an oval-shaped area around the airplane.
8. Deselect all and move the stencil aside. The airplane within an oval shape remains.

9. Before going on, select the oval containing the airplane and click Fit Bounding Box on the Arrange palette to make the oval's bounding box the same size as the sprite. Make a copy of this sprite and set it aside for later use.

Making the Transparency Gradient

Next, you want to make an oval transparency gradient that is transparent at its perimeter and opaque at its center. However, you don't want the airplane to become too transparent, so you will make the transparency gradient oval larger than the peach-colored oval that contains the airplane.

1. Duplicate this oval airplane sprite and scale the copy to 110 percent of its current size. Make a copy and set it aside for later use.
2. Apply a Grayscale Left Gradient effect to the scaled-up oval sprite at 100 percent Opacity.
3. Apply the Radial Sweep effect to the oval sprite at an angle of 0 degrees.

   As in previous projects, you want the opaque white area of the transparency gradient to take up the majority of the oval.
4. With the gradient oval still selected, open the Color Tuning palette and click the Dynamic Range tab.
5. Move the right side vertical slider to the left as shown in Figure 9-11, and click Apply.

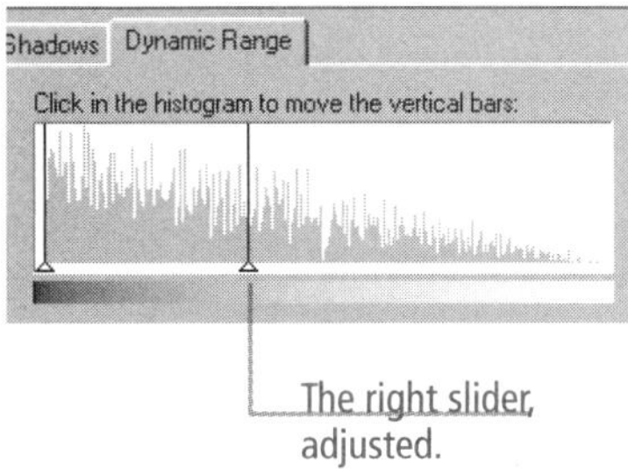

Figure 9-11
Move the right slider to the position indicated in the figure and click Apply.

The opaque white area of the oval is enlarged.

6. Center the oval with the airplane over the gradient sprite. Bring it to the front if necessary. See Figure 9-12 to see how the gradient and the airplane over it look.

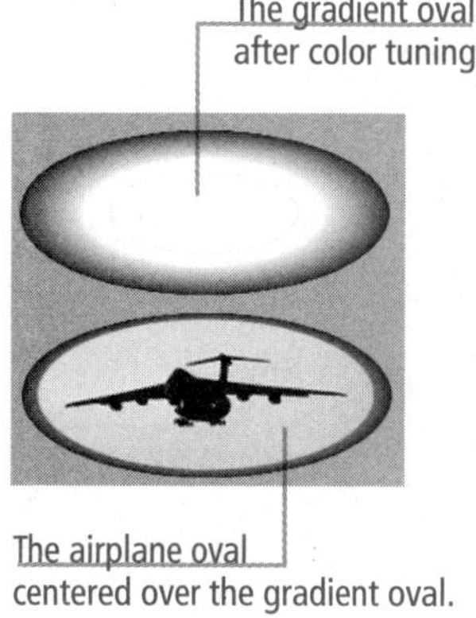

Figure 9-12
The color-tuned gradient and the airplane oval centered over the gradient oval ready for transparency mapping.

7. Deselect all the sprites, select the gradient oval first, and then select the airplane. The gradient is the source. Apply Map Transparency from the Texture Transfer palette twice.
8. Deselect all the sprites and move the airplane onto the composition. Refer to the finished TIF file to see where to position it.

Making the Center Airplanes

The next element you'll make is the group of airplanes that appear to be emerging from the bridge sprite. It's made from the same airplane as the sprite at the upper right corner, but it's flipped horizontally and it has a different transparency mapping. To create this sprite, follow these steps:

1. Make a copy of the oval airplane sprite that is on the Workspace.
2. To another copy of the original oval, scaled up to 110 percent, apply the same Grayscale Gradient as before, followed by the same Radial Sweep. This time, though, leave the gradient as is, without using color tuning to alter its grays.

3. As before, apply transparency mapping to the airplane sprite twice.
4. Flip the sprite horizontally and move it into position over the bridge, as shown in Figure 9-13. The sprite should be placed on the first cross member above the bridge span, on the vertical structural element.

Figure 9-13
Placement of the airplane sprite.

To move the first airplane sprite behind the bridge structure, follow these steps:

1. Select the bridge sprite that has glowing accents. It is on top.
2. Shift-click the airplane sprite. The bridge sprite will be the source.
3. On the Arrange palette, click the Order Behind button. The airplane moves behind the bridge structure.

Now make the copies that give the illusion of movement.

1. Select the airplane and click Duplicate. The copy appears a little down and to the right of the original.
2. While the copy is selected, scale it to 105 percent.
3. Duplicate again and scale the duplicate to 105 percent again. Figure 9-14, on the next page, shows a close-up of these sprites.
4. Select all the sprites and set their home position.

Figure 9-14
Series of airplane sprites emerging from the bridge.

Adding the Text Elements

With the purely graphical elements of the composition finished, you are ready to begin placing the text that will provide the factual information. Keeping in mind that the poster's purpose is to attract people's interest quickly and convey just the information they need, you decide to use just a few, large blocks of text with a simple font.

Beginning with the text at the upper right corner, you select Arial, Bold, 23 points. The color on the Text palette should be 238, 205, 137, a light color that will bring the text visually forward. After you enter "Global Business," place it in its approximate position. You will fine-tune the position of the three text sprites when they are complete.

Make another text element using the same font and size. But this time, the color should be 225, 166, 114, and the text is "means business". The "for you" text element is 30 points with a color of 206, 116, 84.

To all three sprites, apply the Edge effect with a 1 pixel Thickness. The color for the edge should be 138, 21, 252. Now you can move the text elements into the position shown in Figure 9-15.

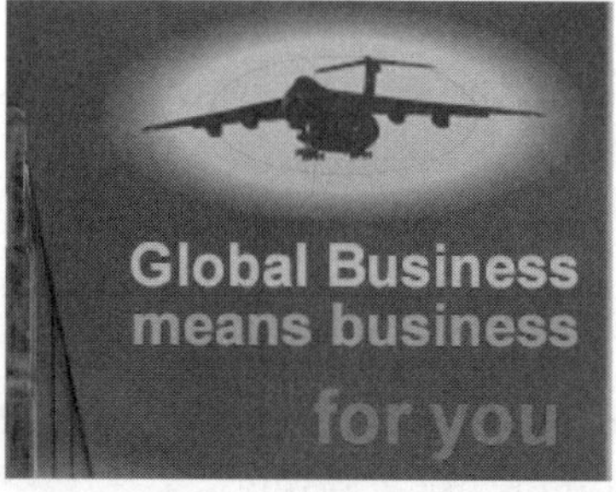

Figure 9-15
The upper right corner text in position.

For the Pacific Rim Expo '98 text, use these settings:

Pacific Rim Expo '98 Text

Pacific rim	Arial	Bold	28 points	Color=0, 0, 80	Edge: 1 pixel, color=141, 46, 252
EXPO	Arial	Bold	50 points	Color=0, 0, 80	Edge: 1 pixel, color=141, 46, 252
'98	Arial	Bold	50 points	Color=0, 204, 177	Edge: 1 pixel, color=141, 46, 252

For the text sprites at the lower right, use these settings:

Lower Right Text Sprite Settings

april 3-17, 1998	Arial	Bold	25 points	Use eyedropper to pick same color as "for you." Edge: 1 pixel, color=138, 21, 252.
san francisco	Arial	Bold	31 points	Same as "april 3-17..."
1-800-expo98	Arial	Bold	16 points	Same as "means business," No Edge
www.pacrim...	Arial	Bold	16 points	Same as "means business," No Edge

Once you've completed the poster, save everything in an Image Composer MIC file, and then save the Composition Space as a TIF file you can hand off to a commercial printer or service bureau to produce your concept piece. The printer or service bureau can also tell you what file you will need to provide when the final poster is produced.

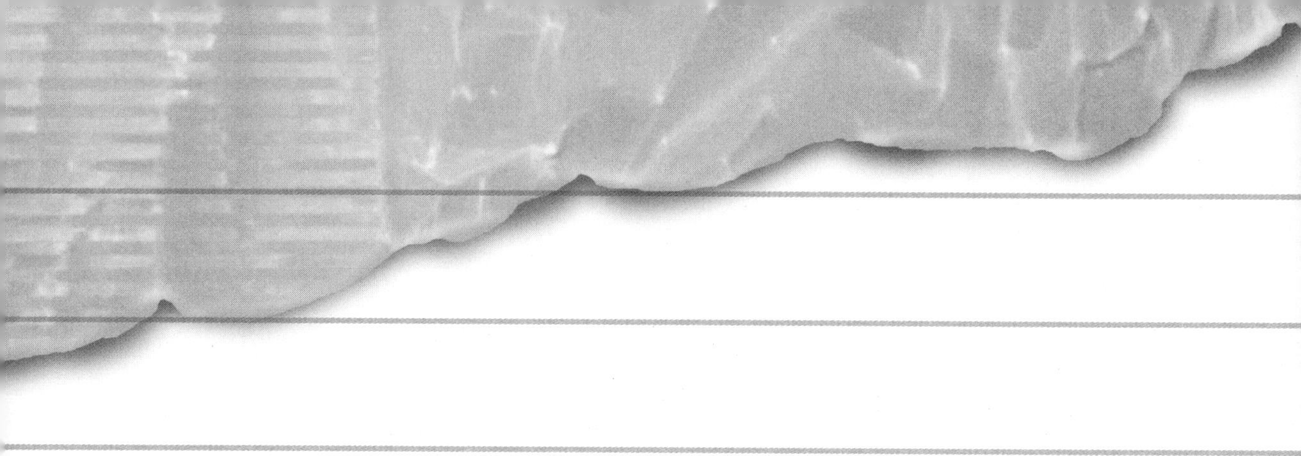

10 CHAPTER

Design of the Day: Creating a Promotional Card

Design of the Day is a project designed to refine your Microsoft Image Composer skills. By now, you realize that doing graphics is much more than selecting which button to click. Your ability to create cool graphics depends in large part on your being able to analyze the raw materials you have and then make informed decisions about which tools to use and how to use them most effectively.

In this project, you make a self-promotion graphic card that does double duty as a trade show hand-out and as a mailer.

Open the file CHAPTER10.MIC, which is in the PROJECTS folder of the CD. On the Workspace, you see a TIF file of the finished project, an image of a butterfly, and another of a sandstone rock surface. The sprites, way over on the left, show the progressive changes that will occur during the project. You will recognize where they fit; you can use them and the finished TIF image as references.

In this project, you will become much more familiar with the RGB color space, where computer monitors and the Color Tuning tools live. You will learn to analyze the needs of an image and tune its colors in a more sophisticated manner. This gives you more control over the tools and translates into your ability to use Image Composer to faithfully communicate your personal vision through graphics for screen or print.

While creating text and other sprites, you will further explore using surface effects and the Impressionist plug-in to make eye-catching graphic design elements. As you work through the project, we will explain some of the design concepts that went into making decisions along the way. That will help you to learn when, and how, to consider those issues in your personal design work.

The Background

Comdex, a major computer industry trade show, is coming up. With the intention of generating some business for your fledgling graphics company, you and some friends have rented one of the small, less expensive booths that line the perimeter of one of the halls.

In addition to the booth, you need a printed promotional handout that will show off your graphics work and tell how to contact your group. You know that the attention span of show attendees is short, so you want this handout to be appealing enough to get a second look after the attendees take it home. You also plan to use it as a mailer after the show, so you decide on a card that has graphics on one side and contact information on the other. Like a typical postcard, the back side must contain space for the address and stamp.

By calling around to local trade printers, you learn that a four by six-inch card is legal to send through the mail. The printer will print 20 cards on one side of 24 by 30-inch paper stock. This leaves room for color bars, registration marks and cutting. You will have to provide to the printer two digital files. A TIF file for the graphic side of the card, and a second TIF for the text side. After the first side dries, the second side of your cards will be printed in a single press run. The turnaround time for printing is four days from the time you deliver the files.

The printer will print at 300 dots per inch, so your final files must be created on a Composition Space of 1200 by 1800 pixels. That will result in a file of 6.48 megabytes. Some facts for the calculation: the final TIF file will be 4 inches by 6 inches by 300 pixels per inch. The number of color channels is three in this case; red, green, and blue (RGB). You don't need a fourth, or alpha channel, in the final TIF file, although you will use the alpha channel during the creation of the files.

Here's the calculation: 4 (inches) multiplied by 300 equals 1200 pixels wide; 6 (inches) multiplied by 300 equals 1800 pixels high. 1200 multiplied by 1800 equals 2,160,00 pixels, or 2.16 megabytes. 2.16 multiplied by 3 (color channels) equals 6.48 megabytes. You'd need something other than a diskette to transport a files of that size, but fortunately, the printer is set up to receive files over the Internet.

You would like to work a bit smaller on the design stage of the project. Remembering about ratios from your recently completed Golden Gate Bridge project, you calculate the ratio for the card and find out it is 1:1.5, the same as the bridge image.

Setting Up the Composition Space

The rock image that will become the background for the design is 512 by 768 pixels. You determine those dimensions by selecting the image and looking at the status bar. Using the 1:1.5 ratio as a guide, you calculate that if one side is 500, then the other side should be 750 to maintain the 1:1.5 ratio. A Composition Space size of 500 by 750 would be proportionate to the size of the final piece, 1200 by 1800. You decide to work at the smaller, less memory-intensive 500 by 750-pixel resolution for the design stage of the project. Later, when the design is final, you will create everything at the higher resolution. You will simply record the settings for all modifications you make during the process in a small notebook.

This is the second time we've mentioned taking notes while working on a project. Taking notes is so valuable that we feel it worthwhile to suggest that you actually do it while you're working through the project. Making this a habit will save you many hours later and speed up your learning process.

The Design

The design you have in mind focuses on a butterfly sitting on a rock surface. The particular rock image you've chosen for this project is suitable because of its balance between an area of deeply wind-eroded texture and a somewhat textured flat space, relatively free of erosions. The smoothness of the butterfly wings will contrast nicely against the textured area of the rock, while the smoother area will be large enough for the name of your group, Channel Graphics, and perhaps even an additional graphic element or two.

Preparing the Images

After setting the Composition Space to the proper 500 by 750-pixel size (we've already done this for you), you set to work preparing the two sprites, the sandstone background and the butterfly.

Color Tuning the Sandstone Image

Although the sandstone image is a great composition, the rock color is somewhat neutral and drab looking. You'd like the background to be warmer and more appealing to the eye, so you plan a color shift toward gold with color tuning.

Earlier in this book, you learned that equal amounts of Red, Green, and Blue make a neutral gray. In this case, you want the rock to be a less neutral color, which suggests separating the color channels a bit.

To begin, you use the Dynamic Range controls to adjust the levels of light and dark in the image.

1. Select the rock sprite.
2. Click the Dynamic Range tab on the Color Tuning palette.
3. Click the Auto Fit button on the Dynamic Range tab and then click Apply.

Auto Fit spreads the light to dark color range in the image from full black to full white. It lowers the lowest dark in the image to black and raises the brightness light in the image to white. In other programs, this function is called Auto Levels or Auto Balance.

To separate the color channels and obtain a golden, less neutral color, you'll work on the Highlight/Shadows of the Color Tuning palette.

Analyzing the Color of an Image

Here's a way to help analyze the color of an image: Zoom in on the rock image, and then open the Color Picker and select the Eyedropper. Without clicking the mouse button, move the Eyedropper across the rock image, stopping at several places. When you stop, look at the numbers next to the RGB sliders in the Color Picker. In almost every case, the red and green numbers will be close or identical. The blue will be more or less different.

Here's how to relate that information to the image. The image is somewhat neutral. If anything, it leans visually toward green. You want a golden tone, which consists of more red than green and more of both compared to blue, so the red channel should be stronger than green, and both red and green should be stronger than blue.

Figure 10-1 shows the settings you want for the Highlight/Shadows curves. Set these curves as close to those in the figure as you can. Your result should be close to the golden rock sprite at the far left of the Workspace. It's not particularly easy to match the figure exactly, so don't worry if you don't get it right the first time. If you have too much trouble setting the three curves, use the sprite provided. You can practice more when you have time.

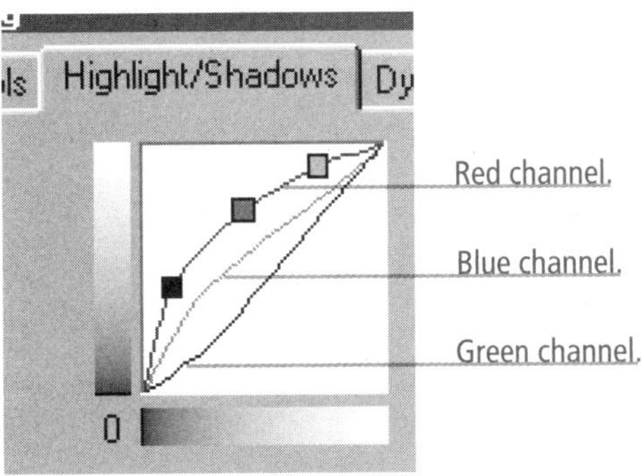

Figure 10-1
The red, green, and blue control settings.

How did we know which settings to use? We determined the settings by analyzing the colors in the sprite with the Eyedropper and experimenting with various settings. Practice will make it easier for you to do the same.

Cropping and Scaling the Sandstone Image

Now zoom in on the sandstone sprite to examine its edges. Notice that a black border needs to be removed which, coincidentally, will square up the sides of the image area.

1. Use the Crop/Extend tool on the Arrange palette to crop away the black border. The final, cropped sprite should be approximately 495 by 735 pixels.

   Cropping the image has made it smaller than the Composition Space. To make the image fit, you'll need to scale it larger, which will produce anti-aliasing around its edges. To allow for cropping away the anti-aliasing later, you should scale the image even a bit larger than you need.
2. On the Arrange palette, turn off Keep Aspect Ratio, and set the Width to 520 and the Height to 770. When you click Apply, the sprite will be just large enough to allow for cropping the anti-aliased edges, and still leave a background that is the correct size.
3. Again, crop the edges. This time crop 8–10 pixels from each side. You can use the status bar information to do this precisely. The resulting sprite should fill the Composition Space exactly and have a hard edge.

Sharpening the Sandstone Image

To create a strong contrast with the butterfly, you want the surface texture of the rock to stand out.

1. Apply the Sharpen effect (not Sharpen Lite) to the rock sprite.
2. On the Arrange palette, click the Align Centers button with Relative To Composition Space turned on. Then set the sprite's home position.

The rock image is now ready to work with. Save the file with any name you'd like.

Cutting Out the Butterfly Sprite

Although the butterfly image is too large, this works to your advantage, because it makes the butterfly easier to cut out.

1. Move the rock image off the Composition Space and move the butterfly image on. Zoom in so the butterfly almost fills your screen.
2. Cut out a sprite using the Curve tool on the Cutout palette. Figure 10-2 shows the shape of the cutout.

We found it best to start just under the left antenna next to the left eye, and then work around counter-clockwise. Take special care around the antennae, and try to keep them thin.

We have provided a template and a full color cutout on the far left of the Workspace. Try doing the cutout without using the template first. Then, if necessary, use the template as a guide by positioning it over the butterfly image and locking the position of both sprites. Remember to select the original butterfly image before using the Cutout tool.

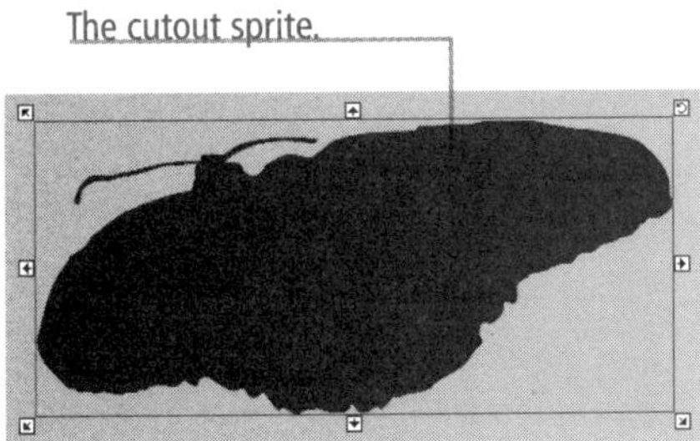

Figure 10-2
The shape of the cutout sprite.

Color Tuning the Butterfly

Now turn your attention to the color qualities of the butterfly. The image appears washed out, with no life to the color and little contrast. You want it to appear alive instead. The body should shine the way butterfly bodies do, and the wings need stronger color.

Making these modifications won't be quite as straightforward as color tuning the rock sprite. You will have to make several adjustments that cumulatively achieve your goal.

First you will remove the somewhat chalky, washed out look of the butterfly by modifying the brightness, contrast and saturation.

1. Select the cutout sprite and, on the Color Tuning palette, set Brightness to –5, Contrast to 3, and Saturation to 10. When you click Apply, the washed-out look disappears.
2. Next, use Auto Fit on the Dynamic Range tab to spread the dark-to-light color range in the image, but don't click Apply yet.

   You'll see that the right marker on the Dynamic Range histogram moves about a quarter of the way to the left to make the light range go all the way to white. But you also want to enhance the blacks, especially in the body of the butterfly.
3. Drag the left side slider to the right as shown in Figure 10-3. This turns the darkest grays to black. Now click Apply. The blacks become more pronounced.

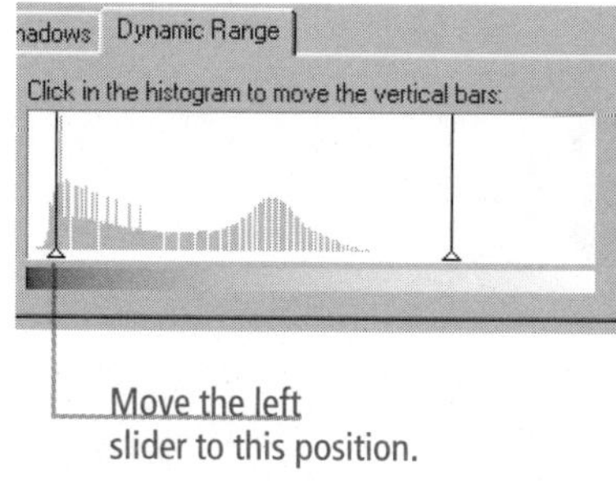
hadows
Dynamic Range
Click in the histogram to move the vertical bars:
Move the left
slider to this position.

Figure 10-3
Dynamic Range settings.

To strengthen the overall color in the image, you can modify the Highlight/Shadows settings.

4. Click the Highlight/Shadows tab of the Color Tuning palette and set the curve as shown in Figure 10-4. When you click Apply, you'll see that the overall color of the butterfly becomes stronger and more vibrant.

For reference, you'll find these color tuned sprites at the far left of the Workspace.

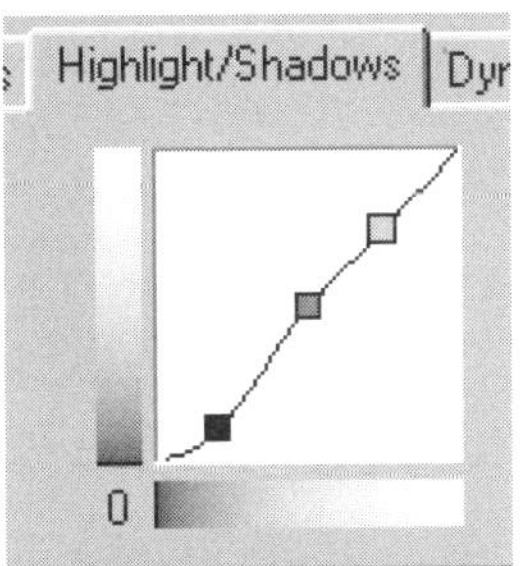

Figure 10-4
Highlight/Shadows settings.

Scaling the Butterfly

Although the butterfly now looks much better, it's still much too large for the background. Open the Arrange palette and, with Keep Aspect Ratio turned on, set the Width of the sprite to 350 pixels. When you click Apply, the butterfly will be scaled appropriately for the composition. Before continuing, make sure you save your file.

Composing the Sprites

Now that the sprites are ready for composing, take a moment to consider the composition. You know that you'd like to place the butterfly on the rough, weathered area of the rock to leave space for the text and perhaps a logo.

With the butterfly off the Composition Space, send the rock sprite home so that it centers on the Composition Space. Now move the butterfly onto the weathered area of the rock, at the upper left. Figure 10-5 shows the positioning of the butterfly on the rock.

Figure 10-5
The butterfly on the weathered part of the rock.

Notice the butterfly, which faces up and to the left, tends to draw your attention away from the overall picture. It would work better in the lower right corner where it would point into the composition.

Flipping the Rock

The solution would be to flip the rock both vertically and horizontally to place the weathered area in the lower right corner.

1. On the Arrange palette, click the Flip Both button, the lower right of the Flip buttons. This inverts the rock diagonally, placing the weathered part in the lower right, and the open area above.
2. Place the butterfly sprite as shown in Figure 10-6, and set its home position.

Figure 10-6
The butterfly in position over the weathered area of the rock sprite.

Creating a Shadow for the Butterfly

The overall composition now works. The butterfly, however, appears to be floating above the rock, not sitting on it as you'd like. Because the weathered areas of the rock have strong shadows indicating a light source from above and to the left, there is no matching shadow under the butterfly, even though the highlight on the butterfly body indicates similar light. To rectify this, you need to make a shadow element with the Drop Shadow effect to link the butterfly with the rock.

1. Select the butterfly, and then select the Drop Shadow effect on the Effects palette.
2. On the Details tab, set the Distance to 35, Angle to 290, Color to 0, 0, 0, Opacity to 90, and the Softness slider one

quarter of the way to the right. By setting the angle, you don't need to click a particular angle button.

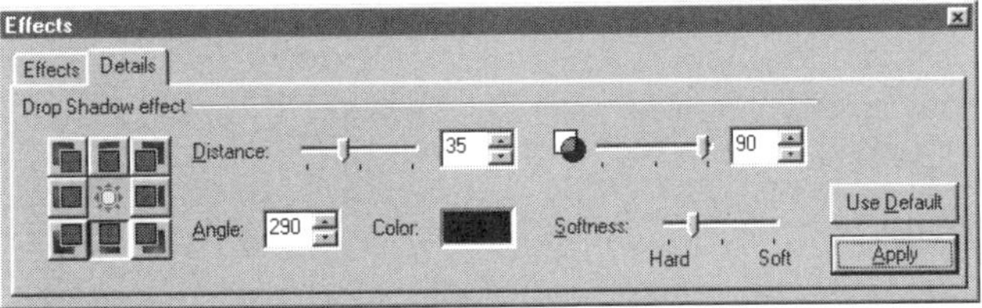

Figure 10-7
The Drop Shadow palette settings.

When you click Apply, you find that the butterfly has a drop shadow and now appears to be sitting in contact with the rock, as shown in Figure 10-8. Save the file once again.

Figure 10-8
The butterfly with a drop shadow.

Adding the Text

Text elements are next in the sequence of creating sprites. Here you have an opportunity to explore the interaction between surface effects and the Impressionist plug-in, to make incredibly cool text.

You want the name of your graphics design company, "Channel Graphics," to stick in people's minds, so you will pull out all the stops, making the text prominent, but in a way that won't overwhelm the rest of the design.

1. Zoom to 100 percent and open the Text palette.

2. On the Text palette, select Snap ITC, Bold, and 90 for the Size. Set smoothing on, set the color to 0, 161, 164, and set Opacity to 100.
3. Drag out a large text box and enter the capital letter "C".
4. Drag out another large text box and enter the capital letter "G".
5. Reduce the text size to 48 points, and make two more sprites, "hannel", and "raphics".
6. Position these sprites near the top of the rock sprite as shown in Figure 10-9.
7. Select the four text sprites and set their home position.

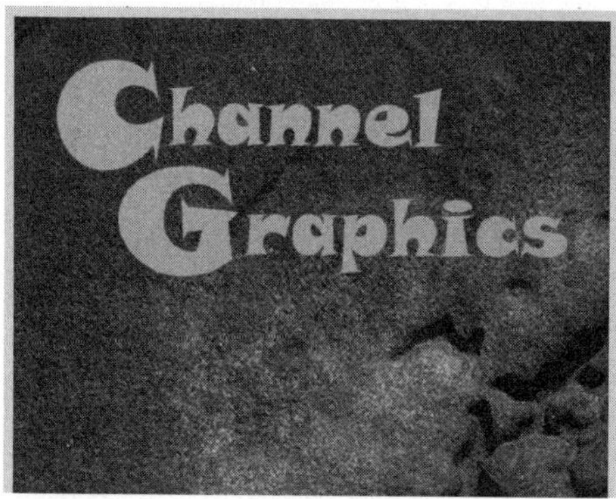

Figure 10-9

Text sprites placed relative to the top of the rock sprite.

Creating the Glowing Outline

To give the first letter of each word a glowing outline, follow these steps:

1. Duplicate the letter "C" sprite and send the duplicate home.
2. Apply the Edge Only effect to the duplicate, which is still selected, with these parameters: Thickness=2, Opacity=100, Color=170, 59, 0 (obtained from the wing of the butterfly).
3. Set the home position of the edge sprite, and then move the original blue-green sprite off the Composition Space.

   Now you want a yellow outline to make the glowing effect.

4. Duplicate the rust-colored outline.
5. Set the current color to 255, 255, 0 and apply it to the sprite with the Color Fill tool.
6. Move the yellow outline off the Composition Space for now.

   Create the blurred, rust-colored outline.
7. Select and duplicate the rust-colored outline and send the copy home.
8. Select and flatten both rust-colored outlines, and set the home position of the resulting sprite.
9. Apply the Edge effect to the flattened outline with these parameters: Thickness=2, Color=170, 59, 0.
10. Apply the Blur effect with a setting of 4, both Horizontal and Vertical.
11. Set the home position of this sprite, and then bring it to the front.

    Now move all the sprites into position.
12. Send the yellow outline home. It slides in under the blurred, rust-colored sprite to make a glowing outline.
13. Select the rust- and yellow-colored outlines (make sure they're both selected—you can tell that they're both selected when the Flatten button on the Arrange palette is no longer grayed out), and then flatten them. Set the home position of the resulting sprite.
14. Select the original blue-green "C" and send it home. It fits under the glowing outline.
15. Repeat this procedure for the letter "G."

Now that you know what you want to do with the text, you can easily repeat it for the second letter, the "G." But when you know what you want to do in advance, you can create a sprite that contains both characters, make the changes to the sprite, and then cut out each character to create two sprites with the same appearance.

You now have large "C" and "G" sprites that look like those in Figure 10-10, on the next page.

Figure 10-10
"C" and "G" sprites with glowing outlines.

Adding a Surface Effect and Drop Shadow

To add an interesting texture to the blue-green "C" and "G", follow these steps:

1. Select the blue-green "C." You can click anywhere on the blue-green portion of the "C" to select it without selecting the edge sprites.
2. Apply Transfer Shape at 50 percent using the rock as the source sprite. This adds some texture to the surface of the letter. The effect you are about to apply will use it.
3. Deselect all the sprites and re-select the blue-green "C."
4. From the Plug-Ins drop-down menu, select Impressionist. Then select Impressionist again on the secondary menu.
5. On the Impressionist dialog box, click Style and choose Geometric, and then Boiling Shiny Bubbles. Set the remaining parameters like this:

Impressionist Dialog Box

Background	Image
Brush size	64%
Coverage	50%
Pressure	98

6. Click Preview to see how the effect will look, and then click Apply.

7. Repeat this procedure for the "G."
8. Apply the Emboss effect with these settings:

Emboss Effect Settings	
Relief	4
Light Position	Top Left
Opacity	80%

9. Apply the Cracked Varnish effect with these settings:

Cracked Varnish Effect Settings	
Crack Spacing	4
Crack Depth	4
Crack Brightness	10
Opacity	85%

10. Click the rust-colored outline of the "C" and "G" sprites (if you have the home positions of all the sprites set, you can move sprites aside temporarily to get to the rust-color outline easily) and apply the Drop Shadow effect using these settings:

Drop Shadow Effect Settings	
Distance	6
Opacity	100
Angle	290
Color	53, 28, 0, obtained from the butterfly wing
Softness slider	One eighth to the right

This lifts the glowing outline away from the textured letters.

The "C" and "G" now have what could be called a magnified version of the surface texture of the rock background. This works to enhance the background and emphasize the letters.

Try this to see how big a difference a small change can make: bring the blue-green letter to the front. Leave the large letters whichever way you like them best.

Save your file to disk.

Treating the Remaining Text Letters

The other two text sprites, "hannel" and "raphics," will get a slightly different surface treatment. While the large letters relate to the surface texture of the rock, the small letters will mimic (in miniature) the feel of the rounded, weathered, blobby looking pieces of rock around the butterfly.

1. Set the current color to 28, 101, 102. This is used by some elements of the following effects.

2. Select the "hannel" and "raphics" sprites and apply the Fine Marker effect using these settings.

Fine Marker Effect Settings	
Stroke length	8
Dark intensity	20
Light intensity	3
Opacity	75

3. Then apply the Stained Glass effect with these settings:

Stained Glass Effect Settings	
Cell size	3
Border thickness	1
Light Intensity	5
Opacity	60

4. Apply the Edge effect with these settings:

Edge Effect Settings	
Thickness	1
Color	118, 0, 173
Opacity	100

5. Apply the Cracked Varnish effect with the settings in the table on the facing page.

Cracked Varnish Effect Settings

Crack spacing	4
Crack depth	4
Crack brightness	10
Opacity	100

6. For the final touch, select each sprite and apply the Drop Shadow effect to it (you can't apply the Drop Shadow effect to multiple sprites simultaneously) with these settings:

Drop Shadow Effect Settings

Distance	25
Angle	290
Color	53, 28, 0
Softness slider	One quarter to the right
Opacity	100

That's it for the text sprites, except for one last item. The drop shadow you just made is on top of the glowing outline of the "G." Select the glowing outline and bring it to the front, unless, of course, you decide you like the letter form in front of the glow.

Save your file to disk.

Adding a Second Butterfly: The Final Touch

Even though your promotional card is looking fine, a few more small graphic elements would add dynamic movement to the composition.

Diagonal lines convey motion and vigor. A modified butterfly would work perfectly to provide just enough movement to pull together the whole composition.

1. Duplicate the original, color-tuned butterfly sprite that is on the Workspace.

   If you forgot to put aside a copy, you can ungroup the group of butterfly sprites we've provided and copy the bottom sprite to use.

2. Flip the copy horizontally and scale it to 180 pixels wide with Keep Aspect Ratio turned on.
3. Place the scaled butterfly sprite as shown in Figure 10-11.

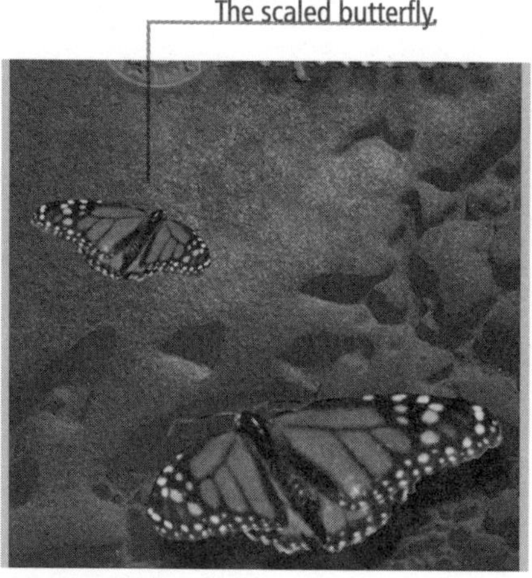

Figure 10-11
Placement of the scaled butterfly.

You want this second butterfly image to become a graphic element, not another representation of a butterfly, which might compete with other graphic elements and make the composition too busy. Applying a surface effect that reduces it to an abstract graphic element will do exactly what you want.

To choose an effect, you want something that provides linear movement. The body shape of the butterfly is a strong linear element pointing like an arrow in a diagonal direction. Something that strengthens the line quality is what you need. Something like the Technical Pen effect.

1. Duplicate the sprite because you will need a copy in a moment.
2. Move the copy, and change the current color to 43, 21, 0.
3. Apply the Technical Pen effect to the first scaled sprite using the settings in the table on the facing page.

Technical Pen Effect Settings	
Stroke Length	15
Stroke Direction	right diagonal
Light Dark Balance	91 (this means there will be more dark than light)
Opacity	100

4. Apply the Drop Shadow effect with these settings:

Drop Shadow Effect Settings	
Distance	18
Angle	290
Opacity	100
Color	53, 28, 0
Softness Slider	one quarter to the right

5. Select the copy of the scaled butterfly you put aside a few moments ago and scale it to 100 pixels wide with Keep Aspect Ratio turned on.
6. Flip the sprite horizontally and place it near the upper right corner of the composition as shown in Figure 10-12.

The second scaled butterfly.

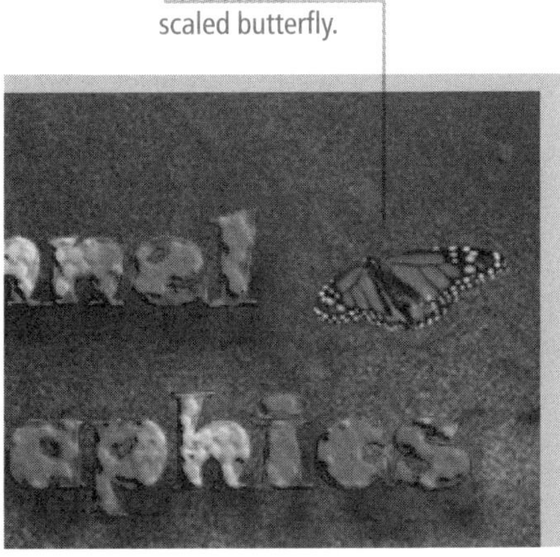

Figure 10-12
Position of the second scaled butterfly.

7. Again, apply the Technical Pen effect. This time set the Stroke to Left Diagonal and the Stroke Length to 8. Everything else remains the same.
8. Add a drop shadow. Change the distance to 10 and leave everything else the same.
9. Now move the small butterfly so that its left wing just overlaps the bottom of the "l" in Channel.
10. Deselect all the sprites, and then select the rock background first so that it becomes the source sprite. Shift-click the small butterfly.
11. On the Arrange palette, click the Order Before button to move the butterfly under the shadow of the "l" and in front of the rock.

Save your file to disk.

The Other Side

The flip side of the promotional card will carry your contact information and a place for a stamp and address label. Unlike the front of the card, its orientation will be landscape rather than vertical, so the Composition Space must now be 750 by 500 pixels rather than 500 by 750.

Open the file CHAPTER10-A.MIC. All the remaining elements that you will make are on the Composition Space. Recreate the layout.

To begin, you'll make a rectangle that outlines the entire text area using the next set of steps. The simplest way to do this is to draw a rectangle using the Shape tools and then apply the Edge Only effect at the thickness you want for the line. For this project, a line thickness of 2 pixels would work well. Later, when you make the full-sized layout, you will want a thicker outline.

To obtain a rectangle that is 25 pixels in from each edge of the card, you can draw a 700 by 450-pixel rectangle. However, you also need to deduct the two-pixel line thickness per edge. That makes the final rectangle 696 by 446 pixels.

1. Draw a 696 by 446-pixel rectangle using the current color and center it on the Composition Space.
2. Apply Edge Only with a 2-pixel thickness and black as the color.

3. Set the home position of the resulting outline and lock its position.
4. Now, as close as possible to the center of the rectangle, draw a vertical dividing line that is 2 pixels thick and 446 pixels high. Remember, you can use the Polygon tool on the Shapes palette with the Close option turned off and Line Width set to 2.
5. Before you click Create to create the line, use Move Points on the shortcut menu, if necessary, to make the line vertical.
6. After you click Create, check the status bar for the X position of the line. The horizontal center of the rectangle is 375 pixels across, so move the line to the right or left to position it at exactly X=375.
7. Use the Text tools to enter imaginary contact information for Channel Graphics at whatever font and font size that you'd like.

Preparing the Final Deliverable

To prepare a full-scale, printer-ready design, you'd scale everything up from a Composition Space size of 750 by 500 pixels to the full size of 4 inches by 6 inches, or 1200 by 1800 pixels. Your goal for the final design would simply be to make everything look the same as it does in the smaller-sized file.

To obtain the very best quality final image, you might even want to scale down copies of the original sprites rather than scale up the small images you've made, so the images go through only one scaling rather than two. Each time you scale an image, especially when you scale it up, the image loses a very small bit of image quality.

To prepare the final image for a service bureau or printer, you would save the composition as a TIF file, which is a bitmap file the service bureau could print from directly.

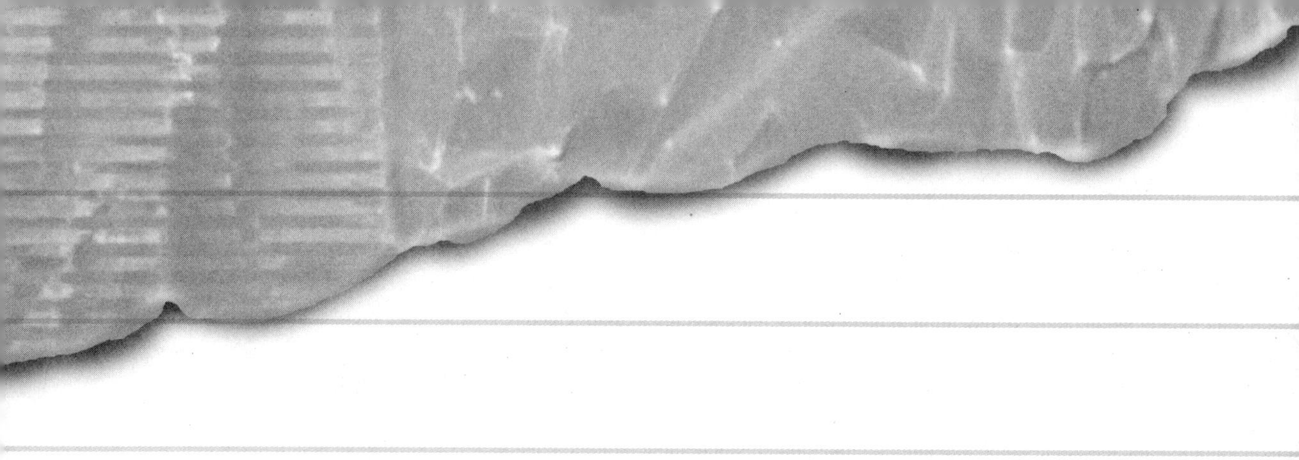

11 CHAPTER

A Web Site Home Page: Cell Fones

Your final challenge in this book will be to create the home page for an imaginary, business-oriented Web site for a company named Cell Fones. This project will require you to use many of the techniques you have learned in earlier chapters.

You will create a tiled background, blend a number of images into a montage, create text with a three-dimensional appearance, use a frame to create the illusion of depth, take advantage of Image Composer's easy control over transparency, and create a set of graphic buttons. Remember to make backup duplicates of all your sprites as you work, because this project is the most complex of all.

You can examine the finished product toward which you will be working by opening CHAPTER11.MIC from the PROJECTS folder on the CD-ROM. Examining the sprites of any project closely, analyzing them, figuring out how they came into being, and then making them yourself is a valuable learning technique. Try it and soon, whatever you see, real or imagined, will be the subject matter for your creations.

Creating the Tiled Background

To begin the project, you'll make the tiled background so you'll be able to create foreground objects that suit the background.

In previous projects, you've made a single tile and then duplicated it and aligned the copies to fill the background of the Composition Space. This time, however, you will use another technique: you will fill a rectangle the size of the Composition Space by transferring the tile with the Tile effect on the Texture Transfer palette. When you are finished, you can set aside a copy of the original tile so you'll have it to deploy on the Web page.

Move the completed image off the Composition Space so you can begin.

1. Set the current color to 187, 210, 195, a pale green.
2. On the Composition Space, draw a 140-pixel square sprite. This is a larger size than you'll need, but the Impressionist plug-in will produce more even color on a larger sprite, so the final image will tile better.
3. From the Plug-Ins drop-down menu, select Impressionist, and then select Impressionist again on the secondary menu. Choose these settings on the Impressionist dialog box:

Impressionist Dialog Box Settings

Style	Ink: Scratchy Pen On Black
Background	Custom Color, RGB 237, 228, 211
Brush Size	56 percent
Coverage	88 percent
Pressure	67 percent

4. Click Preview to see the result of the settings, and then click Apply. The square is filled with a dappled blue-green pattern.
5. Duplicate the sprite and set aside a copy, and then reselect the original.
6. Use the Crop tool on the Arrange palette to crop the square to 121 by 66 pixels. This size tiles properly to the Composition Space.

Remember, to create a tileable sprite, you need to quarter the large tile into smaller sprites that you can transfer switch and reassemble.

1. To make the quarter-sized sprites stand out against the tile, change the current color to 90, 0, 255, a strong blue.
2. Make a 61 by 33-pixel rectangle and a 60 by 33-pixel rectangle.
3. Place the larger blue sprite to the left of the textured sprite, and the smaller blue sprite to the right.
4. Duplicate each of the blue sprites.

Now that you have the four smaller sprites, you can use Transfer Shape to transfer the large sprite's texture.

1. Using the Align tools on the Arrange palette, align one of the larger blue sprites with the lower left corner of the textured sprite and the other with the upper left corner.
2. Select the textured sprite and then select the two blue sprites so that the textured sprite is the source, and Apply Transfer Shape on the Texture Transfer palette at 100 percent opacity.
3. Move the newly textured sprites a little to the left of the source sprite.
4. Align the smaller two blue sprites with the right upper and right lower corners of the textured sprite and Apply Transfer Shape to them also.
5. Move the two smaller sprites to the right, off the textured sprite, and then move the source sprite off the Composition Space.
6. As you've done before, switch the position of the sprites at the the lower left and upper right corners. Switch the upper left and lower right sprites, too.
7. Use the Align tools to align the four sprites so that they make a rectangle that has even outside edges.
8. Flatten the sprites to obtain the completed tile.

As before, use the Transfer tool in the Paint palette to smooth out any obvious lines that go through the tile.

Now you'll automatically tile the sprite you've created.

1. Move the flattened sprite off the Composition Space and make a 605 by 330-pixel rectangle of any color.
2. Align the rectangle with the Composition Space, send it to the back so that you can move the tile sprite onto it, set its home position, and lock its position.
3. Select the tile sprite and align it with the upper left corner of the large rectangle.
4. Click the small sprite to make it the source, and then click Tile on the Texture Transfer palette. Leave Opacity at 100, and set Horizontal Spacing and Vertical Spacing to 0 so there will be no space between the tiles. Click Apply. The tile pattern fills the large rectangle.
5. Deselect all the sprites, and then move the small sprite to the Workspace to save for the Web later.
6. Align the background rectangle with the center of Composition space, set its home position, and lock its position.

   You now have the background for this project, so save your work to a file.

Making the Banner

To create the image for the Web page banner, you'd like to make a montage of several photos that will convey the idea of people talking on cell phones while outdoors. To place the photos in an overlapping arrangement, you can layer the sprites with transparency mapping, which creates the blending among images that you'd like.

To make the finished piece appear to float over the background, you can anchor its corners with photo album-like tabs.

Cropping and Scaling the Images

Before you can work with the images, you need to scale them, and then shape the two images of people.

1. Make a copy of the desert image on the Workspace and then move the copy onto the Composition Space.

   To leave room on the left for images of people, you want the cactus in the desert image to appear on the right.
2. Flip the desert image horizontally.

Now crop and scale the images.

3. To maximize the space available for people in the desert image, crop the flipped image from the right until the Width reading on the status bar is 254. Crop up from the bottom until the Height reading on the status bar is 165.
4. On the Arrange palette, use the Scale control to scale the desert image down to a width of 180. Make sure that Keep Aspect Ratio is turned on so that the height adjusts automatically to 116. Click Apply.
5. Move a copy of the image of a woman using the phone onto the Composition Space, and use the Crop tool to crop up from the bottom of the image until the Height on the status bar reads 195.
6. Scale the sprite to a Width of 100 pixels, making sure Keep Aspect Ratio is turned on.
7. Move a copy of the image of a man using a car phone onto the Composition Space and crop it by cropping the bottom until the Height is 90, cropping the left side until the Width is 190, and then cropping the right side until the Width is 90.

The man's eye, the telephone, and the man's hand are now near the center of the sprite. Figure 11-1 shows the three scaled and cropped sprites on the Composition Space.

Figure 11-1
The three scaled and cropped sprites.

Before going on, move the cactus image near the upper left corner of the background and use the arrow keys to precisely position its upper left corner 10 pixels down and 10 pixels to the right of the upper left corner of the Composition Space. As you move the sprite, check the status bar for the sprite's exact X, Y position. Set its home position.

Preparing the Woman's Head Sprite

To create a sprite for the woman's head that will blend well into the sky background when you apply a transparency gradient to it, you can make the sprite non-rectangular. In this case, you'll make it oval to harmonize with the oval shape of the woman's head. To make the oval sprite you will need a stencil.

Creating and Using a Stencil

1. Set the current color to black, and then make an oval sprite 100 pixels wide by 125 pixels high at 100 percent Opacity. This will be large enough to cover the woman's head and leave enough space around the edges to add transparency mapping later.
2. Use the Crop/Extend tool on the Arrange palette and drag the bottom handle of the oval down 15 pixels so that the status bar Height reading is 140.
3. With the Crop/Extend tool, drag the top crop handle up 15 pixels so that the Height reading is 155.
4. Drag the left Crop/Extend handle until the Width is 115.
5. Drag the right Crop/Extend handle until the Width is 130.
6. On the Cutout palette, click the Stencil button at the far right. Deselect all the sprites.
7. Click directly on the original oval area on the stencil sprite and drag the original oval sprite off the Composition Space.

   You now can see the new stencil sprite that you've created. It's the inverse of the original: its oval center is transparent (alpha channel information) and the surrounding area is opaque.
8. Select the stencil sprite and the woman's head sprite and align their centers, as shown in Figure 11-2. Make sure Relative To Composition Space is turned off when you use the Align commands.

To use the stencil sprite as the source sprite to snip the edges around the woman's head sprite, follow these steps:

1. Deselect all the sprites.
2. Click the stencil and then Shift-click the woman's head sprite. The stencil sprite is the source sprite.

3. On the Texture Transfer palette, choose Snip, make sure Opacity is 100 percent, and click Apply.
4. Drag away the stencil and take a look at the woman's head sprite now. Figure 11-3 shows the result.

Figure 11-2
The stencil and woman's head sprites centered.

Figure 11-3
The woman's head sprite after applying Snip.

Adding the Transparency Gradient

To blend the woman's head sprite with the desert image, you need to use transparency mapping. With transparency mapping, you transfer the gray levels of one sprite to transparency levels in another. In earlier chapters, you used transparency mapping to blend two disparate images in the Big Sur Poster, and to blend three images in the Tropical Fantasy graphic for the Web. You saw that you can use color tuning to adjust the levels of gray in the grayscale gradient before you use Map Transparency, controlling where in a transparency gradient the transparency begins and how quickly the gradient makes the transition from opaque to transparent.

Using Grayscale Gradients

In Image Composer, an 8-bit grayscale has 254 levels of gray, plus black and white. In order for all 256 levels to be displayed, a grayscale gradient sprite must be at least 256 pixels across (at least one pixel for each grayscale level). If the gradient is smaller than 256 pixels across, it can't possibly display all 256 gray levels. Instead, it displays fewer levels with a larger jump between levels, and that produces banding.

To see this for yourself, draw a 10-pixel wide rectangle and then zoom in closely. Apply a Grayscale Left gradient to the rectangle and examine the result. You'll see significant banding. Now draw a rectangle that is 50 pixels wide and apply the same gradient. The banding is still present, but it's less noticeable. If you were to draw a 256-pixel wide rectangle, you would see no banding at all. In other words, you must accept a certain degree of banding for any gradient that is smaller than 256 pixels.

In this case, the image to which you want to transfer transparency is only 100 pixels wide. In fact, because the transparency gradient only runs from near the center of the image to its outside edge, the gradient will be only about 30 to 35 pixels across (from near the center of the image to the outside edge).

A 50-pixel wide gradient will have noticeable banding (see "Using Grayscale Gradients," above) unless you use the following workaround to reduce the number of grayscale levels you are trying to pack into the 50-pixel wide space.

To reduce banding, you can draw the grayscale gradient sprite larger so that it is capable of displaying more gray levels with a smaller increment between each level. However, when you superimpose this grayscale sprite over the sprite to which you want to map transparency, some gray levels at one or both ends of the sprite will not be used, as shown in Figure 11-4.

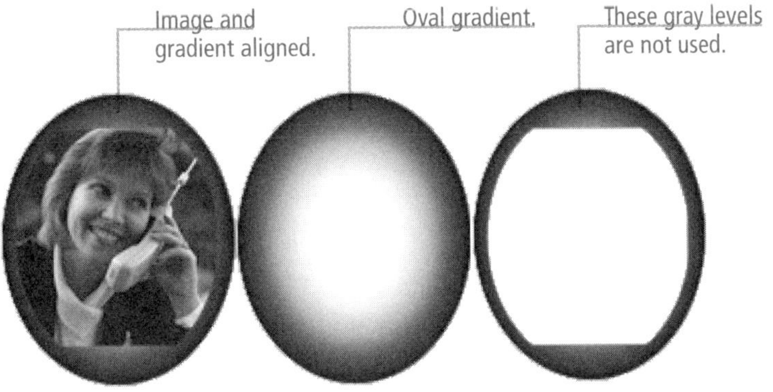

Figure 11-4
Some gray levels are not used when the grayscale sprite is larger than the destination sprite in transparency mapping.

Because the gray levels beyond the edges of the destination sprite are not used in the transparency mapping, the transparency gradient on the destination sprite has fewer than a full 256 levels: it doesn't run from fully opaque to fully transparent. The wider you make the grayscale sprite, the fewer gray levels are used, and the smoother you make the transparency gradient. In other words, you reduce banding by limiting the portion of the gradient to use so you don't try squeezing too many levels into the sprite.

The upshot of all this is that when mapping transparency to the small sprites that you will want to create for the Web, you must balance the smoothness of the gradient against the breadth of the transparency gradient. A transparency that runs all the way from fully transparent to fully opaque in a small sprite may have noticeable banding. Yet another one of life's trade-offs.

For the woman's head sprite, you will find a middle ground.

1. Make an oval 115 pixels wide by 140 pixels high and apply the Gradient effect using a gradient named Grayscale Left on the Details tab, at 100 percent Opacity.
2. To the grayscale sprite, apply the Radial Sweep effect with an Angle of 0 on the Details tab. The result should look like the second grayscale oval down to the left of the woman's head on the Workspace far to the left of the Composition Space.

You now have a grayscale gradient sprite you can use to map transparency to the woman's head sprite, but the gradient of gray levels runs evenly from the center of the oval to the outside edge. You want a larger area covering the woman's face to be opaque, or white in the grayscale gradient. You also want more of the dark area at the outside edge of the gradient to be pure black, or fully transparent, and to push most of the darkest grays outside the area that will be used for transparency mapping. You can achieve this by color tuning the grayscale gradient before you use it to map transparency to the woman's head sprite. This helps smooth out the transparency gradient in the area used for mapping.

Open the Color Tuning palette and click the Dynamic Range tab. The Dynamic Range histogram looks like the histogram shown in Figure 11-5.

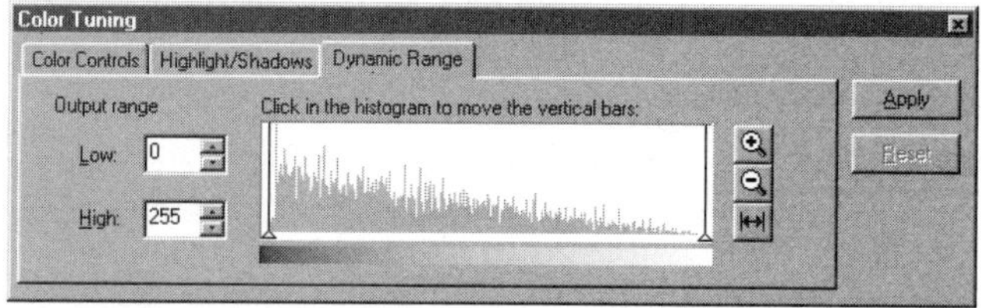

Figure 11-5

The Dynamic Range histogram for the grayscale oval.

Here is how the histogram relates to the grayscale oval: at the left side of the histogram, the gray vertical bars extend more than halfway to the top. Moving to the right, with minor spikes, the gray descends at a constant angle to nothing at the far right. This tells you the relative distribution of pixels from dark (on the left) to light (on the right). More pixels in the sprite are dark gray than light. As you look to the right, you see that fewer and fewer pixels take up the middle and light shades.

Now look at the oval sprite. The outside circumference of the oval, which has the most pixels, is black and dark gray. As you move toward the center, there are fewer pixels and they are lighter and lighter, with white at the center.

Remember that you want a large, center area covering the woman's face to be opaque, or white, and more of the outside edge to be transparent, or black. You also want the gray, middle value area to be strongest toward the dark edge so that the transition to transparency occurs quickly near the edges. Achieving this is a two-step procedure.

1. Move the vertical sliders of the Dynamic Range histogram to the positions shown in Figure 11-6, and click Apply.

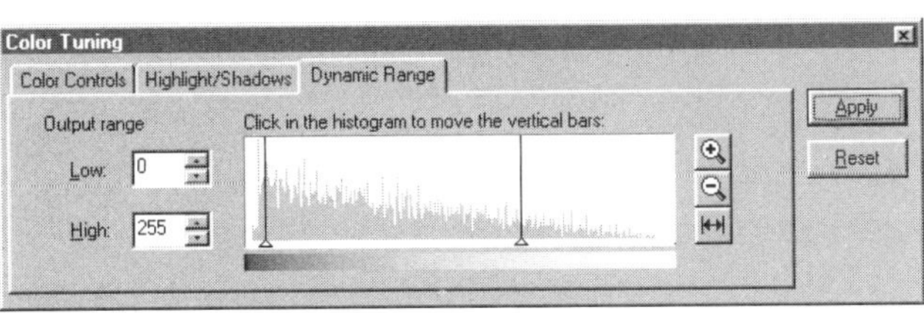

Figure 11-6
The Dynamic Range histogram with the sliders adjusted.

2. Deselect the oval sprite and then select it again so you see the modified histogram.

   Look again at the Dynamic Range histogram. The distribution of values is now more even, with many more mid-level and light pixels, but there's still a slight bias toward the dark. The additional black area you have created by shifting the left slider a little to the right has caused this dark bias.

   Now you want the dark end of the grays to become a little darker. Then you want the grays to quickly become light and then white. You can accomplish this with the Highlight/Shadows control on the Color Tuning palette.

3. Click the Highlight/Shadows tab and adjust the curve to match Figure 11-7. Then click Apply.

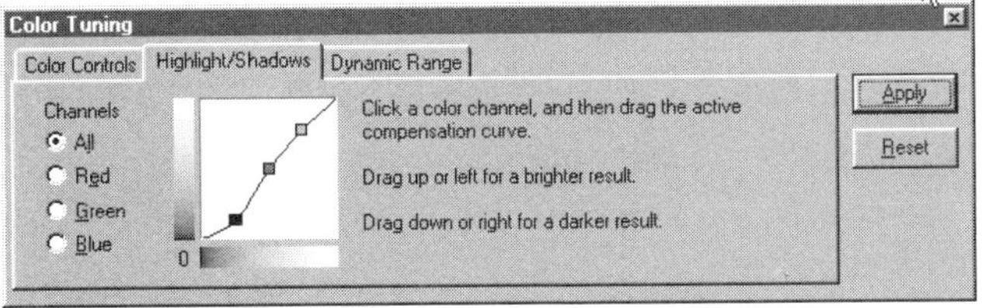

Figure 11-7
Adjustment for the Highlight/Shadows curve.

The black and darkest grays are now a band around the outside edge. Then a gradient of grays moves quickly toward light gray. Most of the gradient is taken up with light grays and white. When applied to the woman's head, this will leave most of her face opaque, with a very translucent area around the edge.

Now look again at the Dynamic Range histogram for the oval to get a sense for how it relates to the distribution of grayscale in the oval. The histogram is shown in Figure 11-8.

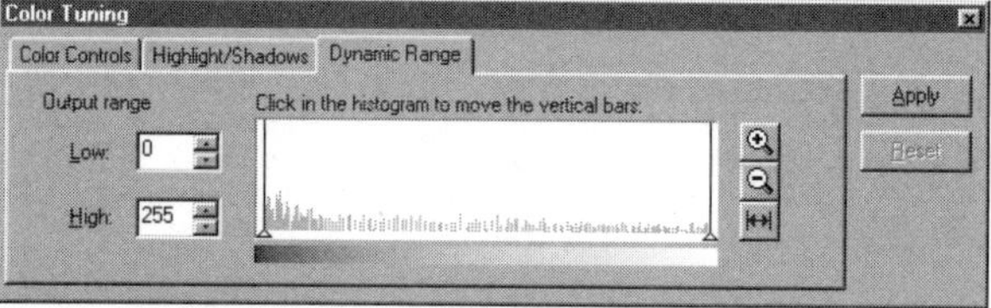

Figure 11-8
The Dynamic Range histogram of the finished oval sprite.

Now, apply the transparency gradient to the woman's head.

1. Select the woman's head sprite and bring it to the front so that you can see how it relates to the gradient sprite.
2. Select the transparency gradient oval you just made.
3. Click the gradient oval again to make it the source sprite.
4. Align the centers of the two sprites with Align Centers.
5. Apply the Map Transparency effect.
6. Deselect all the sprites and move the oval gradient away.
7. Now position the woman's head on the desert image using the finished project image as reference. Set the sprite's home position.

Before proceeding, take a moment to save your file.

Preparing the Cactus and the Man's Head Sprites

To keep the cactus in front when you create the final composition, you need to cut out the cactus shape. Before doing so, you want to enhance the color saturation so the sprites of people contrast well with their surroundings.

1. Select the scaled desert image.
2. On the Color Controls tab of the Color Tuning palette, increase Saturation to 5, and click Apply.

Cutting Out the Man's Head Sprite

This time, you want to end up with a sprite consisting of the man's head, shoulders, and hand holding the telephone, not like the woman's head sprite. But you can define the limits of this sprite by making a circular cutout using the same procedure you used with the woman's head sprite.

1. Draw a 90-pixel circle.
2. Extend the bounding box 15 pixels on all four sides using the Crop/Extend tool.
3. Make a stencil with the Stencil tool.
4. Select the man's head sprite and the stencil, and align their centers.
5. With the stencil as the source, apply Snip from the Texture Transfer palette to the man's head. Move the stencil away.

   Here, you will veer off in a different direction. Snipping to a circle defined the extent of the man's back and left arm. Now you will cut out a sprite that contains the rest of the man's head.
6. Use the Curve tool on the Cutout palette to cut out the sprite shown in Figure 11-9. Leave a pixel or so of the background around the head for blending.

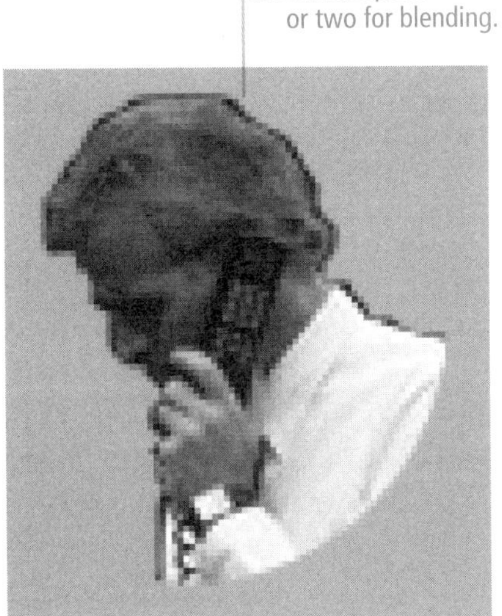
Leave a pixel
or two for blending.

Figure 11-9
Cutout shape of man's head.

7. Soften the edges of the cutout sprite with the Eraser tool on the Paint palette. First, use a soft, small brush of 3 pixels with an opacity setting of 6. Work your way around the

edge of the sprite, softening the pixels so they will blend into the background. Then use a soft, 12-pixel brush with an Opacity setting of 12 to shape the lower right area of the sprite. See the reference sprite for the shape, if necessary.

Cutting Out the Cactus

Next, cut out a sprite of the cactus with the Curve tool on the Cutout palette to place in front of the man's head. Remember to select the desert sprite prior to starting with the Curve tool. You might want to refer to the cutout cactus sprite to the left of the Composition Space to see how much to include around the bottom. After you cut out the cactus, set its home position and move it aside for now.

Composing the Banner Sprites

To place the sprites in their final arrangement, follow these steps:

1. Place the man's head in position, as shown in the completed project.
2. Apply the Transparent effect with an Opacity setting of 85.
3. Select the cactus cutout, send it home, and bring it to the front.
4. Select all the sprites you have made for the banner image, group them, copy and set aside the copy. Then flatten the original group.

   If, when you flatten the sprites, the bounding box grows larger than the desert image, there may be edges of the various sprites protruding beyond the edges of the desert background. If so, use the Crop tool to crop the image edges evenly with the edge of the desert image.
5. Using the status bar, make note of the width and height of the cropped sprite. Or, if you did not crop it, make note of its size now.
6. If necessary, reposition the banner sprite to 10 pixels in from the left and 10 pixels down from the upper left corner of the Composition Space.
7. Set the home position of the sprite, and save the file.

A Different Kind of Frame: Making the Banner Float

In the WalkRight project, the image in the banner worked best when it was framed to give the illusion that it was a window opening to an outdoor space. This time you want to make the sprites of people seem more immediate by giving the image the feeling of being raised in front of the background. A dark background will produce the separation. Then the illusion of having the corners in picture tabs, like a photo album's tabs, but softer, will produce a visual tension that pushes the banner sprites forward. This happens because the dark underneath the banner pushes the whole banner forward, while the corner pieces anchor the corners to the background.

1. Draw a rectangle of any color that is 5 pixels larger on every side than the flattened banner sprite. It should be 10 pixels wider and 10 pixels taller, overall.
2. Align the centers of the banner image and the rectangle, making sure the banner image is the source when you use Align Centers on the Arrange palette.
3. Send the rectangle behind the banner by clicking Behind on the Arrange palette. Set the home positions of the sprites.
4. Deselect all the sprites and then re-select the rectangle.
5. Shift-click the background sprite, and then click it again to make it the source sprite.
6. On the Texture Transfer palette, apply Transfer Shape at 100 percent Opacity. The rectangle takes on the texture of the background and seems to disappear.

NOTE

If the sprite does not seem to disappear, you have come across the bug in Image Composer that sometimes applies only partial opacity (rather than the full 100 percent that you have specified) when you are using one of the Transfer tools. The solution is to undo the change, move the Opacity slider on the Texture Transfer palette to zero and then move it back to 100 percent. Then try using Transfer Shape again.

7. Deselect all the sprites, and click next to the banner image to select the rectangle sprite.
8. On the Color Controls tab of the Color Tuning palette, drag the Brightness slider left to –100 and click Apply. The rectangle becomes darker.

While the rectangle still has the background texture, you want to cut out a sprite from which to make the corner pieces.

1. Zoom in on the upper right corner of the banner area and select the rectangle sprite, if it is not still selected.
2. Use the Curve tool on the Cutout palette to cut out a corner from the rectangle, shaped as in figure 11-10, on the next page. The cutout sprite in the figure is shown as black so that you can clearly see the shape. Your sprite will have the same texture as the rectangle.

Figure 11-10
The corner sprite cut out.

3. Set the home position of the cutout sprite.
4. Deselect all the sprites, re-select the new corner sprite and apply the Blur effect at 2 pixels both Horizontal and Vertical.
5. Apply the Transparent effect at 85 percent Opacity.
6. Make three copies of the sprite, one for each corner.
7. Flip one sprite horizontally for the top left corner. Flip another sprite vertically for the bottom right corner, and use Flip Both to flip the last sprite both horizontally and vertically for the bottom left corner.
8. Move the corner sprites near their corners, but not on the corners yet.
9. Set the current color to black if it is not black already. Then select the rectangle sprite and click Color Fill to make the rectangle black.
10. Apply the Blur effect at 4 pixels both Horizontal and Vertical, and then apply the Transparent effect at 90 percent Opacity.

11. Place the corner sprites over the corners of the banner image, using the finished project as a reference.
12. Select all the banner area sprites and flatten them. Figure 11-11 shows how the completed banner image looks. Set the banner image's home position.

Figure 11-11
The finished banner image.

That's it for the banner. Save your file.

Creating the Standing Man Sprite

The next element to create is the standing man who is talking on the telephone and looking at his watch. Copy this image and move the copy onto the Composition Space.

Cropping, Scaling, and Cutting Out the Image

1. Use the Crop/Extend tool to crop the image from the bottom, so the bottom of the sprite is barely touching the elbow of the man's right arm (the man on the telephone). Then crop in from the left, stopping just before touching the hand with the telephone. The cropped image should look like the image in Figure 11-12, on the next page.
2. Scale the resulting sprite to 85 percent.

3. Use the Curve tool on the Cutout palette to cut out a sprite containing the shape of the man. Leave a small margin around the outside, 1 or 2 pixels, for cleanup.

Figure 11-12
Cropped image.

Now use the following technique to clean up the edges of the cutout sprite:

1. Make a dark-colored rectangle larger than the cutout sprite.
2. Select and bring the cutout sprite to the front. Then place it on the dark rectangle so that you can see the edges that need to be cleaned up. If the image had been on a dark background, you would use a light-colored rectangle for contrast.
3. Use the Eraser and Paintbrush tools at very small sizes (1 or 2 pixels) and opacities of 6 to 12 percent to clean and touch up the edges of the image. Figure 11-13 shows the sprite after cleanup. Delete the dark rectangle that you used for contrast.

   Although another approach would have been to carefully cut out the sprite without leaving a margin for cleaning up, this procedure fixes the inevitable glitches that occur. By using the Eraser on the margin with partial opacity, you also introduce some blending, or anti-aliasing, with the background.

4. Refer to the finished image to position this sprite.
5. Set the home position, make a backup copy and move the copy aside.

Figure 11-13
Sprite after cleanup.

Creating a Blurred Recess for the Sprite

With a few steps, you can create a recess to surround the sprite you've just created.

1. Extend the bounding box of the original cutout man sprite 20 pixels on all sides, set the sprite's home position and make a stencil. The color of the stencil does not matter.
2. Set the home position of the stencil.
3. Apply Transfer Shape to the stencil at 100 percent Opacity using the background as the source sprite.

NOTE

If the Stencil darkens but does not disappear, you have come across the Transfer tools bug again. Remeber to undo the change, move the Opacity slider on the Texture Transfer palette to zero, set it back to 100 percent, and then try Transfer Shape again.

4. Make a copy of the stencil and move the copy aside.
5. To the original stencil that is still on the Composition Space, apply the Blur effect at 4 pixels both Horizontal and Vertical.
6. Apply the Recess effect to the blurred sprite.
7. Crop the outside, recessed edges off the recessed sprite. See figure 11-14.

Figure 11-14
Blurred, recessed sprite with edges cropped.

Notice that the blurred sprite no longer shows the texture that you transferred from the background. To restore this texture, follow these steps:

1. Select the copy of the textured stencil you put aside.
2. Send the copy home and to the front.

   The copy appears to restore the texture to the surface around the man's silhouette, but it also cuts slightly into the recessed halo around him. To restore the recessed halo and retain the textured surface, follow Step 3.

3. Carefully use the Eraser with a soft brush (9 pixels or so) at 35 percent Opacity to erase the interior edge of the textured stencil sprite around the man's silhouette. You want the full width of the recessed edge of the sprite underneath to become visible all around, as shown in Figure 11-15.

Figure 11-15
Man with recessed edge and textured background around the recess.

4. Select the recessed sprite, the textured sprite, and the man sprite. Flatten them into a single sprite and set the sprite's home position.

Creating the Main Text Element

Here you'll make text that gives the illusion of being three-dimensional. Because this process is somewhat convoluted, we occasionally ask you to make extra copies along the way as insurance in case something doesn't quite work.

Creating the Basic Sprites

1. On the Composition Space, make two text sprites: "Cell" and "Fones". The font is Viner Hand ITC, 60 points, and the color is black.
2. Move the Fones sprite off the Composition Space for now. You will work through the whole procedure with the Cell sprite and then repeat it with Fones.
3. Position the Cell sprite as it is in the finished reference image, and set its home position.
4. Duplicate Cell, and move the copy off the Composition Space.

Zoom in closely to the edges of the letters and you'll see considerable anti-aliasing. To make the 3-D effect, you first need to make the anti-aliasing opaque, and then thicken the letters.

5. Copy the Cell sprite and send it home. Do this twice more. This builds up opacity on the edges of the letters.
6. Select these sprites and flatten them. Set their home position, and then apply the Edge effect with a Thickness of 1, and the color set to black.

   This produces semi-transparent pixels between the original letter and the new edge.
7. Set the home position of the sprite, and then copy and send the copy home three times. Flatten the sprites and then set the home position again. This step has filled the transparency.

Creating a Stencil

Next, you'll create a stencil that you can use to begin the 3-D effect.

1. If you're not already zoomed in, zoom in so that the Cell sprite is large, and select it. Notice the bounding box extends quite a bit above and below the letterforms.
2. Extend the left and right sides of the bounding box an equal amount with the Crop/Extend tool.
3. Set the home position of the sprite. Make a backup copy and set it aside.
4. Blur the Cell sprite 3 pixels in both directions so that when you make a stencil from it, it will have a nice, smooth edge with which to Snip.
5. Make a stencil from the Cell sprite, set the home position of the stencil, and then move the text sprite away for now.
6. With the background as the source, apply Transfer Shape to the stencil at 100 percent Opacity. The stencil disappears.

NOTE

Remember, if the Stencil darkens but does not disappear, undo the change, move the Opacity slider to zero and then move it back to 100 percent. Then try using Transfer Shape again.

The stencil will protrude above the background. Use the Crop/Extend tool to crop it down so its top edge is 4 or 5 pixels inside the top edge of the background.

7. Deselect all the sprites and re-select the stencil.
8. Apply the Blur effect at a setting of 3 in both directions. Then apply the Recess effect. Set the home position of the sprite. Figure 11-16 shows the sprite now.

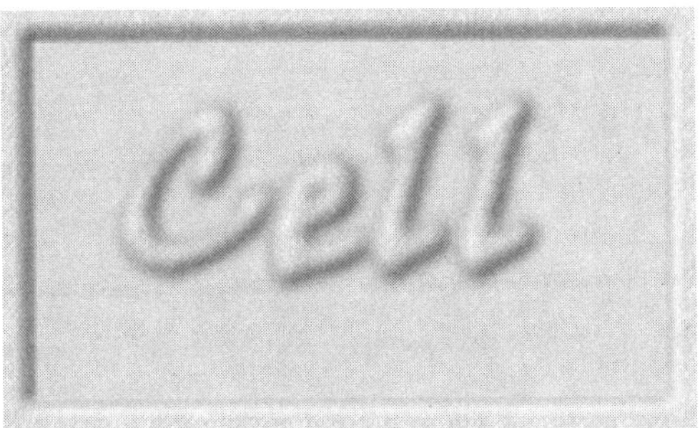

Figure 11-16
The stencil after Blur and Recess.

That looks cool by itself, but you want color, so continue.

9. Select the last, extended text sprite you put aside, copy it, and apply the Gradient effect to the copy using these settings for the color:

Gradient Effect Settings

Top two color swatches	133, 133, 133
Bottom two swatches	95, 0, 164

10. In the Gradient Name field on the Details tab of the Effects dialog box, enter "cellfones_text," and click the small disk icon to save the gradient to disk. It is now available for you to use again.

    The text sprite now has a purple to gray gradient.
11. Select the recessed sprite and bring it to the front.
12. Select the gradient text, and send it home. It moves into position under the stencil.

13. Select and flatten both sprites, and then crop the sides of the resulting sprite enough to completely remove the recessed outside edges. Set the home position of the sprite and move it aside for now.

Isolating the Letterforms

To make the text appear 3-D, you need to remove the blurred texture from around it. You'll create a stencil in the same shape as the letterforms but slightly larger, to use as the source to erase the blurred texture. Here's how:

1. Select the text sprite copy you made before you applied the gradient. Bring it to the front and send it home.
2. Copy the sprite and send it home. Copy and send it home again, and then select the original and the copies and flatten the sprites.
3. Make a stencil from the resulting sprite and set its home position.
4. Move the text sprite away.
5. Select the text sprite with the blurred texture and gradient color. Send it home and bring it to the front so that you can see it.
6. Shift-click the stencil and click it again to make it the source.
7. Apply Snip on the Texture Transfer palette at 100 percent opacity.

NOTE

If Snip does not work as you expected, you've hit the Texture Transfer tool bug again. Again, the solution is to undo the change, move the Opacity slider on the Texture Transfer palette to zero, and then move it back to 100 percent. Then try using Snip again.

8. Move the stencil away.
9. Select the newly snipped text sprite, apply Fit Bounding Box, and set its home position.
10. Apply the Drop Shadow effect with the settings on the facing page.

Drop Shadow Effect Settings	
Angle	315
Distance	15
Color	68, 34, 93
Softness	A little less than ¼ to the right of hard
Opacity	85

11. To make the text really stand out, apply Saturation at 15 on the Color Tuning palette.
12. Set the home position of the text, repeat the procedure for the "Fones" sprite and check Figure 11-17 to see how the final text should look.

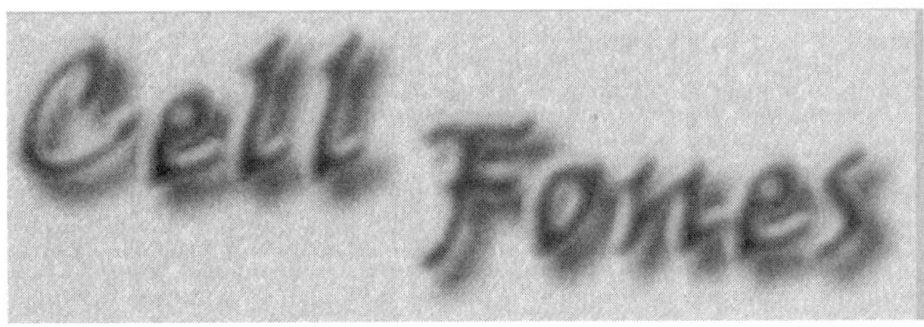

Figure 11-17
The final text.

Before going on, be sure to save your file.

Making the Horizontal Rule

You can use a similar technique with some slight modifications to make the horizontal rule.

1. Make a 260 by 50-pixel oval of any color, Opacity at 100 percent, just below the banner area on the Composition Space.
2. With the oval selected, drag the Interactive Scale handles evenly at all four sides of the sprite's bounding box to make the oval 560 pixels wide by 8 pixels high, as shown in Figure 11-18, on the next page.

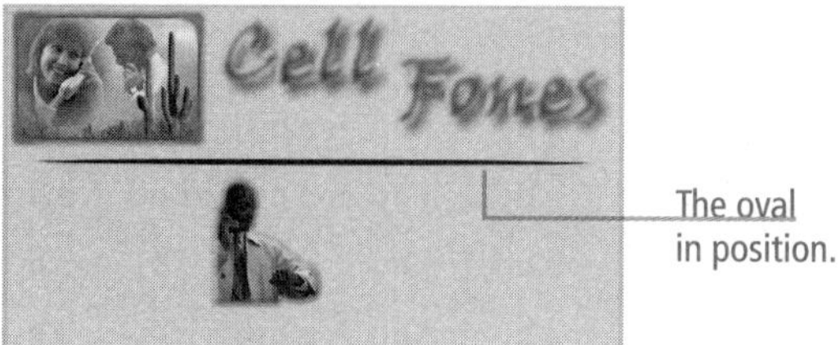

Figure 11-18
560 by 8-pixel oval in position.

3. Using Crop/Extend, extend the scaled oval out on all sides by 3 pixels.
4. Make a stencil, and then move the oval away.
5. Apply Transfer Shape to the stencil at 100 percent Opacity with the background as source.
6. Deselect all the sprites and then select the stencil. Even though you can't see the stencil, apply Blur at 1, Horizontal and Vertical, and then apply Recess.
7. Crop in from all four sides, making sure the recessed edges are gone, leaving only the recessed oval.
8. Starting at the left side of the oval, make a separate 180 by 20-pixel rectangle.
9. Apply a Grayscale Right gradient to the rectangle.
10. Select the oval and bring it to the front, and then position the rectangle as shown in Figure 11-19.

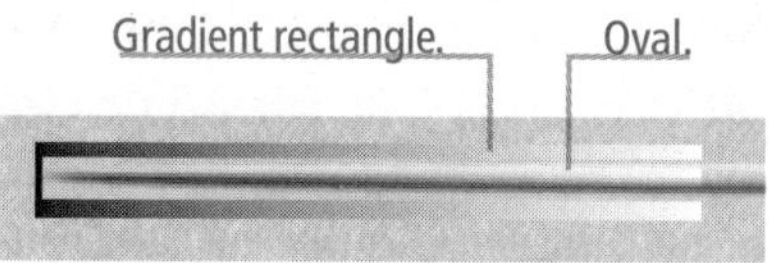

Figure 11-19
Rectangle with gradient in position under the oval.

11. Select both the rectangle and the oval. Make the rectangle the source.
12. Apply Map Transparency on the Texture Transfer palette.

13. Flip the rectangle horizontally, move it to the right side of the oval, and then apply Map Transparency as you did to the left side. Check Figure 11-20 for the result.

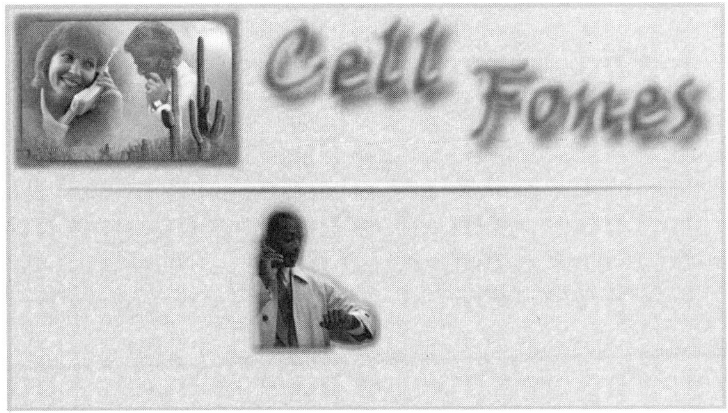

Figure 11-20
Horizontal rule with transparency mapping.

Creating the Buttons and Small Text Elements

Now that you have all the major compositional elements finished, it's time to make the buttons and small text elements for the Web page. Although we'll give you the steps that you need to follow to create these elements, we won't go into any depth with the procedures because you have used them many times throughout the book.

On the text buttons and for the small text, we used 20-point Tempus Sans ITC, but you can use any font you'd like. Try several fonts to get a feel for how different typefaces might work with the design. Remember that small text elements should be doubled and flattened to make them more solid and legible.

The starting point for the text buttons along the bottom is a copy of the original 140-pixel square with the background texture. Make a duplicate of that square and move it just below the Composition Space. You might want to make the buttons on the Workspace.

1. Set the current color to 84, 34, 143.
2. Leave the width of the square as is, but crop the height to 40 pixels.

3. Shift the color of the rectangle toward blues by changing the Hue setting on the Color Tuning palette to 100.
4. Make the sprite darker with a Brightness setting of –15.

   On the sample image, look closely at the "Personal Service" button below the man looking at his watch. The face of the button has a soft, dark gray outline around its edge, where the bevel meets the flat face.

5. To make the largest of the buttons, use the soft, gray outline as a guide, and create a shape with the Curve tool just inside the gray outline. Be sure you have Close and Fill selected before you click the Curve tool. You can then use the same shape to make all the smaller buttons.

   You should end up with three copies of the sprite you've just made. One copy as is, one copy with a black outline and the Blur effect applied, and a third copy of the outlined sprite with the Relief effect applied.

6. Place the shape over the 140 by 40-pixel rectangle and apply the Transfer Shape effect at 100 percent Opacity using the rectangle as the source. Make a copy and set it aside.
7. To the original, apply a black Edge that is 1 pixel thick.
8. Blur this sprite with a setting of 2.
9. Copy the sprite and apply the Relief effect to the original that the copy was made from.

   Now you will position one sprite on top of the other to make a finished button.

10. Place the blurred sprite with the black edge on the sprite that has the Relief effect. Bring it to the front, if necessary, and center it so the Relief effect is visible evenly around the edges.
11. Select the first, unblurred copy. Bring it to the front, then place it centered on top of the other two sprites. Use the arrow keys to position it precisely, if necessary. You should now have an unblurred button face with a dark border and a 3D look.
12. Select the three sprites and flatten them. This button is now ready for text.

To make the smaller text buttons, first make the text sprites to determine how large the buttons must be. Duplicate the large button you just made and cut out a left half and a right half for the smaller button. Then position the two halves next to each other, flatten them, and use the Paint tools for any minor cleanup. With this technique, you get the same shape without the edge degradation that would have been caused if you scaled the original sprite. When you have a full set of buttons, position them and place their text.

To make the small diamond-shaped buttons, follow these steps:

1. Make the shape with the Curve tool. Make a copy and set it aside.
2. Apply a gradient that is the opposite of the Cell Fones gradient. The two lower colors should be 95, 0, 164, and the upper two colors should be 133, 133, 133.
3. Make two Edge Only sprites using copies of the shape you made a few minutes earlier. Their color should be 118, 0, 173. One sprite should be 1 pixel thick. The other should be 2 pixels thick.
4. To the 2-pixel, Edge Only sprite, apply Blur at a setting of 2.
5. Apply Recess to the same sprite.
6. Apply Transparent at 50 percent to the same sprite.
7. Apply Transparent at 50 percent to the gradient shape sprite.
8. Arrange the sprites in the following Z order: the gradient shape on the bottom, the recessed sprite next, and the single pixel outline on top.
9. When you have these in place and aligned by eye, flatten them and then copy as many as you need.

Congratulations, you've completed the final project in your study of Image Composer. Be sure to check out the important information you'll find in the appendix about GIF Animator, color palettes, and other technical topics.

Have fun with Image Composer!

Appendix

In this appendix, we have gathered information about some of the more technical aspects of using Image Composer. Here you'll find information about GIF Animator, scanning effectively, and using PhotoCD files and color palettes.

Using GIF Animator

GIF Animator is a free utility that works along with Image Composer to automate most of the procedure for making an animated GIF file. About the only thing it doesn't do for you is the artwork.

You can add eye-catching motion to your Web sites with animated GIFs (the G is pronounced like a J), but you must use them with constraint. If the viewer's system is not powerful enough, large animated GIFs may not display the way you intended. Whether they work properly depends on the user's system resources, the number of frames in the GIF file, the number of colors used, and the size of each frame.

We have included in the PROJECTS directory of the CD two animated GIF files, SPINNER.GIF and SPINNER2.GIF, with slightly different display settings. Figure A-1 shows the GIF Animator window, which offers a standard Windows toolbar, but no menu. One frame is available and ready to receive a sprite.

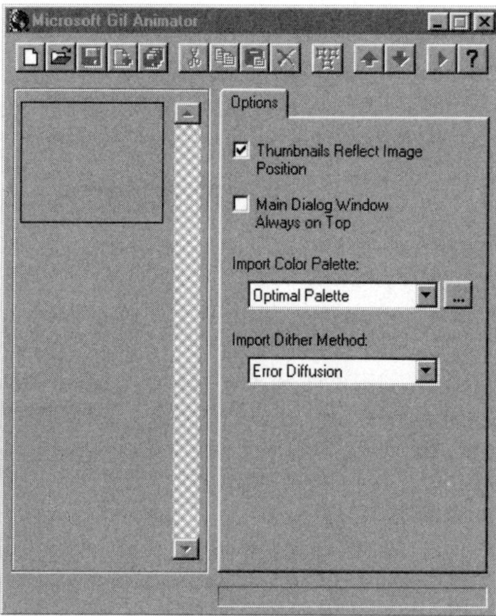

Figure A-1
The GIF Animator window.

The following exercise will familiarize you with the basics of making a working animated GIF.

First, open GIF Animator by clicking Microsoft GIF Animator on the Start menu. You can open a sample animation by following these steps:

1. Click the Open icon on the toolbar.
2. Using the controls in the Open dialox box, navigate to the PROJECTS folder of the CD-ROM and open SPINNER.GIF. The frames of the file are placed into GIF Animator.
3. Click the Preview button near the right end of the toolbar. The preview window appears and displays the animation over and over. Figure A-2 shows the Preview window.

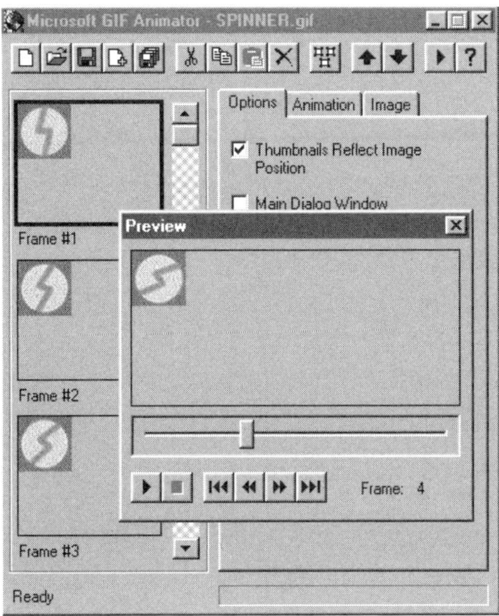

Figure A-2
SPINNER.GIF loaded into GIF Animator with the Preview window open.

4. After you've seen the animation, click the Stop button in the Preview window and close the window.
5. Now load SPINNER2.GIF and preview it. This second animation runs slower. You will make both of these animations to learn the difference.

GIF Animator literally works side by side with Image composer. You create images in Image Composer, drag them into GIF Animator, and set a few parameters. It's that simple.

Creating Sprites for the Animation

Before you create an animation, you must create the sprites for it. In the PROJECTS directory, open the file GIFANIMATOR.MIC in Image Composer. All the sprites used to make the two spinner GIF files are in the MIC file so you can refer to them.

First, decide on the size of the sprites based on the overall design of the Web page. For this project, you'll make sprites that are 40 pixels square.

Ten frames seemed enough to make a smooth turning spinner, and ten divides evenly into the 360 degrees of a circle. You will use a gray background to separate the animation from the Web page background, but the background of the sprite could be transparent, too.

To create the basic sprites, follow these steps:

1. Make ten 40-pixel gray squares and put them in a horizontal row, as shown in the MIC file. Don't worry about aligning the squares precisely.
2. Make one 36-pixel diameter light green circle.
3. Use an open polygon to make the dark green line.
4. To thicken the line, set its home position, copy it, and send it home twice.
5. Flatten the three line sprites with the circle, and align the flattened sprite with the center of the gray square. Then set its home position. The flattened circle/line sprite (which is not flattened with the gray background) is now what is called the "original" circle-line sprite in step 1 below.

To make a full circle with ten sprites, you must rotate each sprite 18 degrees more than the sprite before. To make the rotated circles, follow these steps:

1. Copy the original circle-line sprite and place the copy onto the first gray square, aligning the centers of the sprite and the square.

   Now make the first rotated sprite.

2. Select the original circle (the one from step 5 above) and enter "18" into the Rotation field on the Arrange palette and click Apply. Duplicate the rotated sprite and center the duplicate on the second square. You will use the original for the next step.

You must flatten the circle and line sprites before you can rotate them. Until the sprites are flattened, the Rotation control will be grayed out.

3. Select the first circle again (the one that has been rotated 18 degrees) and click Apply next to the Rotation control. This rotates the sprite another 18 degrees.
4. Duplicate the sprite and center the duplicate on the next available square.
5. Return to the first circle again, rotate it another 18 degrees, and then place a duplicate on the next square.
6. Repeat until you have filled all 10 squares with rotated circles.
7. Select each square/circle combination and flatten them. Then, move the sprites into two vertical columns, keeping them in order.

Opening GIF Animator Alongside Image Composer

Now open GIF Animator and arrange it side-by-side with Image Composer. Here's the easiest way to get a working arrangement of windows:

1. Open Image Composer and GIF Animator if they aren't already open. Make sure they are the only windows open. Other programs can be minimized to the Windows taskbar.
2. Right-click the Windows Taskbar at bottom of the screen and choose Tile Windows Vertically from the shortcut menu. Open windows are automatically tiled.
3. Use Image Composer's tools to position the vertically placed sprites where you can see them while you work. Figure A-3, on the next page, shows the two windows arranged next to each other.

You may want to close any palette that is open.

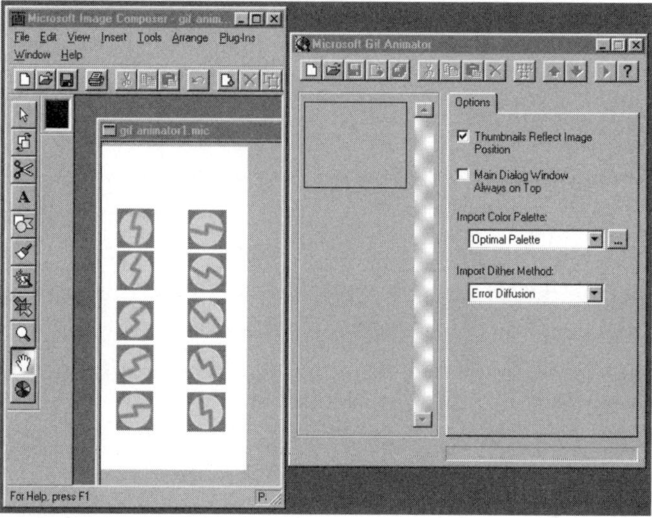

Figure A-3

Image Composer and GIF Animator open side by side.

Inserting the Sprites into GIF Animator

To make an animated GIF, you can drag sprites from Image Composer into GIF Animator frames one-by-one.

1. In the Image Composer window, click the top sprite in the left column and drag it onto the frame near the top of the left column in GIF Animator.

If the sprite doesn't seem to go into GIF Animator, click the New button on the GIF Animator toolbar and try again.

   A copy of the sprite is placed into the frame, which now has a heavy, dark blue border and is labeled Frame #1. The sprite automatically positions itself in the upper left corner of the frame, and a second blank frame appears.

2. Drag the next sprite into the second frame in GIF Animator.
3. Repeat with the rest of the sprites until all the sprites are in numbered frames. Don't worry about the blank, unnumbered frame after Frame #10. GIF Animator always adds a blank frame.

Selecting GIF Animator Settings

The settings on the three tabs in the GIF Animator window determine how the animation images are imported and how they will play.

The Options Tab

The settings on the Options tab, shown in Figure Appendix-1, above, determine how GIF Animator displays images, and how it handles color in the images. When Thumbnails Reflect Image Position is turned on, the frames in the left column display the actual position of the images within the animation frames (you change this position on the Image tab). When Main Dialog Window Always On Top is turned on, GIF Animator will always stay on top of other windows on your screen. When this option is on, you cannot use drag-and-drop to drag images from Image Composer to GIF Animator, though.

The Color Palette control lets you determine the color palette that GIF Animator will use to display the images. Browser Palette uses a single palette for all the images that best displays them in Web browsers. Optimal Palette creates a separate palette for each image, which produces a better display, but a slower one.

The Import Dither Method setting allows you to determine how colors in images are dithered. The finest quality images are produced with the Error Diffusion Setting.

For this exercise, leave the settings as shown in the figure Appendix-1.

The Animation Tab

The settings on the Animation tab, shown in Figure A-4, let you change the width of the animation frame and how it repeats.

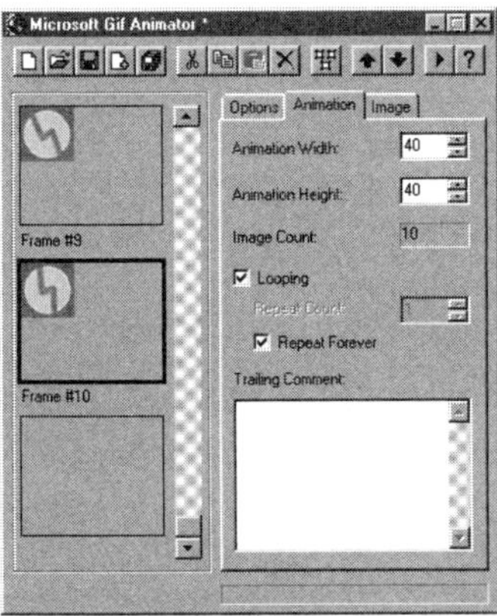

Figure A-4

The Animation tab settings.

The Animation Width and Animation Height fields tell you the size of your animation. Image Count tells you how many frames are in your animation. You can click the Looping check box and then, in the Repeat Count field, enter the number of times to repeat the image.

For this animation, click the Repeat Forever checkbox so the animation will repeat over and over continuously.

The Image Tab

The settings in the Image tab, shown in Figure A-5, allow you to control the position of the image within the frame, specify how long each frame stays on the screen, and how the frames replace each other.

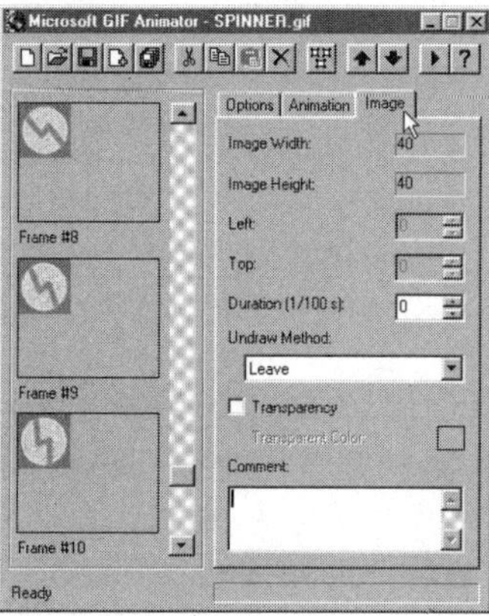

Figure A-5

The Image tab settings.

Before you change these settings, click the Save As button on the toolbar and save the file to your disk. The file you have created is identical to SPINNER.GIF on the CD. Play it to see.

Now you will change some settings and make a file that runs slower, like SPINNER2.GIF.

Changing the Duration

After saving the first animated GIF, make sure the Frames slider is all the way at the top so that Frame #1 is showing. Then follow these steps:

1. Click Frame #1 to select it.
2. Click in the Duration field and enter 2.
3. Repeat this step for each frame.
4. Preview this file to see that it runs slower.

The duration field determines the time in hundredths of a second that each frame displays. You can set a different duration for each frame.

GIF Animator offers a few more advanced options which determine how it will draw each successive frame, and which color in a GIF to make transparent. You can experiment with these using the file you just created.

Scanning

Scanning lets you bring any image into Image Composer, where it appears as a new sprite ready for modification. Flatbed scanners work best when they scan flat artwork, such as photographs. But they are also good for scanning other substances that are relatively flat and that can provide interesting background textures, such as pieces of polished wood, stone, pebbles, coffee beans, lentils, sand, and many other common, easily obtainable items.

You can even use a flatbed scanner to scan three-dimensional objects, such as seaweed, shells, small pieces of driftwood, plant life, leaves, interesting tropical fruit and vegetables, rocks, and just about anything else that fits on the bed of your scanner.

To help control the outcome of these explorations, you might want to obtain several flat pieces of black foam, each a different thickness and size. When you position objects on the scanner bed, you can use the foam to hold things in place and to completely cover the object and the flatbed so no light gets in. Why use black foam? Because when you scan, the light from the scanner bounces around, reflecting off light objects. The black foam absorbs much of this light and provides more controllable results. We even use a thin sheet of black foam over photographs when we scan.

A large, soft paint brush is useful to have on hand for cleaning the glass surface of the scanner bed. Follow this with liquid window cleaner applied with a soft cloth.

To create an interesting background effect, take Saran Wrap or another similar translucent food-wrapping substance, crumple it, and place it between two pieces of polarizing filter material that have been rotated 90 degrees from each other. When the polarizing material is properly rotated, the wrinkles in the food wrapping material take on rainbow colors that create amazing, abstract patterns. Polarizing filter material is available in sheets at good photographic supply stores or from mail order houses that sell to hobbyists who are interested in scientific exploration.

Until recently, each scanner manufacturer provided a software driver and special scanning software to accompany each scanner model. To use a scanner, you had to use the scanner's proprietary scanning software, save the scanned image to a bitmap graphics file, and then import the file into your graphics software, in a three-step process.

Now, most scanner manufacturers support the TWAIN specification, so graphics programs, such as Image Composer, can communicate directly with the scanner's scanning software. The result is that you can start a scan from within Image Composer and bring the image directly into Image Composer without interim steps.

Before you can scan, you must select the scanner by following these steps:

1. Make sure your scanner is turned on, of course.
2. From the File menu, click Scan Image, then choose Select Scan Source from the secondary menu.
3. On the Select Scan Source dialog box, click a scanner from the list.
4. Click Select.

To scan an image, follow these steps:

1. From the File menu, click Acquire Scan. A dialog box opens with scan settings for your particular scanner.
2. Choose the scan settings you'd like, such as brightness, contrast, number of colors, and resolution.
3. Click Final.

The image you scan is inserted into the upper-left corner of the Composition Space.

Choosing a Scanner

Scanner models are generally flatbed or hand-held. Professional service bureaus use another type of scanner, a drum scanner, which costs many thousands of dollars more.

Flatbed scanners let you scan anything from a single sheet or page in a book to a three-dimensional object. Hand-held scanners are acceptable for quick-and-dirty scans of flat objects, but they are difficult to use with any precision.

Scanners that can provide acceptable color and resolution for Web site graphics are easy to find, and they are relatively inexpensive. Because you will be using Image Composer, you won't need to purchase a scanner/ software bundle. You should also avoid a scanner that requires its own, special add-in board for your computer. It's better to connect a scanner to a SCSI interface to which you can connect other devices, such as hard disks, CD-ROM drives, and removable disks.

Getting the Best Scan

The "best" scan is the scan that works for your purposes. Become familiar with your scanner and use Image Composer to fine-tune your scanning technique. It's usually best to scan and work on images in 24-bit color, then reduce them to the Web palette when you save them for the Web in Image Composer. It's also better to scan at a resolution that is slightly higher than you need rather than lower because scaling algorithms work better when removing pixels than when adding them.

All consumer scanners have slight inconsistencies in how they scan. To find out how your scanner scans, scan a white object that is the size of your scanner bed at 72-dpi screen resolution. Look at the resulting image. Is it pure white? Probably not. This gives you some idea about how your scanner will affect a scan of a photo. When you scan, place your original material within the area on the scanner bed that has proven to be most even in value.

Learning More about Scanning

For those who really want to get into the topic of scanning further, here are some resources that we have found on the Web. At the first Web address, you can register for a free subscription to *Scanner World*, an online magazine dedicated to scanning. The second address provides more general information.

www.dpi-scanner-authority.com/288int/swiss1/swreg.html
www.dpi-scanner-authority.com/228int/swiss1/swiss1-main.html

Using PhotoCDs

A PhotoCD holds a collection of images that have been scanned by a service bureau and placed on the CD in Kodak PhotoCD format. Having a service bureau put your collection of photographs, slides, or negatives on a PhotoCD can be easy and economical. At this writing, a service bureau near us will scan 75 or more images for only $1.49 per image. They provide the CD, containing five levels of resolution for each image, and a printed index card that shows color thumbnails of the images and their filenames. Having a service bureau produce a PhotoCD is something you should consider if you would not be scanning often enough to justify the purchase of a scanner.

To insert an image into an Image Composer composition from a PhotoCD, choose From PhotoCD on the Insert menu. We have found, though, that the error message shown in Figure A-6 appears intermittently.

Figure A-6
PhotoCD error message.

This error usually occurs when an MIC file is already open when you insert the PhotoCD disk into the CD player. Inserting the PhotoCD before you start Image Composer usually causes no problem, so put the PhotoCD disk in your CD player, then start Image Composer and insert into a new MIC file all the image files you'd like. Then copy and paste the images into your project or save them as TIF or PNG files so they are readily available. Starting a new file and then choosing From Photo CD, on the Insert menu, usually also works.

About Color Palettes

If you could be sure that every viewer of your Web site had a 24-bit graphics card running in 24-bit (True Color) mode, and that every viewer had a high-speed communications line fast enough to download very large graphics files almost instantaneously, you'd never have to worry about color palettes. But the reality is that most people still use graphics cards that display only 8-bit color, 256 colors at a time, and most people use 14,400 or 28,800 baud modems.

For the bulk of your viewers, you need to make smaller images so that the graphics files will download quickly. You also need to reduce the size of your graphics files by using fewer colors, 8-bit color (256 colors) rather than 24-bit color (16.7 million colors).

Creating 8-bit color files also helps to reduce the problems that occur when Web browsers attempt to display 24-bit color images on 8-bit graphics systems. To try to faithfully represent colors that are not in their limited color palette, these Web browsers dither colors by mixing pixels of colors that they do have in their palette. But because you cannot control this dithering when it occurs in the browser, you cannot be certain that your viewers will see your images as you intend them to be seen. Dithering can be a problem especially when images are smaller and therefore have fewer pixels to mix.

To get around this problem, it's a good idea to reduce the number of colors in an image before you place it on the Web by using Image Composer's Web (Dithered) palette. If you apply this palette when saving a graphic file, you can see for yourself how it dithers the colors, and you can make adjustments as you see fit. Because the Web (Dithered) palette contains the same 216 colors that both Internet Explorer and Netscape can display, you can be confident that your viewers will see your graphics the same way you do. By the way, the Web (Solid) palette will also reduce an image to 216 colors, but it won't allow dithering of the colors, so your images will probably show unwanted bands of solid color.

When 24-Bit Color Isn't Really 16.7 Million Colors

When you work in the True Color color format in Image Composer (24-bit color), you have access to a palette of over 16 million colors. But the number of colors your computer's graphics system (its graphics card and monitor) can produce in theory is much more than the number of pixels it can display in reality because a screen cannot display more colors than it has pixels.

For most graphics systems, resolutions are 800 by 600, 1024 by 768, or 1280 by 1024. Doing the math, you find that 800 x 600 is 480,000 pixels, 1024 x 768 is 786,432 pixels, and 1280 x 1024 is 1,310,720 pixels on the screen in total. Any of these pixel totals is far less than the 16.7 million color palette of 24-bit color.

Visit Our Web Site

For more information about the book and Image Composer, visit our Web site for the book at www.studioserv.com.

Index

Numbers

A

B

C

L

M

N

O

P

T

U

V

W

X

Z

About the CD

The CD that accompanies this book contains a 90-day trial version of Image Composer, files for the projects, sample files and photos taken by Will Tait, and images provided by PhotoDisc. The files are organized into folders.

The Images Folder

In the IMAGES folder, you will find more than 100 24-bit color photos of various subjects taken by Will Tait and licensed to Microsoft Press. You can use these images in your own compositions and artwork, but you may not sell them individually or in collections. You are free to use them as elements in design projects for which you will receive payment.

Try applying the Web (Dithered) palette to these photos by inserting the image and then choosing Web (Dithered) from the Color Format drop-down list on the toolbar.

The Additional Folder

In the ADDITIONAL folder, you will find two grayscale photographic images, 18 texture files and 11 conceptual images. The textures and conceptual images were created in Image Composer using the techniques you have learned in the projects. These files are included so you can see additional examples of how you might employ Image Composer's tools. Feel free to use them as integrated parts of your own projects, if you'd like. Trying to figure out how they were made can lead to some interesting explorations.

The PhotoDisc Folder

The images in the PHOTODISC folder have been supplied by PhotoDisc, a leading supplier of digital stock images. Copies of these images have been used in the Tropical Fantasy, Blendo, and Cell Fones project files. You can contact PhotoDisc at the following address: PhotoDisc, Inc., 2013 Fourth Avenue, Seattle, WA 98121. Phone: 1-800-528-3472. www.photodisc.com. All PhotoDisc images: © 1997 PhotoDisc, Inc.

The Projects Folder

The PROJECTS folder contains the Image Composer files and TIF files you will need to use in the book's projects. All photographic images used in projects other than Tropical Fantasy, Blendo, CellFones, Wind World, and the photo retouching project in Chapter 4 were taken by Will Tait. Rebecca Fogg and John Mason took photos of the male figure in the color section.

Installing the Trial Version of Image Composer

To install the 90-day trial version of Image Composer, follow these steps:

1. From the Start menul, choose Run.
2. Type X:\imgcomp\enu\setup (where X is the letter of your CD-ROM drive.

   Note that the License Agreement presented during Setup outlines the legal use of Image Composer and of the sample images contained in the folder \imgcomp\common.

   This trial version of Image Composer is not supported by Microsoft Technical Support. Any attempts to circumvent the 90-day expiration date will cause the software to expire immediately.

Installing MSN 2.5

The enclosed CD also contains the client software for Microsoft Network, or MSN, which is Microsoft's Internet online service. When you install MSN, you get *one month free* unlimited access to MSN and the Internet. To install MSN 2.5, you must run Setup by following these steps:

1. From the Start menu, choose Run.
2. Type X:\msn\setup and click OK (where X is the letter of your CD-ROM drive.

Will Tait was born in Edinburgh, Scotland, and came to America at an early age. His interest in art led him to study drawing and painting at the Art Students League of New York. In addition to painting, he has worked extensively in printmaking, a discipline perfectly suited as a background for creating art on computers. He has been involved in various educational projects. They include developing an art program for schools in Berkeley, California, printmaking and multimedia programs through the Oregon Coast Council for the Arts, for the Lincoln county schools, and the initial interface design curriculum for the San Francisco State University Multimedia Studies Program. His personal artwork is included in the Achenbach print collection at the California Palace of the Legion of Honor in San Francisco, as well as many private and corporate collections. Currently, he produces multimedia at Intuit, where he uses Image Composer extensively as his primary image creation tool.

Steve Sagman is the New York-based author of more than a dozen books on the subjects of graphics, Windows, business applications, and online communications, and he has contributed chapters to several additional books. His books have sold well over a million copies worldwide, and they have been translated into Chinese, Dutch, German, Greek, Hebrew, Italian, Japanese, Portuguese, Russian, Spanish, and Thai. His book, *Traveling The Microsoft Network*, also published by Microsoft Press, was the winner of the Award of Excellence from the International Society of Technical Communicators (STC). When he's not writing books, he runs Studioserv, a technical communications company that offers user documentation, software training, interface design, and book editing and production. And when he's not writing or running his business, he plays jazz piano and toils in the fertile loam of his garden. He can be reached at steves@studioserv.com. His Web site is www.studioserv.com.

The manuscript for this book was prepared and submitted to Microsoft Press in electronic form. Text files were prepared in Microsoft Word. Pages were composed by Studioserv in PageMaker 6.5 for Windows. Graphics were prepared in Adobe Illustrator 7.0. The text is set in Garamond with display type in Frutiger. Composed pages were delivered to the printer as color-separated electronic prepress files.

Cover Designer
Greg Erickson

Cover Illustrator
Patrick Lanfear

Interior Graphic Designer
Kim Eggleston

Typographer
Studioserv

Proofreader
Eric Weinberger

Indexer
Audrey Marr

Make your presence **felt** on the **Internet** or within your own **intranet.**

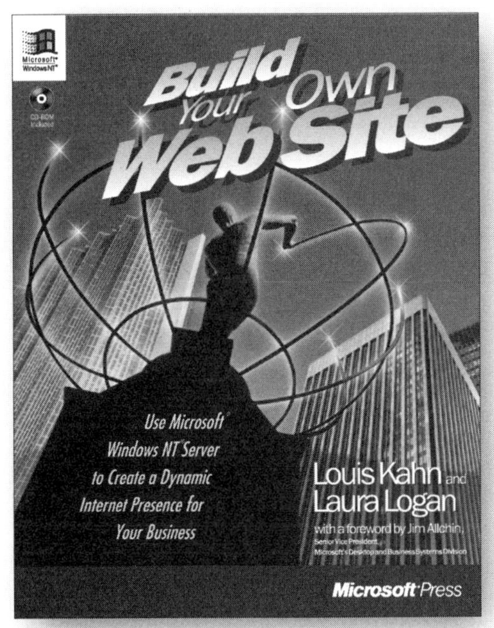

U.S.A. **$29.95**
U.K. £27.99 [V.A.T. included]
Canada $39.95
ISBN 1-57231-304-8

Unlike so many books on the market, this book is not about developing Web site content (although it touches on it). BUILD YOUR OWN WEB SITE shows you how to publish your content on the Internet or your corporate intranet using Microsoft® Windows NT® Server and Microsoft Internet Information Server—even if you have little or no programming or networking experience. In this helpful guide, you will find everything you need to know about:

- How the Internet and intranets work
- Why Windows NT Server is the platform to choose
- How to calculate choices of hardware, connections, security, bandwidth, and routing
- How to set up your system, maintain security, create content, and observe Internet etiquette
- How to configure your system, deal with maintenance issues, and plan for the future
- How to become an Internet service provider

BUILD YOUR OWN WEB SITE also familiarizes you with hot new technologies such as Java and ActiveX™.

If you're ready to establish a presence for your organization on the Internet or set up your own intranet, BUILD YOUR OWN WEB SITE is the smart place to start.

Microsoft Press® products are available worldwide wherever quality computer books are sold. For more information, contact your book or computer retailer, software reseller, or local Microsoft Sales Office, or visit our Web site at mspress.microsoft.com. To locate your nearest source for Microsoft Press products, or to order directly, call 1-800-MSPRESS in the U.S. (in Canada, call 1-800-268-2222).

Prices and availability dates are subject to change.

Microsoft® Press

Welcome to the next dimension in C++ programming.

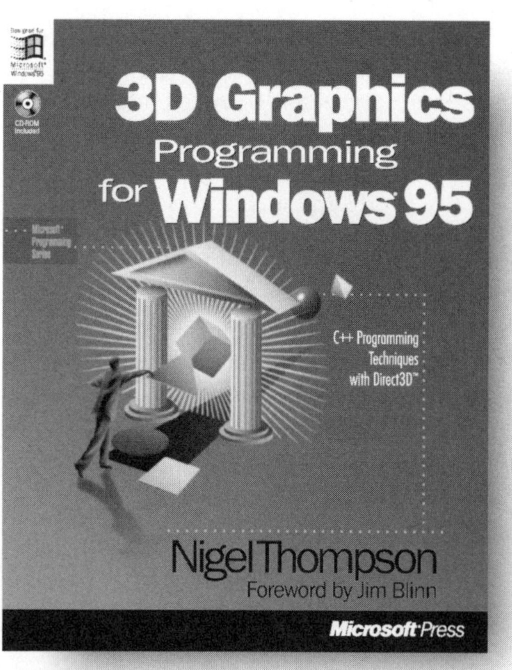

U.S.A. **$34.95**
U.K. £32.99 [V.A.T. included]
Canada $46.95
ISBN 1-57231-345-5

If you're a C++ developer who's eager to add all kinds of 3D effects to the Windows®-based applications you're creating, this book is for you. With 3D GRAPHICS PROGRAMMING FOR WINDOWS 95, you can learn to use the Direct3D® API to deliver real-time 3D graphics to mainstream PC users. The book's hands-on approach and effective samples also make it great for other developers (and even students) who want clear information about the basics of 3D graphics programming. Three-dimensional graphics are powerful—and this is the book that can help you harness that power.

Microsoft Press® products are available worldwide wherever quality computer books are sold. For more information, contact your book or computer retailer, software reseller, or local Microsoft Sales Office, or visit our Web site at mspress.microsoft.com. To locate your nearest source for Microsoft Press products, or to order directly, call 1-800-MSPRESS in the U.S. (in Canada, call 1-800-268-2222).

Prices and availability dates are subject to change.

Microsoft Press

To really **understand** Dynamic HTML, go to the source.

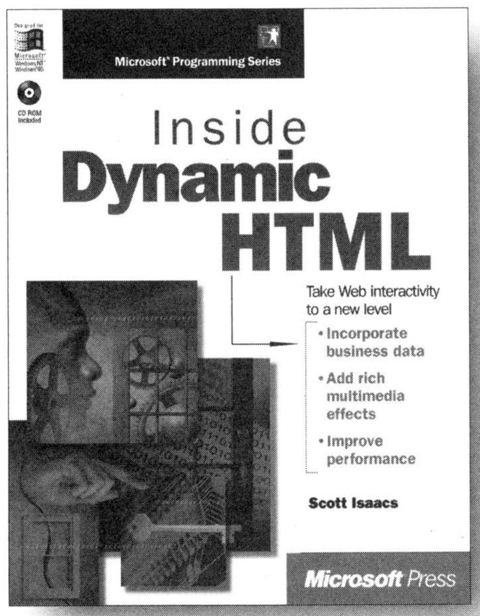

U.S.A. **$39.99**
U.K. £37.49 [V.A.T. included]
Canada $55.99
ISBN 1-57231-686-1

Web sites developed for Microsoft® Internet Explorer 4 can offer the most advanced, most exciting interactive features, thanks to Dynamic HTML—a technology that author Scott Isaacs helped create. Now he's written the programmer's bible on this important subject. Part technical manifesto, part application sourcebook, INSIDE DYNAMIC HTML starts by laying out core concepts and tools—HTML, cascading style sheets, and scripting fundamentals. Subsequent chapters explain the object model and element collections.

But beyond presenting the technical blueprint to Dynamic HTML, this book delivers what you need most—provocative, reusable techniques that demonstrate key benefits of the new object model. What's more, the companion CD-ROM supplies you with a copy of Microsoft Internet Explorer 4.0, the Internet Client Software Development Kit (SDK), sample scripts, and more. INSIDE DYNAMIC HTML is for Web developers, sophisticated content providers, users of JavaScript and other scripting tools, and anyone else who wants the lowdown on this widely embraced approach to a livelier Web. Give your pages the power of dynamic content. Get INSIDE DYNAMIC HTML.

Microsoft Press® products are available worldwide wherever quality computer books are sold. For more information, contact your book or computer retailer, software reseller, or local Microsoft Sales Office, or visit our Web site at mspress.microsoft.com. To locate your nearest source for Microsoft Press products, or to order directly, call 1-800-MSPRESS in the U.S. (in Canada, call 1-800-268-2222).

Prices and availability dates are subject to change.

Microsoft® Press

IMPORTANT—READ CAREFULLY BEFORE OPENING SOFTWARE PACKET(S). By opening the sealed packet(s) containing the software, you indicate your acceptance of the following Microsoft License Agreement.

MICROSOFT LICENSE AGREEMENT

(Book Companion CD)

This is a legal agreement between you (either an individual or an entity) and Microsoft Corporation. By opening the sealed software packet(s) you are agreeing to be bound by the terms of this agreement. If you do not agree to the terms of this agreement, promptly return the unopened software packet(s) and any accompanying written materials to the place you obtained them for a full refund.

MICROSOFT SOFTWARE LICENSE

1. GRANT OF LICENSE. Microsoft grants to you the right to use one copy of the Microsoft software program included with this book (the "SOFTWARE") on a single terminal connected to a single computer. The SOFTWARE is in "use" on a computer when it is loaded into the temporary memory (i.e., RAM) or installed into the permanent memory (e.g., hard disk, CD-ROM, or other storage device) of that computer. You may not network the SOFTWARE or otherwise use it on more than one computer or computer terminal at the same time.

2. COPYRIGHT. The SOFTWARE is owned by Microsoft or its suppliers and is protected by United States copyright laws and international treaty provisions. Therefore, you must treat the SOFTWARE like any other copyrighted material (e.g., a book or musical recording) except that you may either (a) make one copy of the SOFTWARE solely for backup or archival purposes, or (b) transfer the SOFTWARE to a single hard disk provided you keep the original solely for backup or archival purposes. You may not copy the written materials accompanying the SOFTWARE.

3. OTHER RESTRICTIONS. You may not rent or lease the SOFTWARE, but you may transfer the SOFTWARE and accompanying written materials on a permanent basis provided you retain no copies and the recipient agrees to the terms of this Agreement. You may not reverse engineer, decompile, or disassemble the SOFTWARE. If the SOFTWARE is an update or has been updated, any transfer must include the most recent update and all prior versions.

4. DUAL MEDIA SOFTWARE. If the SOFTWARE package contains more than one kind of disk (3.5", 5.25", and CD-ROM), then you may use only the disks appropriate for your single-user computer. You may not use the other disks on another computer or loan, rent, lease, or transfer them to another user except as part of the permanent transfer (as provided above) of all SOFTWARE and written materials.

5. SAMPLE CODE. If the SOFTWARE includes Sample Code, then Microsoft grants you a royalty-free right to reproduce and distribute the sample code of the SOFTWARE provided that you: (a) distribute the sample code only in conjunction with and as a part of your software product; (b) do not use Microsoft's or its authors' names, logos, or trademarks to market your software product; (c) include the copyright notice that appears on the SOFTWARE on your product label and as a part of the sign-on message for your software product; and (d) agree to indemnify, hold harmless, and defend Microsoft and its authors from and against any claims or lawsuits, including attorneys' fees, that arise or result from the use or distribution of your software product.

DISCLAIMER OF WARRANTY

The SOFTWARE (including instructions for its use) is provided "AS IS" WITHOUT WARRANTY OF ANY KIND. MICROSOFT FURTHER DISCLAIMS ALL IMPLIED WARRANTIES INCLUDING WITHOUT LIMITATION ANY IMPLIED WARRANTIES OF MERCHANTABILITY OR OF FITNESS FOR A PARTICULAR PURPOSE. THE ENTIRE RISK ARISING OUT OF THE USE OR PERFORMANCE OF THE SOFTWARE AND DOCUMENTATION REMAINS WITH YOU.

IN NO EVENT SHALL MICROSOFT, ITS AUTHORS, OR ANYONE ELSE INVOLVED IN THE CREATION, PRODUCTION, OR DELIVERY OF THE SOFTWARE BE LIABLE FOR ANY DAMAGES WHATSOEVER (INCLUDING, WITHOUT LIMITATION, DAMAGES FOR LOSS OF BUSINESS PROFITS, BUSINESS INTERRUPTION, LOSS OF BUSINESS INFORMATION, OR OTHER PECUNIARY LOSS) ARISING OUT OF THE USE OF OR INABILITY TO USE THE SOFTWARE OR DOCUMENTATION, EVEN IF MICROSOFT HAS BEEN ADVISED OF THE POSSIBILITY OF SUCH DAMAGES. BECAUSE SOME STATES/COUNTRIES DO NOT ALLOW THE EXCLUSION OR LIMITATION OF LIABILITY FOR CONSEQUENTIAL OR INCIDENTAL DAMAGES, THE ABOVE LIMITATION MAY NOT APPLY TO YOU.

U.S. GOVERNMENT RESTRICTED RIGHTS

The SOFTWARE and documentation are provided with RESTRICTED RIGHTS. Use, duplication, or disclosure by the Government is subject to restrictions as set forth in subparagraph (c)(1)(ii) of The Rights in Technical Data and Computer Software clause at DFARS 252.227-7013 or subparagraphs (c)(1) and (2) of the Commercial Computer Software — Restricted Rights 48 CFR 52.227-19, as applicable. Manufacturer is Microsoft Corporation, One Microsoft Way, Redmond, WA 98052-6399.

If you acquired this product in the United States, this Agreement is governed by the laws of the State of Washington.

Should you have any questions concerning this Agreement, or if you desire to contact Microsoft Press for any reason, please write: Microsoft Press, One Microsoft Way, Redmond, WA 98052-6399.

Register Today!

Return this
Official Microsoft® Image Composer Book
registration card for
a Microsoft Press® catalog

U.S. and Canada addresses only. Fill in information below and mail postage-free. Please mail only the bottom half of this page.

1-57231-593-8A ***OFFICIAL MICROSOFT® IMAGE COMPOSER BOOK*** ***Owner Registration Card***

NAME

INSTITUTION OR COMPANY NAME

ADDRESS

CITY STATE ZIP

Microsoft® Press
Quality Computer Books

For a free catalog of Microsoft Press® products, call
1-800-MSPRESS

NO POSTAGE NECESSARY IF MAILED IN THE UNITED STATES

BUSINESS REPLY MAIL
FIRST-CLASS MAIL PERMIT NO. 53 BOTHELL, WA

POSTAGE WILL BE PAID BY ADDRESSEE

MICROSOFT PRESS REGISTRATION
OFFICIAL MICROSOFT®
IMAGE COMPOSER BOOK
PO BOX 3019
BOTHELL WA 98041-9946